D0761077

DISCARD

Desiring Discourse

Desiring Discourse

The Literature of Love, Ovid through Chaucer

Edited by
James J. Paxson
and Cynthia A. Gravlee

SUP

Selinsgrove: Susquehanna University Press
London: Associated University Presses

Associated University Presses
440 Forsgate Drive
Cranbury, NJ 08512

Associated University Presses
16 Barter Street
London WC1A 2AH, England

Associated University Presses
P.O. Box 338, Port Credit
Mississauga, Ontario
Canada L5G 4L8

'NDEXED IN *EGbf*

The paper used in this publication meets the requirements of the American National Standard for Permanence of Paper for Printed Library Materials Z39.48–1984.

Library of Congress Cataloging-in-Publication Data

Desiring discourse : the literature of love, Ovid through Chaucer / edited by James J. Paxson and Cynthia A. Gravlee.
    p. cm.
    Includes bibliographical references and index.
    ISBN 1–57591–013–6 (alk. paper)
    1. Love in literature. 2. Courtly love in literature. 3. Literature, Medieval—History and criticism. 4. Literature, Comparative—Themes, motives. I. Paxson, James J. II. Gravlee, Cynthia.
PN682.L68D47   1998
809'.933543—DC21   97–39577
                                                                 CIP

PRINTED IN THE UNITED STATES OF AMERICA

Contents

Part 3: Chaucerian Discourses of Desire

Preface

The literature of love—represented in the works of Vergil, Ovid, the troubadours, the Old French romance and *lai* composers, Dante, Boccaccio, and Chaucer—has by now enjoyed critical treatment both broad in scope and profound in detail. The essays in *Desiring Discourse: The Literature of Love, Ovid through Chaucer* therefore hope to capture a representative sense of the latest work being done on these authors, providing a cumulative document that promises to be of interest and use to students of the Middle Ages in general and to specialists on the psychology, phenomenology, and discourses of love and desire.

This volume had its beginnings in a National Endowment for the Humanities Summer Seminar for College Teachers in 1989. The seminar, "Chaucer's *Troilus and Criseyde* and the Literature of Love," afforded new directions in the work of several of the seminar participants. Those of us who've benefited from these new directions (not in the least we two editors) have a debt of gratitude to Robert W. Hanning, director of the seminar, who inspired and invigorated such work and who subsequently encouraged a number of that seminar's complement—those located in the New York City area—to continue meeting on a monthly basis at Columbia University in order to create a forum for the sharing of research and writing on subjects medieval or theoretical. This group (most often self-ascribed as "NY Club Med"), in conjunction with nonlocal participants from the original NEH seminar, kept alive the idea of presenting a unified volume on Ovid's legacy in the Middle Ages. The essays collected here thus represent long and careful engagements—indeed continued and augmented, scholarly and discursive *desires*—concerning the medieval literary culture of love. Thus our thanks and warm wishes to the original members of the 1989 NEH seminar (Liz Bernstein, Marge Davlin, Sealy Gilles, Victoria Guerin, Joan Haahr, Priscilla McKinney, Nancy Reale, Anne Schotter, Sidney Vance, and Elizabeth Walsh).

7

We also wish to thank guest members of the original seminar and its later incarnation—some of whom dropped in during visits to New York and others of whom still make their homes there (William Askins, Richard K. Emmerson, Joan Ferrante, John Ganim, Simon Gaunt, Charlotte Gross, H. Marshall Leicester Jr., Joseph Solodow, Martin Stevens, and Peter Travis). And we most heartily thank those new recruits who permanently joined the Columbia Club Med group during the course of the 1990s (Christopher Baswell, Sandra Pierson Prior, Robert M. Stein, and Sylvia Tomasch).

But we especially thank Bob Hanning for his vision, his dedication, his wit (those puns indeed!), his astute critical and theoretical sensibility, and his voluminous knowledge of and love for the Middle Ages. This volume certainly represents a concerted and ongoing group effort; but Bob's care and guidance shine through, we believe, on just about every page.

Desiring Discourse

The Medieval World of Desire, Discourse, Reception, and Writing: An Introduction

JAMES J. PAXSON

We have grown familiar with the array of terms used to organize our sense of the literature of love in the Middle Ages: the rhetorical institution of persuasion and seduction, the Ovidian heritage, *aetas ovidiana*, the language of amatory trial, the genealogy of the romance, the conventions of courtly love, the tradition of *fin amors*. These terms or subtitles continue to identify books, essays, anthologies, conferences, and specialized research seminars; they thus indicate a burgeoning and healthy universe of critical production in contemporary medieval studies that tries to articulate the medieval discourse of desire.

The late classical and medieval literatures of desire or love have indeed spurred a field so vast that historians and critics working on them now turn to very precise topical or formal problems. That is, few studies are published today that have the sweep or certainty of such earlier critical touchstones to the literature of love as W. P. Ker's *Epic and Romance*, C. S. Lewis's *The Allegory of Love*, Denis de Rougement's *Love in the Western World*, or Alexander J. Denomy's *The Heresy of Courtly Love*.[1] Such touchstone studies serve up an aesthetic and historical richness that is unrivaled, but they take love as an epistemological and ontological "given." De Rougement or Denomy focuses on how medieval literature's fictional lovers indeed have problems; but the structure of desire in such love goes unproblematized.

Even though much has been said and written on the conventional discourse of enamorment, seduction, adoration, and loss in medieval literature, only recently has critical or theoretical attention pointed to the problematic nature of *desire*—that is, on its psychological, phenomenological, and gendered bases—and on the corollary problem of the historical reception concerning desire's monumental texts. The literature of love obviously involves people yearning for, pursuing, or in love with one another; it involves both sexuality and gender. Yet how spare or nonexistent has been critical recognition of the discursive or ideological nature that undergirded this literature of desire and pursuit from its classical representations through its later vernacular heritage. Scholars who treat the psychologically latent or gendered underpinnings of the discourse of desire have indeed helped enlarge and enrich the critical domain of the love literature tradition; few would dispute the value of work done by people like E. Jane Burns or Roberta Krueger on medieval images of sexual repression or the dehumanization of women.[2] This volume, *Desiring Discourse: The Literature of Love, Ovid through Chaucer*, wishes to join that theoretical enrichment.

The essays in *Desiring Discourse* acknowledge desire as a very powerful and dominant discourse in medieval culture. They treat desire's often ambiguous nature as a topic both theologically charged and socially central. Like Alexandre Leupin's general thesis in *Barbarolexis*, the point in common of the essays in *Desiring Discourse* involves the interdependence of sexual desire, spiritual desire, and the desire to make language itself.[3] Desire urges writing—and rewriting, reappropriating, rereading. It is now seen, in Evelyn Birge Vitz's words, as the "primary way in which the subjects of medieval narrative are represented in relation to other people and things in the medieval *récit*."[4] Desire, Vitz continues, "is virtually the *sole* characterological principle" in medieval narrative.[5]

The textual representation of desire in Western culture, of course, finds its wellspring in Ovid. The terms or subtitles tallied at the outset of this Introduction underline the roles of Ovidian topoi, style, formal and generic structures, and ideology for the literature of love in the late Middle Ages and especially in the work of Chaucer. In particular, the modern critical commentary on Old French poetry, neo-Latin scholastic verse, Dantean allegory, didactic moralized mythography, and Chaucerian romance narrative hinges on the recognition and articulation of Ovid's prime cultural and textual legacy. The field of medieval studies has come to enjoy a strong treatment of "medieval Ovids," as witnessed by the special issue of the journal *Mediaevalia* in 1987, titled *Ovid in Medieval Culture*, or by the contributions in Charles Martindale's lively collection *Ovid Renewed*. Ralph Hexter's *Ovid and Medieval Schooling* demonstrates Ovid's textual primacy as didactic or heuristic master-model in the schools.[6] For classicists and medievalists, Ovid scholarship has enjoyed an indisputable boom in the last twenty or so years, one rivaling those in, say, *Beowulf* or Chaucer scholarship.[7]

Yet, despite the progress that feminism and poststructuralism have begun to make in medieval studies, the critical reception of Ovid maintains a characteristic uniformity and conventionality regarding the gender implications for the structure and phenomenology of suasive discourse. That is to say, Ovid's prominent pretexts on the social theory of love and seduction (the *Amores*, *Remedia amoris*, and *Ars Amatoria*) are taken at times as a kind of ground zero that one readily apprehends. Above all, Andreas Capellanus's great imitation of Ovid, the *De amore*, has fostered this perception. Persuasion and seduction at first seem to involve a no-holds-barred binary structure: the male enacts a verbal attack, the female resists (if even strategically) but is overcome. One might say that the barest Jakobsonian duplex works as the structural armature of this universal seeming state of affairs: for Roman Jakobson, all "communicational acts" (including linguistic, gestural, or social ones) are constituted in part by an "addresser" and an "addressee," a sender and a receiver.[8] The persuading and seducing male functions as sender while the female functions as receiver. This spare structuralist paradigm found its historical articulation in the widely held grammatical allegory representative of human social dynamics: the male is active "subject," while the female is passive "object." The grammatical allegory, which served as the conceptual template for the binarizing of persuasion and seduction and thus for the subsequent simplification of Ovid's coded model, enjoyed fullest expression in the declarations of Alan of Lille and of the "speculative grammarians" like Thomas of Erfurt; it was, as Jan Ziolkowski has shown, a predominant paradigm for social reality in medieval Europe.[9] But this mechanical structural allegory far from describes the full social, psychological, ideological, and structural dynamics that are more and more being perceived in Ovidian love situations[10]—or indeed in all human acts of passionate interaction as they have been taken up by semiologists like A. J. Greimas.[11] Given developments in recent theory, the uni-directional and binary paradigm seems less and less to serve as an effective descriptive tool.

The essays in this volume seek to explore further and to overturn many of the prior critical conclusions concerning the aforementioned binary and "linear" model of verbal or rhetorical persuasion. On the whole, they accommodate a poetics of female response and the commensurate assertion of (potential) female rights or power; they locate the rhetorical scene of persuasion and the admirational discourse of desire not just as acts of immediate and contained male-controlled verbal act and social praxis, but as universal figures for human cognition and ontology in general. Even at the barest semantic level, the rhetorical aura of "persuasion" and "enamorment" does reveal the latent assertion or

intrusion of feminine experience and ontology into the "masculine."
Writing on *ravissement* or ravishment, enamorment, Roland Barthes
declares that:

> in the ancient myth [of the abduction of the Sabine Woman], the ravisher is
> active, he wants to seize his prey, he is the subject of the rape (of which the
> object is a Woman, as we know, invariably passive); in the modern myth (that
> of love-as-passion), the contrary is the case: the ravisher wants nothing, does
> nothing; he is motionless (as any image), and it is the ravished object who is
> the real subject of the rape; the *object* of capture becomes the *subject* of love;
> and the *subject* of the conquest moves into the class of loved *object*. (There
> nonetheless remains a public vestige of the archaic model: the lover—the one
> who has been ravished—is always implicitly feminized.)[12]

Barthes's analysis invokes the vocabulary of grammar, of subjects and
objects, to demonstrate how the predictable ontic and social state of
affairs (male → female) articulates instability and self-dismantling. The
feminine is always already implicit in the masculine; the linear or binary
model of gender (and grammar) deconstructs itself.

Barthes's observations of course invite a danger. The basic structural
conditions of enamorment occlude what Barthes's thematic inversion of
male and female roles presages: woman as "ravishing subject"
incorporates in germinal form the negative concept, ultimately central to
amatory (and misogynistic) culture, of the destructive or cruel female
who does seem to enjoy a kind of "power." The beloved woman as cruel
or flippant mistress, as *domina*, indeed as murderess or "blood-sucker,"
really functions to justify further repression and erasure of female voice,
presence, power; as was suggested above, much of this conviction stems
from the receptional node built around the *De amore*.[13] But discursive,
rhetorical, and social realities exist as mutual terms. For this reason these
essays consider *real* social problems between the sexes in medieval
culture—problems like rape, abduction, servitude or slavery, silencing—
as adjuncts to the preponderantly *rhetorical* or poetic problem of amatory
discourse. Such an essay collection, which centralizes female cognition
and voice, female ontology, *and* female suffering in amatory literature,
sponsors the critical academy's ongoing sophistication and consequent
revitalization of, in particular, Ovidian themes, topoi, and protocols.

The title of this volume points up the problems in characterizing the
continuity between original Ovidian and, ultimately, Chaucerian texts.
Why "Desiring Discourse"? The volume's title reflects the concurrent
critical meditation on the "discourse of desire," an oft repeated
formulation in the study of amatory literature. However, the yoking of

the participle "desiring" to "discourse" in our title indicates a reflexive and ambiguous ontological situation that the essays in various ways take up (recall how Alexandre Leupin recognizes the slipperiness of grammar when it involves desire). "Discourse" is certainly the object of those who are in a state of desiring, of those who desire; but it can also be the subject who *does* the desiring. Discourse desires and is desired. People in a mimetic narrative produce discourse; yet discourse, like a sentient agent, generates a semiotic or rhetorical field wherein human agents are produced, constructed, or arranged. Discourse determines and disposes the social world and formal structure of the literary text invested in desire and love. It determines that most fundamental category called "gender." Already in our volume's title, the fixed ontology of grammar—with its privileging of subject over object, active over passive, masculine over feminine—inches towards readjustment, rupture, deconstruction.[14]

In turn, the essays address a historical (but not necessarily genetic) continuity of amatory texts, a chronological continuity that runs *"from Ovid through Chaucer."* Yet this continuity also reaffirms the problematics of reception always constitutive of the Chaucerian tradition. This receptional state of affairs demands an awareness of "Ovid *through* Chaucer," of Ovid inside Chaucer; Ovid as pretext or subtext to Chaucer; Ovid as what Harold Bloom would call the "strong" anterior poet who is prior to and therefore inside Chaucer.[15] The essays therefore treat a number of intermediaries in medieval literature that appropriate and struggle with the Ovidian pretext and that presage the Chaucerian poetics evident in certain of *The Canterbury Tales* and in *Troilus and Criseyde*. Ovid orders desire's formalization in texts including Andreas Capellanus's *De amore*, the *Pamphilus*, various troubadour lyrics, the lais of Marie de France, the *Roman de la rose*, Boccaccio's *Filostrato*, and Dante's *Commedia*; but in often strange and striking ways these very texts in turn reorder and realign Ovidian protocols. The shifted receptional horizon of the later Middle Ages, with its emerging models of the self, the individual, and the feminine, accounts in particular for such a decisive realignment.[16]

In the ubiquitous terms of Hans Robert Jauss's conceptual scheme,[17] the genealogical *rezeptionsästhetik* established among these former and posterior texts hinges on powerful but often subtle representations of the feminine stakes in and responses to the rhetorical structures that constitute masculine amatory discourse. The essays in this volume seek to demonstrate how masculine discourse that is seductive, laudatory, suppressive, or elegiac does not flat out determine the roles or registers of the desirous male and the beloved female, but is also shaped by the powers of feminine consciousness, language, phenomenology, and experience, however latent or implicit they may be. In other words, most of the essays are oriented towards a critical epistemology based on a feminist or gender poetics, although Jaussian imperatives underwrite virtually all of the pieces as well. Several of the essays employ historical approaches or address political realities; others focus on rhetorical tropes and generic forms; some take up textual or codicological matters; and others explore the psychological compositions of female consciousnesses locked in love or seduction situations. The volume does not offer a particular theoretical or critical approach but rather a general awareness of and homage to the contributions that theoretical thinking has made in medieval studies over recent years. It is in this way that *Desiring Discourse* seeks to enrich and vary the voluminous critical literature on Ovid and on the subsequent poets of love.

As noted at the outset of this introduction, the essays presented in this volume already fit into an established critical pedigree. Yet the topics addressed in several of the essays touch precisely upon some common-places of theoretical work exclusive to the 1990s. For instance, the matter of physical as well as metaphorical *wounding* experienced by male figures engaged in the activities of pursuit, seduction, or amorous inter-change establishes a critical track resonant with the theoretical "poetics of the body" concurrent in today's critical theory. If the 1970s can be said to be the theoretical decade of climactic formalism (with decon-struction as the terminal procedure) and the 1980s can be said to be the theoretical decade of culminational historical awareness (with Marxism, New Historicism, and Cultural Studies as the dominant discursive formations), then the 1990s mark the establishment of a "personalist" criticism, a criticism of the body, a criticism or theory of somatic hyper-awareness, demarcation, and identity; as some would have it, a "bodytheory."[18] Some of the essays in *Desiring Discourse* make an investment in such a rhetoric or poetics of the physical body. Suasive discourse, as Robert W. Hanning asserts, can no longer be separated from the narrative imaging of actual physical bodies—human *and* nonhu-man—in medieval texts centered on love and seduction. Hanning's essay, entitled "The Talking Wounded: Desire, Truth Telling, and Marie de France's Androgynous Deer," turns on the wounding of a personified deer in *Guigemar*. While exploring the rhetorical imperatives of male and female eloquence, the essay exemplifies the tight poetic and struc-tural juncture of hunt/wound/persuasion/lovesickness. Robert Stein's "The Conquest of Femenye: Desire, Power, and Narrative in Chaucer's *Knight's Tale*" provides a semiological balance sheet of "five series" that order the poem: "political action," "storytelling," "desire," "explanation," and "suffering flesh." The final series affirms the tale's inscription of the

erotic, the rhetorical, and the political in a narrative of desire and pleasure and in one of corporeal ruin and decay. Stein furnishes a psychoanalytical and sociopolitical poetics of the mortal body, a poetics evocative
of some of the most important contemporary work now produced on the
Knight's Tale—for instance, H. Marshall Leicester Jr.'s analysis of the
erotics and violence that constitute both the poem's social institution of
chivalry and the chivalric subject's psychological quality.[19] And in
semiological terms at times reminiscent of those offered in "The Conquest of Femenye," James Paxson's essay, "The Semiotics of Character,
Trope, and Troilus," inspects the embodied condition and textual
"construction" of the suffering male lover, Chaucer's Troilus, in terms of
a de Manian deconstructive program that focuses on the master tropes
prosopopoeia and apostrophe. The depiction of figurative encasement,
interiority and exteriority, and of somatic (and literal) stasis or catatonia
simultaneously depicted along with frenzy, indeed derives from Ovid but
also configures Troilus as Slavoj Žižek's notion of "the sublime object of
desire." This imagery in turn invokes the cultural notion of encased or (as
a recent *Exemplaria* issue devoted to feminism and medieval texts has it)
"skirted" feminine phenomenology.[20]

Reflective of these tropological discussions, other essays in the
volume deal directly with the rhetorical or tropological purview of
suasive discourse and the literary language of unbridled desire and loss.
Some pieces thus attend to traditional matters drawn from rhetorical
theory while others promote feminist models of trope deployment and
self-reflexivity. Joan Haahr's "Justifying Love: The Classical *Recusatio*
in Medieval Love Literature" posits the rhetorical and tropological
centrality of the Ovidian *recusatio*, the figure of "refusal" whereby a poet
rejects a prior and overriding convention. According to Haahr, Ovid's
often tongue-in-cheek rhetorical legitimization of amatory subjects and
forms subverted or displaced other Roman poetic values. For medieval
amatory writers, however, the *recusatio* went beyond the ornamental or
facetious, often functioning both structurally and thematically as a kind
of master trope of amatory discourse. And whereas enamorment and
recusatio name tropes effectual in the enabling of poetic love situations,
the corollary rhetorical moment can be found in the direct plea for
release. In "The Transformation of Ovid in the Twelfth-Century
Pamphilus," Anne Schotter studies that brief neo-Latin poem not only for
the representation of actual rape in medieval culture but for the
realization of female defensive eloquence in defiance of (and in ratio to)
male offensive, sexual assault. The female attempt to fend off rape in
medieval literature marks the often ignored, hidden, or erased structural
counterpart to the initiatory rhetoric of discovered male desire and

subsequent persuasion. If the whole inventory of rhetorical tropes and the modes of invention or disposition constitute the domain of "rhetoric" that hinges on the persuasive act, then the defensive female response charted by Schotter constitutes a corollary domain of antirhetoric.

As some of the matters touched upon so far indicate, reception theory (shaped primarily around the Ovidian legacy) governs many of the pieces in this volume. Warren Ginsberg's essay, "*Ovidius ethicus*?: Ovid and the Medieval Commentary Tradition," provides a sweeping and powerful receptional program that considers how the hedonistic, pagan poet of imperial Rome became an ethical and conceptual pillar for so much medieval textual production. In showing how Ovid's *Ars Amatoria* is really an art of love-making, Ginsberg rewrites desire—with its embedded, counterintuitive logic of required and sustained *resistance*— as the ironic precursor element in an economy of resistance-centered, and thus "ethical," intergender relations. According to Ginsberg, a logic of reversal programs desire's self-shaped identity in the Ovidian commentary tradition. In similar terms, Charlotte Gross's "*Loc Aizi/ Anima Mundi*: Being, Time, and Desire in the Troubadour Love Lyric" demonstrates how Platonic materials reshaped by twelfth-century philosophers (including William of Conches) find further and bolder receptional molding in the *cansos* of Jaufre Rudel, Bernart de Ventadorn, and Raimbaut d'Aurenga. This final reception works in the service of bridging the sensuous world of the singer or lover and the transcendent world desired in Platonic thought. The rhetorical or poetic act of bridging, materialized in the *canso* itself, serves as analog to the Platonic notion of the "intermediary" *anima mundi* central to twelfth-century ruminations on the *Timaeus*.

Yet the absolute hegemony of Ovid in medieval reception warrants scrutiny, as do all decisive claims about the primacy of any monumental source for the propagation of a subsequent literary tradition. Our volume pays heed to this wisdom by commencing with a *remedia* of its own: Sarah Spence's "The Judgment of Aeneas, the Judgment of Paris, and the *Roman d'Eneas*" challenges the volume's (and the critical field's) receptionist enshrinement of Ovid's texts. She locates the problematic convergence of elegiac and amatory elements not in Ovid but in Vergil. Already in the *Aeneid*, and in advance of Ovid, Vergil has plotted a self-contrary discourse of desire that serves as ideological foundation (rather than the *formal*, epic prototype) for the twelfth-century *roman d'antiquité Eneas*. It is Vergil's problematic discursive confluence (one that uncannily anticipates Ovid)—and *not* the generic nature of epic—that takes part in shaping the equally strange character of the *Eneas*. Spence's analysis therefore disrupts our canonized precepts regarding genre, literary monuments, and reception.

Just as reversal can be taken as a pervasive process in the model of desire and ethics located by Warren Ginsberg and others in Ovid's amatory texts and their medieval commentary, so *displacement*, an allied tropological effect, controls the narrative structure of Marie de France's *Eliduc*. According to Sandra Pierson Prior's essay, "'Kar des dames est avenu / L'aventure': Displacing the Chivalric Hero in Marie de France's *Eliduc*," a series of spatial, physical, syntactical, narratological (especially regarding the textualist matter of poem titling), and psychological displacements in Marie's poem overrides the Ovidian impulse at the core of her amatory apparatus. Rather, the poem reinstates aesthetic and ideological properties consonant with the Breton or Celtic, orality-based, para-ecclesiastical traditions and values that underlie her material. Similarly, Nancy M. Reale's "Reading the Language of Love: Boccaccio's *Filostrato* as Intermediary between the *Commedia* and Chaucer's *Troilus and Criseyde*" rethinks ecclesiastical or religious elements that anchor Boccaccio's cultural place and his aesthetic contributions in terms of how they reflect Dantean precursors and Chaucerian postcursors. And on the note, once again, of displacement and reception, Cynthia Gravlee's "Presence, Absence, and Difference: Reception and Deception in *The Franklin's Tale*" begins with a look at the efficacy of Hans Robert Jauss's hermeneutics and then posits an open text for the modern receptor of Chaucer: the tale undoes the Franklin's attempts to provide a definitive discourse on gender, love, desire, courtship, and marriage. The ethical constants on which these institutions base themselves for the Franklin find the continual foregrounding, and therefore the demystification, of their binary oppositions.

In addition, the volume offers work that takes up the discursivity of desire and persuasion in terms of the new textualist or new philological treatment of manuscripts containing the literature of love's paramount texts. In "Discourse Desired: Desire, Subjectivity and *Mouvance* in *Can vei la lauzeta mover*," Simon Gaunt studies a problematic manuscript tradition—that of Bernart de Ventadorn's most famous lyric, which, with virtually no medieval witnesses, has been made canonical through Carl Appel's 1915 edition alone. By examining the documentary legacy of various medieval manuscripts of *Can vei*, and in conjunction with Amelia Van Vleck's theory of the *canso* as a "moving text," a text that fluctuates in form among its manuscript witnesses,[21] Gaunt extrapolates a theory of how Bernart's lyrical subject is constructed and empowered through his discourse of desire. In turn, modern editorial practices, themselves acts of "discourse desired," determine Bernart's construction as the literature of love's prototypical desiring subject.

The foregoing tally of capsulizations accords with an order based more or less on methodological approach or thematic concurrence; yet the actual sequence of essays in the volume accords with chronological and linguistic or national tradition. Again I note that this is an heuristic device, one of convenience, rather than an assertion of genetic continuity among texts or historical periods. As the Contents indicates, we have grouped together pieces on Ovidian topoi or on the medieval Latinistic legacy of Ovid in part 1; pieces on the Old French *canso* and *lai* traditions in part 2; and pieces on the Chaucerian efflorescence of the fourteenth century in part 3. Despite the chronological, national, or linguistic lines of demarcation used here, connections and echoes felicitously occur among several of the pieces in the collection or among the three symmetrical book sections.

Taken together, the essays work to reshape modern readers' receptional horizon regarding the currency of Ovid in medieval and postmedieval Western culture in particular and of the "lovers' discourse" in general. This discourse, preeminently among all discourses, persists at first *appearing* to be self-evident while it is in truth fraught with complications, confusions, disjunctions, and aporias in need of affirmation and reconstitution. Such was the position of Barthes, who began his own *ars amatoria*, *A Lover's Discourse*, by noting:

> This discourse is spoken, perhaps, by thousands of subjects (who knows?) but warranted by no one; it is completely forsaken by the surrounding languages: ignored, disparaged, or derided by them, severed not only from authority but also from the mechanisms of authority (sciences, techniques, arts). Once a discourse is thus driven by its own momentum into the backwater of the "unreal," exiled from all gregarity, it has no recourse but to become the site, however exiguous, of an *affirmation*.[22]

Desiring Discourse does not of course exhaust the possibilities of the concurrent critical or theoretical meditation on the literature of love; no doubt, coverage of *all* the important examples of problematic love literature prior to Chaucer escapes the scope of any one volume. Our volume does, however, aim to push out the frontiers of those critical possibilities. And this is itself an "affirmational" and a political activity, for nowhere in the study of medieval literature has there been (until so recently) such an institutional drive for complacency—a drive for the collective notion that one particular tradition, that of the literature of love, existed according to apodictic and unilateral terms. Such a complacent view never held for, say, the literature of allegory or the metapoetic frame narrative, or for the epic supercharged by historiographic, philological, and ethnological forces or interventions.[23] The institutional bearings of this volume's response to the literature of love have come to reflect the heightened consciousness of gender in Western culture in large.

Notes

1. For the field of English studies in particular, Lewis's discussion of courtly love in *The Allegory of Love* (Oxford: Oxford University Press, 1936), 1–43, has long served as the most sweeping and powerful program of introduction to the literature of love. See also W. P. Ker, *Epic and Romance: Essays on Medieval Literature*, 2nd. ed. (London: Macmillan, 1926); Alexander J. Denomy, *The Heresy of Courtly Love* (New York: D. X. McMullen, 1947); and Denis de Rougement, *Love in the Western World*, rev. and aug. ed. (New York: Pantheon, 1956).

2. The scholarship of feminism, gender, and sexuality that treats the literature of love is already voluminous in itself. One exemplary essay collection that well represents such scholarship and thereby serves as a model for this volume is E. Jane Burns and Roberta L. Krueger, eds., *Courtly Ideology and Woman's Place in Medieval French Literature*, special issue of *Romance Notes* 25.3 (spring 1985). Note too that the current critical institution's reshaped apprehension of amatory literature involves not only redefinitions and rediscoveries of the feminine in relation to the masculine, but redefinitions of same-sex sociality as well. For historical foundations see John Boswell, *Same-Sex Unions in Pre-Modern Europe* (New York: Villiard, 1994).

3. See Alexandre Leupin, *Barbarolexis: Medieval Writing and Sexuality* (Cambridge, Mass., and London: Harvard University Press, 1989), 6–7, where Leupin writes: "Beginning with the prescriptions of rhetoric and the desire of woman (in all of the senses implied by the genitive), literature turns [the double lack of language's 'unfitness' to name God and the desire of female climax] into the resources of its own production: the literary text transforms a dual impossibility into an affirmation of the desire to write."

4. Evelyn Birge Vitz, *Medieval Narrative and Modern Narratology: Subjects and Objects of Desire* (New York and London: New York University Press, 1989), 3.

5. Vitz, 3. It is important to note, however, that Vitz's fine study ultimately treats "desire" in broad narratological terms rather than in the thematic terms (amatory literature) that interest the essays in this volume. Her chapter titled "Desire and Causality in Medieval Narrative: the *Roland*, Thomas's *Tristan*, and *Du segretain moine*" (176–212) deals more with the narratological functions of plot generation. This generation depends on what characters *want* rather than on their interior motives and constitutions.

6. Marilynn R. Desmond, guest ed., "Ovid in Medieval Culture," *Mediaevalia: A Journal of Medieval Studies* 13 (1987); Charles Martindale, ed., *Ovid Renewed* (Cambridge: Cambridge University Press, 1988); Ralph J. Hexter, *Ovid and Medieval Schooling* (Munich: Bei der Arbeo-Gesellschaft, 1986).

7. See Joseph Solodow, *The World of Ovid's "Metamorphoses"* (Chapel Hill: University of North Carolina Press, 1988); Peter Allen, *The Art of Love: Amatory Fiction from Ovid to the Romance of the Rose* (Philadelphia: University of Pennsylvania Press, 1992); and Molly Myerowitz, *Ovid's Games of Love* (Detroit: Wayne State University

Press, 1985) for a sampling of some of the voluminous and strong work now produced in Ovid studies.

8. For an accessible description of Jakobson's communicational schema (which contains the components "addresser," "addressee," "contact," "message," and "code"), see Terence Hawkes, *Structuralism and Semiotics* (Berkeley: University of California Press, 1977), 82–87.

9. See Jan Ziolkowski, *Alan of Lille's Grammar of Sex* (Cambridge: Medieval Academy of America, 1985); and Dennis Baron, *Grammar and Gender* (New Haven: Yale University Press, 1986).

10. Central to the essays in this volume is the idea that Ovid's love situations, particularly in the amatory poems (but less so in the *Metamorphoses*), transcend this mechanical social relationship. Already in Ovid we find the coded social representation of women in love situations as active agents. The resolute simplification of Ovidian social protocols comes with their idiosyncratic medieval reception, especially in the work of Andreas Capellanus. See Michael Calabrese, *Chaucer's Ovidian Arts of Love* (Gainesville: University of Florida Press, 1994), passim, for Chaucer's selective salvaging of Ovid's sophisticated and subtle social apparatus concerning rhetoric and seduction.

11. Structuralism, however, has since attempted to work through a far more thorough semiology of desire and love. See for example Algirdas Julien Greimas and Jacques Fontanille, *The Semiotics of Passions: From States of Affairs to States of Feelings*, trans. Paul Perron and Frank Collins (Minneapolis: University of Minnesota Press, 1993). The study provides a complicated but stunning semiotic analysis of emotions in general and of canonical literary texts that thematize strong passions. Vitz's study, cited above (see n.4), is one of the more lucid and innovative applications of structural semiotics to the medieval literature of desire; it is also a forthright and sustained critique of the method's shortcomings. See especially 6–9.

12. Roland Barthes, *The Lover's Discourse*, trans. Richard Howard (New York: Hill and Wang, 1982), 188–89.

13. Toril Moi's analysis of this configuration has proven indispensable. See her "Desire in Language: Andreas Capellanus and the Controversy of Courtly Love," in *Medieval Literature: Criticism, Ideology & History*, ed. David Aers (Brighton: Harvester, 1986), 11–33.

14. In short, the title of this volume echoes the grammatical instabilities inherent in the gendered poetics of desire or in the structural allegory spoken of above.

15. Harold Bloom's theoretical descriptions of influence and misprision are now commonplace. See for instance his *The Anxiety of Influence* (Oxford: Oxford University Press, 1973).

16. I need not rehearse the vast scholarship on the ideological or literary development of selfhood, individuality, and bourgeois culture in the twelfth century. As for modifications in Europe's ideology of the feminine, R. Howard Bloch's appraisal of post–eleventh-century improvements in women's economic and legal standing and the ensuing emergence of the courtly love tradition serves as a fine overview. See his *Medieval Misogyny and the Invention of Western Romantic Love* (Chicago and London: The University of Chicago Press, 1991).

17. Hans Robert Jauss, *Toward an Aesthetics of Reception*, trans. Timothy Bahti (Minneapolis: University of Minnesota Press, 1982).

18. The work, for example, of Jane Gallop or Nancy K. Miller well represents this trend in modern cultural and literary studies; Caroline Walker Bynum has made the most incisive interventions regarding the ideology of the female body in medieval theology and

historiography. See Jane Gallop, *Thinking Through the Body* (New York: Columbia University Press, 1988); Nancy K. Miller, *Getting Personal* (New York and London: Routledge, 1991); E. Jane Burns, *Bodytalk: When Women Speak in Old French Literature* (Philadelphia: University of Pennsylvania Press, 1993); and Caroline Walker Bynum, *Fragmentation and Redemption: Essays on Gender and the Human Body in Medieval Religion* (New York: Zone Books, 1991). My thanks to Jeffrey Williams for formulating the "successivist" model I employ here for tracking recent movements in theory.

19. See H. Marshall Leicester Jr., *The Disenchanted Self: Representing the Subject in the "Canterbury Tales"* (Berkeley and Los Angeles: University of California Press, 1990), 221–382.

20. See Barrie Ruth Straus, guest ed., *Skirting the Texts: Feminism's Re-Readings of Medieval and Renaissance Texts, Exemplaria* 4.1 (spring 1992).

21. See Amelia E. Van Vleck, *Memory and Recreation in Troubadour Lyric* (Berkeley: University of California Press, 1991).

22. Barthes, 1.

23. Narratology, for example, has thrived on the formalist articulations of framed or embedded narratives; such critical production enjoyed the inevitable link with the critical institution's idolization or fetishizing of Chaucer and *The Canterbury Tales*. Allegory theory has moved through several arcane and self-promoting, self-mystifying discourses—from Romanticist aesthetics through Benjaminian cultural materialism and (in turn) demanian deconstruction. Such institutional movements have always proclaimed their own complexity, arcaneness, and centrality to the critical field in large. Contemporary discussion of the literature of love now needs to do the same.

1
Desiring through Ovid, Ancient and Medieval

The Judgment of Aeneas,
the Judgment of Paris, and the *Roman d'Eneas*

SARAH SPENCE

When Aeneas kills Turnus in the scene that ends Vergil's *Aeneid*, he poses a moral question that remains unresolved to this day: Did he do the right thing? Was there any way to avoid the brutal slaughter of his enemy, and thereby follow his father's advice to spare the suppliant, while still remaining true to earlier vows of loyalty made to his ally Evander? Yet to read the end of the first great literary reworking of the poem, the *roman d'antiquité*, *Eneas*, the ending would seem to have made little impact, for there the poet makes only vague and unsatisfactory allusion to the end of the Augustan epic. While Vergil's poem remains poised on the horns of a moral dilemma, the *Eneas* poet lands squarely on sure, if somewhat pedestrian, moral ground:

> Eneas ot le mialz d'Itaire,
> une cité comence a faire,
> bons murs i fist et fort donjon.
> Albe mist a sa cité non;
> molt par fu riche, molt fu granz,
> ses anpires dura molt anz. . . .
>
> (10131–36)

> Molt furent tuit de grant pooir
> et descendirent d'oir an oir.
> desi que nez an fu Remus,
> de cel linage, et Romulus;
> frere furent et molt fort home.
> Cil firent la cité de Rome,
> que Romulus li anposa
> son nom, que primes li dona.
>
> (10149–56)

[Eneas had the best part of Italy, and began to build a city; strong walls he made there and a sturdy fortress. His city was called Alba. It was very rich and big and his rule lasted a long time. . . . They were all powerful rulers and descended from heir to heir until Remus came from this line, together with Romulus. They were brothers and very strong men. They founded the city of Rome to which Romulus first gave his name.][1]

All recent critics of the *Eneas* would argue that its author was a remarkably good reader of Vergil, armed with his own agenda, without a doubt, but still a very perceptive and intelligent critic. To read the ending, however, one would have to say that the author fumbled, that he missed the enigmatic importance of the ending as Vergil proffered it. It is in part because of this apparent lapse that critics have argued that the *Eneas*, while borrowing much of the epic apparatus from Vergil, in fact takes little of the content, especially at the end; that, really, the poem is divided in its provenance, drawing form from Vergil and content largely from the elegiac works of Ovid.[2] As the English translator of the *Eneas*, John Yunck, insightfully points out, the *Eneas* is not the least bit interested in Roman or even epic issues; its true concern seems to lie with the love ultimately shared between Eneas and Lavine.[3] But this, to my mind, raises a larger question, namely, why use Vergil at all? Why use a genre and rely on a source that ostensibly has little to offer him? This, in fact, can be taken as the critical formulation of the problematics of reception in medieval amatory literature.

While the ending of Vergil's poem apparently offers little to the conclusion of its twelfth-century offspring, it, arguably, offers a great deal to its beginning. One of the most striking innovations made in the *Eneas* is the lengthy digression at the start of the poem on the Judgment of Paris, an addition so obviously important and underscored that it has been used as a programmatic approach to the poem as a whole. I would suggest a different tack, however. My reading will propose that the Judgment of Paris is important not as innovative but as renovative, in that it represents a reworking of the central moment of judgment in the *Aeneid*, the choice Aeneas makes at the end between Evander's son Pallas and Turnus. But whereas the choice made by Aeneas is really a non-choice, a damned-if-you-do, damned-if-you-don't scenario, in the *Eneas* it becomes a forum for self-creation and expansion.[4]

Simon Gaunt has recently argued that the poem is an example of the transition between epic and romance; he bases his thesis on the changing relationships asserted among men and between men and women.[5] He states that "the *Eneas* provides a bridge between epic and romance, between two ideologies, enacting a conscious movement towards an ideology in which love and sexuality regulate the bellicose tendencies of the medieval aristocratic male rather than male bonding within a male brotherhood."[6] Gaunt sees the poem dividing at the death of Camille: the lines preceding her death belonging to the epic section, those following, the romance. Eneas, in short, becomes a romance hero, but only at the end of the story.

I would like to follow in Gaunt's footsteps and offer a reading that, likewise, divides the poem at the death of Camille, but my argument will follow slightly different lines. It is my contention that the *Eneas* poet chose the *Aeneid* as his primary source precisely because he saw the Latin poem as one in which the epic and the elegiac were unresolved. In the section preceding Camille's burial, the author discusses this problem in the context of his source; in the section following Camille's burial, he offers up a new resolution for the epic and the elegiac by forging the outlines of a new genre, romance. In making this point I will also argue that he uses Vergil not for his epic form but because he reads the *Aeneid* as the exploration of the uneasy place allotted love and elegy in the world of the epic.[7] He sees Vergil, in other words, as an author of desire, before Ovid. And he sees his own work as offering an answer to the Vergilian dilemma of epic or elegy by suggesting a way to combine love and war and so to resolve Vergil's ultimate dilemma.

* * *

It is, in fact, the impossibility of making a good moral choice that freights the ending of the *Aeneid* with such tragedy. For, as Vergil has set it up, Aeneas qua Aeneas can only lose. As he stands face-to-face with the suppliant enemy Turnus, we hear the echo of Priam appealing to Achilles for the return of his son Hector's body in book 22 of the *Iliad,* even as Aeneas hears as well the voice of his own father instructing him in the Underworld of book 6 that sparing the suppliant will be what makes the Romans different, unique, even, and powerful. But the sight of Pallas's buckle on Turnus's shoulder, and the memory of the young boy killed by Turnus and the promise Aeneas made and subsequently broke to Pallas's father Evander to protect him and return him home (again, reverberations of the *Iliad*) echo back and leave Aeneas with an impossible moral choice: kill Turnus and give up all hope of being the first Roman hero or show Turnus mercy and leave unavenged the wrongful death of his friend, surrogate son, and, some have argued, represssed erotic attachment.[8] This is truly a horrible choice, and at its other side rest consequences no less significant than those resulting from Paris's fateful choice of Venus.

Moreover, the consequences for Aeneas are more dire than those faced
by Paris because the choice has been internalized. Whichever choice
Aeneas makes, some part of him will die; Turnus and Pallas each
represent aspects of Aeneas's self. Killing either will also kill Aeneas
because he is defined throughout the text in terms of just this tension.
Especially if the attachment with Pallas is allowed its full erotic weight,
the choice between Turnus and Pallas becomes a choice between his
public and private selves, between duty and desire. Whatever choice he
makes, he will suffer, and the hero as defined in the *Aeneid* will cease to
exist. The text of the *Aeneid* had no alternative but to end here, with the
demise of its epic/elegiac hero. Whether you read his decision as right or
wrong, optimistic or pessimistic, Aeneas as Aeneas is destroyed by the
judgment he makes.[9]

In the *Eneas*, by contrast, the hero thrives at the end. He is happily
married; has children, land and riches; and lives out the classic, romance,
comic end. How can this be? Somehow, what led to the destruction of the
hero in the *Aeneid* is turned to his creation in the *Eneas*. The theme of
choice—the right choice—that is rung so loudly at the start of the
romance by the long exposition on the Judgment of Paris is clearly one
that carries through to the end.

The key to the difference, I think, lies in an observation made, but not
elaborated on, by Simon Gaunt. In the midst of a section on the
parallelism that the *Eneas* author asserts between Pallas and Camille,
Gaunt observes that "Camille's death is specifically an act of revenge for
Pallas's."[10] He cites as evidence line 7388; I will quote 7388–91:

> Molt est Pallas chier comparez,
> un chevalier que lor ocis;
> molt lo m'ont or bien an lou mis,
> lo contrepan m'an ont randu

[Pallas is very dearly bought, a knight of theirs whom I killed. Now they have
given me this instead; they have reimbursed me with his equivalent.]

But here the *Eneas* poet swerves noticeably from his source, for in the
Aeneid it is not Camilla but Turnus who is killed out of revenge for
Pallas's death: the much-discussed last lines of the epic focus precisely
on this act of seeming vengeance:

> Pallas te hoc vulnere, Pallas
> immolat et poenam scelerato ex sanguine sumat.

(12.948–49)

[Pallas sacrifices you with this wound; Pallas takes compensation from this guilty blood.][11]

In the *Aeneid*, Camilla's death, by contrast, is not related specifically to that of Pallas; rather, if anything, it is assimilated to the deaths of Nisus and Euryalus, who, like Camilla, die for love of booty (9:384–85). Yet, while there is no connection made between Camilla and Pallas in the *Aeneid*, and therefore no connection asserted between their deaths, there is a connection made at the end of the *Aeneid* between the death of Camilla and the death of the character Vergil does blame for the death of Pallas, namely Turnus. The last line of the poem, "vitaque cum gemitu fugit indignata sub umbras," is, as many critics have noted, the same line used for the death of Camilla in 11:831.[12] For Vergil, this identification merely serves to underscore a quasi-erotic relationship he has developed throughout the poem between Camilla and Turnus in their roles as general and soldier, as well as a possible further relationship in the cause of their deaths by *furor*. But for the author of the *Eneas* I would propose that something very different is taking place. By assigning to Camille the Vergilian motive for the death of Turnus, the author of the twelfth-century text folds his source in on itself, collapsing the figures of Camille and Turnus and allowing the final scene of the *Aeneid* to play itself out in the center of the *Eneas*. The end of the *Eneas*, in other words, is not flat because the author missed the point of his source. On the contrary, it is flat relative to its source because he transposed the moral issues presented there to the central portion of his work. Camille, in short, replaces Turnus and, in so doing, frees up both the hero and his text.

The displacement of the ending to the middle of the poem is not the only displacement of its kind that occurs. Rather, even as Camille takes on the onus borne by Turnus of Pallas's death, so Pallas's burial is linked by juxtaposition to Dido's death and lack of proper mourning. As with Camille and Turnus, there is precedent in the *Aeneid* for this as well. There the reader is allowed a catharsis of sorts as the text moves abruptly from Dido's death on the funeral pyre in Carthage to the funeral games Aeneas and his men engage in on Sicily to celebrate the anniversary of his father's death. A similar catharsis is perpetrated in the *Eneas,* but this time instead of funeral games we get an actual funeral, and the laments Aeneas pours over Pallas can be readily understood as applying equally to Dido:[13]

> ja mes n'iert jors, ne me repente
> que ça venis ansanble moi.
> Malvese garde ai fait de toi,

quant tu sanz moi recoillis mort;
g'en ai les corpes et le tort;
. . . .
Bele faiture, gente chose,
si com soloil flestist la rose,
si t'a la morz tot tost plessié
et tot flesti et tot changié.
De tant est plus mes cors dolanz,
quant tu ne m'oz ne m'entenz;
tu ne me respondroies mie.

(6148–52; 6193–99)

[I will never not regret that I brought you here with me. Poor care have I
shown you, since without me you received your death; I bear the guilt and the
shame . . . Handsome, refined one, as the sun withers the rose, so has death
rapidly unraveled you and withered and changed all. So much the more does
my heart sorrow, since you neither see nor hear me; nor will you ever answer
me.]

If nothing else, Pallas's burial represents a narratological completion
of Dido's story that enables the story to progress. Linking Pallas and
Dido in this way also allows the text to suggest, gently, that Camille's
death is payment not only for Pallas but also, in some indirect way, for
Dido as well.

But if Camille's death is payment for the deaths of Pallas and Dido,
then it is possible to see the entire first part of the romance as a playing
out not of the Judgment of Paris but rather of the Judgment of Aeneas.
That is, if Camille's death is conflated with Turnus's as revenge for
Dido's memory as well as Pallas's, then the whole first part of the poem
can be seen as a gloss on the final scene of the *Aeneid*.

By conflating Turnus and Camille—giving Camille the moral baggage
Vergil saves for Turnus—the *Eneas* poet grants to Camilla weight that
Vergil specifically denies her. It is obvious on any reading of the
romance that Camille is unlike her Latin counterpart. Critics from
Auerbach to Huchet have granted her priority, as, of course, the text itself
does, both in its extended description of her and the lengthy and
marvelous description of her tomb.[14] The question that forces itself on
any reader is, What textual justification is there for granting Camille such
pride of place, especially when we consider that as described, she is
neither Vergilian nor, in any elegiac sense, Ovidian? And, given that she
never meets the hero of the work, Eneas, how can we justify her lengthy
inclusion? Unlike Dido, her role in the text is explained neither by her

source nor by her function within this text so focused on love. In short, what is she doing there?

In order to show further how Camille functions, we need to look again at Gaunt's suggestion that the poem divides between epic and romance at the burial of Camille. If what is implied by this assertion is not that the two genres are opposed but rather that they are defined in terms of each other—that we are to see epic, in other words, through the lens of romance—then it offers us a new way of studying the work in relation to its source. For, with some legitimacy, one can approach Vergil's poem in exactly this way, as an epic understood in terms of romance, or as a pastoral elegy of epic length. From the opening line, "arma virumque cano," where the verb, *cano*, is drawn not from an epic lexicon but, rather, a pastoral one, through the love stories of Dido and Aeneas, Turnus and Lavinia and even Nisus and Euryalus, to, finally, the choice Aeneas makes at the end when he is faced with the memory of the death of his Arcadian friend Pallas, an emblem of innocence and purity, the epic plays frequently with the suggestion that epic and elegy, especially pastoral elegy, present a potentially unresolvable tension and that Vergil's aim is to bring the two into some sort of harmony.

Let me be clear about this. The *Aeneid* is not a romance; nor is it really an elegy. But neither is it "pure" epic. Rather, it constantly brings together the themes of elegy with those of epic—of Italy with Troy—and works toward a synthesis of the sets of values each represents. With the death of Turnus the text suggests that such a synthesis is, for the moment, beyond the grasp of the poet, his genre, and perhaps his ruler. If there is, in fact, an emblem for this synthesis, it is, significantly, Camilla herself, whose final attribute in her opening description is "pastoralem praefixa cuspide myrtum" [pastoral myrtle pike tipped with steel] (7:817).[15] Yet she too, in both the Roman and French versions, dies a tragic and morally enigmatic death.

If the first half of the *Eneas* is perceived, as Gaunt suggests, as the epic of romance, then it represents a decent and fair reading of the whole of the *Aeneid*. By the same token, if the second half of the poem is seen as pure romance, then it quite possibly represents a resolution to the problems posed at the end of Vergil's work. What one might reasonably expect, given this, is that the first half of the twelfth-century work would set up a reading of Vergil's uneasy alliance of epic and elegy that the second half can then resolve. More specifically, the first half of the poem might be seen as a reading of the Augustan epic; the second half a solution to its perceived problems.[16]

Yet the displacement that suggests a blurring of Paris's and Aeneas's judgments—in which the leading figures of choice become women instead of men—provides a mediation that distances that judgment from the hero. By focusing the work on the women killed, the deaths, in short, become less tragic. What is being killed off is not a part of the hero but, rather, his negative others. In mediating the choice by focusing it on women instead of men, the text presents a series of defining and negative others whose deaths serve not to destroy the hero but rather to construct him.

I would propose that Camille is allowed to become as central as she does—more central even than Dido—because she represents a mediated version of Eneas. That is, she is allowed such a major part in the text because she represents a playing out of one version of Eneas and so is, in fact, ultimately derived from Vergil. Moreover, her death and burial loom as large as they do because they come to symbolize the action that enables the *Eneas* and its eponymous hero to progress beyond the point where the Latin source breaks off.

For Camille is not only Turnus but, arguably, Aeneas as well, as he is when he leaves Dido. At that point Dido seems to suggest that Eneas can only perceive things in terms of war, whereas she sees things in terms of love. In a sense, her parting words indicate that she thinks he is leaving her because she has not been interested enough in battle:

> Sire, por coie m'avez traie?
> —Ge non ai, voir, la moie amie.
> —Mesfis vos ge onques de rien?
> —Moi n'avez vos fait el que bien.
> —Destruis ge Troie?—Nenil, Greus.
> —Fu ce par moi?—Mes par les deus.
> —Ai ge vos vostre pere ocis?
> —Nenil, dame, gel vos plevis.
>
> (1749–56)

[Lord, why have you betrayed me? —Really I haven't, my sweet—Have I ever caused you any harm?—You have done only good for me—Did I destroy Troy—No, the Greeks did—Was I the cause [read, am I Helen?]—No, the gods were—Did I kill your father?—No, my lady, I promise you.]

Camille, by contrast, presents herself as having prowess only on the battlefield:

> mialz sai abatre un chevalier
> que acoler ne dosnoier;
> ne me sai pas combatre anverse.
>
> (7123–25)

[I know how to fight a knight better that I do to hug him or love him; I do not know how to fight on my back.]

Camille is precisely what Dido is not; but more importantly, she is presented here as the perfect match, even double, for Eneas as he was when he left Dido. Through allowing Camille to play out that aspect, or version, of Eneas to its logical extreme, and then to kill her off, the text, once again, as in the case of Dido, uses the female, rejected character as a means of allowing the hero to develop away from the imbalance of epic and into the moderative synthesis of romance.

In *Speculum de l'autre femme,* Luce Irigaray speaks to exactly this issue, as she critiques Freud's depiction of women as man's mirror and defining, negative other. Referring to the feminine as "le noir" and a "sorte d'alter ego inversé,"[17] she explains how man's subject is dependent upon the feminine object as its ground. Perhaps clearest is her assertion that the concept of penis envy is constructed out of the need to reassure the male of the existence, even preeminence, of his penis by virtue of the fact that she is lacking one, that she, in Irigaray's reading of Freud, is a castrated male. Her very castration ensures the male of the presence of his penis, as she reflects him while also constructing him out of her lack. This dual emphasis on sameness (she mirrors him in his maleness) and difference (while pointing out his presence through her lack; what Irigaray calls "la dialectique phallocentrique" [60]) places the feminine in the shadow of the male even as it makes her essential to his existence. As she says, "Le *rien* de sexe, le *ne pas* de sexe, et de sexuel, sera supporté par la femme" (60).

It is along these theoretical lines that I would argue that Eneas as a character is constructed out of three negative, female others: Dido, Camille, and Lavine. Even as Eneas's rejection of Dido merely serves to redefine him in terms that come to reflect—create?—Camille, so Camille's enactment of the role Eneas has chosen and the death that results from its very limitations and two-dimensionality serve to redefine him yet again. To put it slightly differently, Dido and Eneas are similar when they meet; when they part, he has separated himself from her and is quite alive while she lies dead. The figure of Camille is allowed then to play out the values he has purportedly espoused in leaving Dido and to play them out to their logical, read mortal, end. Both Dido and Camille are versions of Eneas, even as Pallas and Turnus are versions of Aeneas, but because the French characters are feminized, they are removed from him as object from subject and so in being killed they merely help to refine as they redefine his subject.

The epic choice of Aeneas that marks the close of book 12 and the

destruction of the Trojan hero becomes in the *Eneas* a romantic choice as
the objects of that choice are displaced from men to women. As a result,
the elegiac thread of the *Aeneid* is emphasized and the epic is presented
in terms of elegy. By shifting the emphases (and, again, it is only that
elegy and epic are equally present in the *Aeneid*), the synthesis between
the two that Vergil was seeking in his text is, in fact, presented as
achievable in the romance. The burial of Camille, like the burials of Dido
and Pallas, represents the final repression of aspects of the hero and his
text that ultimately serve to create, or re-create, him as the ideal romance
hero. Yet, while the *Aeneid* forces its hero to choose between the two
polarized figures of Pallas and Turnus, the *Eneas* offers its knight three
possibilities, represented by Dido, Camille, and Lavine. What
distinguishes Lavine from the other two is that she is able to see, and thus
construct, Eneas as a synthesis of both love and war. The famous
passages in which she describes falling in love with him clearly bring
together the amatory and the martial as love is seen, finally, as a form of
sublimated warfare:

> Lavine fu an la tor sus,
> d'une fenestre garda jus,
> vit Eneam qui fu desoz,
> forment l'a esgardé sor toz.
> Molt li sanbla et bel et gent
> . . . .
> Amors l'a de son dart ferue;
>
> (8047–51; 8057)

[Lavine was up in the tower and from a window looked down and saw Eneas
who was below; deeply she stared at him over all. He seemed the most
handsome and refined to her . . . Love struck her with his arrow.]

It is the combined effects of looking with rapture and being struck by
Love's arrow that create the romance between Lavine and Eneas or, more
specifically, enable Lavine to create the romance hero. The rejection of
Eneas's extreme representations in Dido as pure elegy and Camille as
pure epic have opened the space for his construction out of the
intermediate representation of Lavine in love.

By calquing the final choice of Aeneas onto the expanded triple
choice, or judgment, of Paris, the author of the *Eneas* is able to use his
text to offer a new interpretation of his source. While the *Aeneid* ends
with an image of implosion, as its hero is forced to self-destruct, Eneas
emerges from this ordeal unscathed, bettered even, as the full
embodiment of the romance hero who can modulate readily between love

and war. The social, psychological, and narratological construction of Eneas depends upon the mutual construction of the three main female figures, with Camille and then Lavine taking primacy. The figures who represent Eneas throughout the text, because they are all women, are able to be sloughed off as so many snakeskins. Aeneas should have been so lucky.

Notes

1. The text of the *Eneas* is that of J.-J. Salverda de Grave, 2 vols. (Paris: Classiques Français du Moyen Age, 1929). The translation is mine.

2. See, particularly, Edmond Faral, *Recherches sur les sources latines des contes et romans courtois du Moyen Age* (Paris: Champion, 1913), 119–57.

3. *Eneas: A Twelfth-Century Romance*, trans. John A. Yunck (New York: Columbia University Press, 1974), 81 n. 29; 97 n. 47.

4. Several recent studies have pointed to the way in which the poem seems to focus on the three goddesses involved in the Judgment of Paris—Juno, Minerva and Venus—and their mortal counterparts—Dido, Camilla and Lavinia. While I disagree with this reading as a formulaic program for the work as a whole, I do agree that the twelfth-century work foregrounds the role of women and female goddesses more than its source. Best among these is the article by Michelle A. Freeman, "The Roman d'Eneas: Implications of the Prologue," *Medioevo Romanzo* 8 (1983): 37–50. For a list of other studies that assert such a relationship, see Simon Gaunt, "From Epic to Romance: Gender and Sexuality in the *Roman d'Eneas*," *Romanic Review* 33 (1992): 1–27, esp. 10 n. 24

5. See Gaunt, passim. A similar argument is made by William Burgwinkle, "Knighting the Classical Hero: Homo/Hetero Affectivity in *Eneas*," *Exemplaria* 5 (1993): 1–43.

6. Gaunt, 9.

7. Stephen G. Nichols argues that the text "pointedly depicts the onset of love, then quickly deflects it." See "Amorous Imitation: Bakhtin, Augustine and Le Roman d'Eneas," in *Romance: Generic Transformations from Chrétien de Troyes to Cervantes*, ed. Kevin Brownlee and Marina Scordilis Brownlee (Hanover: University Press of New England, 1985), 71. Reading the romance against the double background of Vergil's *Aeneid* as filtered through Augustine's *Confessions*, Nichols argues that "for all the success of the Eneas-poet in transcoding Augustine's conversionary theoretic into a confessional doctrine of human love, he still could not entirely control the markers of desire" (72).

8. See Michael Putnam, "Possessiveness, Sexuality and Heroism in the *Aeneid*," *Vergilius* 31 (1985): 1–21.

9. It is this quality of the text, no doubt, that has led to its widespread allegorization. On this, see, above all, J. W. Jones Jr., "The Allegorical Traditions of the Aeneid," in *Vergil at 2000: Commemorative Essays on the Poet and his Influence* (New York: AMS, 1986), 107–32.

10. Gaunt, 12.

11. The text of the *Aeneid* is that of R. A. B. Mynors (Oxford: University Press, 1974). Translation is mine.

12. Servius was probably the first to note this fact: *Servii Grammatici qui feruntur in Vergilii carmine commentarii*, ed. Thilo and Hagen (Hildesheim: Olms, 1961), 2: 649–50.

13. Eneas's eulogy to Pallas may even be derived in part from two speeches of Aeneas to Dido in the *Aeneid*, one from book 4: 333–61, in which Aeneas states that he will never regret remembering Dido, the other from book 6: 456–71, when he laments the fact that she refuses to speak to him in the Underworld.

14. Erich Auerbach, *Literary Language and Its Public in Late Antiquity and in the Middle Ages* (London: Routledge and Kegan Paul, 1965), 184–333; J.-C. Huchet, *Le Roman médiéval* (Paris: Presses Universitaires de France, 1984), esp. 76–78.

15. See Michael C. J. Putnam, *The Poetry of the Aeneid: Four Studies in Imaginative Unity and Design* (Cambridge: Harvard University Press, 1966; rpt. Ithaca: Cornell University Press, 1986), 192.

16. For further information on the *Eneas* as offering solutions to problems in the *Aeneid*, see Marilynn Desmond, *Reading Dido: Gender, Textuality and the Medieval Aeneid* (Minneapolis: University of Minnesota Press, 1994), chap. 3.

17. Luce Irigaray, *Speculum de l'autre femme* (Paris: Edition de minuit, 1974), 20.

Justifying Love: The Classical *Recusatio* in Medieval Love Literature

JOAN G. HAAHR

Quare hec tria, salus videlicet, venus et virtus, apparent esse illa
magnalia que sint maxime pertractanda, hoc est ea que maxime sunt ad ista,
ut armorum probitas, amoris accensio et directio voluntatis.

—Dante, *De Vulgari Eloquentia*[1]

In the *proem* to the third and most erotic of the five books of *Troilus and Criseyde*, Chaucer invokes not only Venus, the natural symbol of benevolent love and generation, but also Calliope, the muse of epic poetry and traditional first and "optimae vocis" of the nine sisters:[2]

> Caliope, thi vois be now present,
> For now is nede: sestow nought my destresse,
> How I mot telle a-non right the gladnesse
> Of Troilus, to Venus heryinge?

(3.45–46)[3]

While adequate inspiration for the lover, in that she vanquishes even the most powerful opponents in love's wars ("Ye fierse Mars apaisen of his ire . . . ," [3.22ff]), Venus is apparently not powerful enough for the love-*poet*, who is inevitably forced to consult non-amatory poetic models for formal and thematic inspiration and support. Chaucer, like amatory poets from the time of "Venus clerk Ovide,"[4] must acknowledge that the literature of love, even while it displaces authorized ideas (as Venus, the goddess of love, overpowered Mars, the god of war), tends to remain dependent on authorized forms, often mimicking, as it subverts, these more conventional narrative and poetic structures.[5] In this paper, my purpose is to explore ways in which classical and medieval amatory poets—in what Moshe Lazar has designated "a general aesthetics of the subversive"—asserted the priority of erotic themes, even while acknowledging their deviancy, and worked to confound literary expectations. In so doing, I will focus on the rhetorical device called *recusatio* (or, "refusal" to obey convention) by means of which Ovid and other Roman amorists introduced the issue of the poetic legitimacy of amatory subjects. I will further argue that what was, for Ovid and the classical elegists, an explicitly rhetorical tactic became, for medieval poets, part of a much broader process for creating new types of courtly literature emphasizing private and secular experience.

In raising the issue of Calliope's service to Venus, Chaucer is alluding to the distinction between public and private poetic discourse (that is, between epic and lyric), of which love poets had been conscious from earliest times. A well-known (indeed perhaps the most famous) example of the *recusatio* occurs at the beginning of the *Amores,* where Ovid—impudently echoing the first line of the *Aeneid*—playfully admits that Cupid has undermined the poet's epic ambitions by "laming" him and acknowledges his thematic and formal violations of conventional poetic values:

> Arma graui numero uiolentaque bella parabam
> edere, materia conueniente modis.
> par erat inferior uersus; risisse Cupido
> dicitur atque unum surripuisse pedem.

(1.1.1–4)

[Arms and violent wars, I was prepared to sound forth, in solemn numbers, with meter suited to matter—the second verse equal to the first. But, as they say, Cupid, laughing, stole away one foot.][6]

Ovid's characteristically tongue-in-cheek "confession" admits to two kinds of impropriety: topical and formal. It questions both the superiority of epic (with its presumed articulation of serious public values) over elegy (with its focus on private passions) and the supposed superiority of the epic hexameter (with its dignity and flexibility) over the elegiac distich.[7]

Ovid's lines playfully introduce the issues surrounding the poetic legitimacy of private concerns that engaged amatory poets—both classical and medieval—for the next fifteen hundred years. Like Ovid, these poets relied on the *recusatio* to generate alternative rhetorical and narrative strategies for justifying dissent from ostensibly more serious collective and institutional principles embodied in epic and other moral poetry. It is no accident that the medieval literary tradition of *fin'amors* is coincident with early signs of humanism, love and its discourses invariably inspiring a poetics of individualism and subjectivity.[8]

Although the *recusatio* was to prove particularly useful as an amatory trope, it first appeared as a subspecies of the *captatio benevolentiae* (the so-called "modesty topos"), frequently with political overtones.[9] Originating in the Alexandrian Callimachus's contemptuous rejection of stock mythological and historical subjects, the Augustan *recusatio* more commonly lamented the poet's feelings of inadequacy to celebrate the character and deeds of a *contemporary* political or cultural hero—the modest disclaimer characteristically serving as a pretext for doing the thing disclaimed. For example, Horace, in *Epistles* 2.1, first proclaiming himself incapable of praising Caesar, goes on to enumerate the emperor's accomplishments.[10] In *Odes* 4.2 (*Pindarum quisquis*), Horace praises Pindar's "daring dithyrambs and . . . measures freed from rule" ("seu per audaces nova dithyrambos / verba devolvit numerisque fertur / lege solutis"), disclaiming his own verses "fashion(ed) . . . with excessive toil"; yet he then projects his own panegyric to Caesar through Pindar's imagined voice. A similar *recusatio* opens *Odes* 1.6 (*Scriberis Vario*), where Horace, extolling Varius's heroic verses as better implements for panegyric than his own lyric voice, continues with praise of Agrippa formulated in language as extravagant as the Varian "Homeric flight" ("Maeonii carminis aliti").[11]

Gordon Williams suggests that the political *recusatio*, while it may initially have been inspired by Augustus's proclaimed eagerness for epic celebration of his rule, was ultimately a rhetorical stratagem for writing about imperial politics from personal rather than epic perspectives.[12] Increasingly, however, the *recusatio* was employed to assist poetic entry into the erotic. Vergil, for example, begins *Eclogue* 6 by apologizing to his friend Varus for his inability to write of great events; he can write only bucolic poetry. The bucolic, however, subtly fades into the erotic when Silenus's song is linked with Apollo's lament for Hyacinthus.[13] Horace devotes the first three stanzas of *Odes* 2.12 to a rejection of epic themes as inconsistent with lyric style, which, he proclaims, is better served by "sweeter" subjects, with "longa ferae bella Numantiae / nec durum Hannibalem" [fierce Numantia's tedious wars or doughty Hannibal] (2.12.1–2) more suited to narrative prose:

> me dulces dominae Musa Licymniae
> cantus, me voluit dicere lucidum
> fulgentes oculos et bene mutuis
> fidum pectus amoribus.

(2.12.13–16)

[Me the Muse has bidden to celebrate the sweet singing of Mistress Licymnia, her brightly flashing eyes, and her heart right faithful in mutual love.]

The poem ends, as Williams notes, with "a frank and sensual description of the pleasures of love-play . . . unique in the *Odes* of Horace."[14] *Odes* 1.19 clearly contrasts epic and amorous topics: "[E]namored of (the) sweet forwardness" ("urit grata protervitas") of the beautiful Glycera, the poet is forbidden by Venus "to sing of the Scythians, of the Parthians bold in flight, or of aught irrelevant" ("in me tota ruens Venus . . . / nec patitur Scythias / et versis animosum equis / Parthum dicere nec quae nihil attinent").[15]

A mainstay of erotic elegy beginning with Tibullus, the *recusatio* is most often associated with Propertius and Ovid and their lively skepticism towards imperial themes. But, whereas Propertius used the *recusatio* to introduce a serious evaluation of the often conflicting imperatives of love and war, recognizing, for example, the ways in which amorousness can undermine ambition, Ovid often asserted his subversive claims through parody of epic or political poetry. Inherent in this parodic transformation, however (as Warren Ginsberg has noted), is the paradox that the poet thus elevates his love poetry "to the same position as epic or poems of political consequence."[16] Therefore, *Amores* 1.1, which opens, as we saw above, with Cupid's derisive crippling of the epic hexameter, concludes when the poet-narrator—his objections to Cupid's intervention silenced by a well-aimed arrow—enthusiastically submits to Cupid's power:

> uror, et in uacuo pectore regnat Amor.
> sex mihi surgat opus numeris, in quinque residat;
> ferrea cum uestris bella ualete modis.
>
> (1.1.26–28)

[I am on fire, and Love reigns in my empty heart. Let my work rise in six feet and sink again in five; farewell iron wars, with your hexameters.]

With Cupid as his inspiration, Ovid can then confidently assume "the artistic gravity and pre-eminence claimed by the vatic Augustans."[17]

Amores 1.2 introduces the image of love as a form of war and the bed as surrogate of the battlefield; via elaborate mock-heroic imagery, *sub specie militaris*, the lover debates the effects of surrender.[18] Ending with an audacious analogy—that Cupid extend to the fallen lover the same magnanimity that Caesar offered his captives—Ovid slyly implies that

Caesar's military achievement (and, by implication, Rome's imperial glory) has importance primarily as an exemplar for Love:

> aspice cognati felicia Caesaris arma:
> qua uicit, uictos protegit ille manu.
>
> (1.2.51–52).

[Look at the happy arms of your kinsman Caesar: by that hand with which he conquered, he shields those whom he conquered.]

When, in *Amores* 1.9, love itself becomes a heroic activity preoccupying the most valiant warriors (Achilles, Hector, Agamemnon, even Mars), its respectability as a subject seems unquestionable—until Ovid, completing his formal dissociation with comic and subversive posture intact, proclaims that *his* wars take place only between the sheets:

> Militat omnis amans, et habet sua castra Cupido. . . .
> inpulit ignauum formosae cura puellae,
> iussit et in castris aera merere suis.
> inde uides agilem nocturnaque bella gerentum:
> qui nolet fieri desidiosus, amet.
>
> (1.9.1; 43–46)

[All lovers are soldiers, and Cupid has his own camp. . . . Love for a beautiful girl drew me from my sluggish ways with orders to serve in her camp. So now you see me nimbly waging nocturnal wars: let him love who wishes to forswear idleness.]

In a characteristically Ovidian subversion, love—usually viewed as a source of *otium* and a cause of military and civil failure, is here offered as a cure, with Ovid underlining the paradox that "no one is less lazy, day and night, than the lover."[19]

The opening elegy of *Amores* 2 is similarly concerned with establishing a respectable pedigree for a poetics of private concerns. Interrupted in his composition of an epic *gigantomachia* by his beloved's violently slamming her door just as Jupiter is about to loose his lightning, the poet-narrator precipitously abandons Jupiter and—"blanditias elegosque leuis, mea tela, resumpsi" (2.1.21)—"resumes his old arms, the smooth and flattering verses" of the love elegist. Therefore:

> . . . heroum clara ualete
> nomina non apta est gratia uestra mihi;
> ad mea formosos uultus adhibete puellae
> carmina, purpureus quae mihi dictat Amor.
>
> (2.1.35–38)

[Farewell heroes of illustrious name! Your graces are not suited to me. Turn
your beautiful faces, girls, to my songs which rosy Love dictates to me.]

No epic prowess can equal the poet's song in soothing a woman's anger
("carmina" suggesting both "poems" and "spells"); thus epic is useless
for actual (as opposed to mythological) amatory persuasion.

In the *Amores*, Ovid not only substituted erotic for more traditional
poetic subjects but also used conventional elegiac tropes with
unconventional impudence. For example, in employing the *priamel*
(wherein the speaker lists a series of commonplace examples, only to
differentiate his own situation by means of an epigrammatic
conclusion),[20] Ovid—employing unorthodox metaphors and ribald
puns—richly exploits the erotically subversive possibilities of language:

> induat aduersus contraria pectora telis
> miles et aeternum sanguine nomen emat;
> quaerat auarus opes et, quae lassarit arando,
> aequora periuro naufragus ore bibat;
> at mihi contingat Veneris languescere motu,
> cum moriar, medium soluar et inter opus;
> atque aliquis nostro lacrimans in funere dicat
> "conueniens uitae mors fuit ista tuae."

(Amores 2.10.31–38)

[Let the soldier expose his breast to the enemy's darts and buy eternal glory
with his blood; let the greedy person seek wealth, and the one who has been
shipwrecked drink with his perjured mouth the waters which he has made
weary with ploughing. But let it befall me to be overcome by Venus's
motion, when I die, to dissolve amid that work; and, at my funeral, let a
mourner say, "Yours was a death appropriate to your life."]

Heroic acts are transformed into sensual ones, and Ovid asks us to
recognize the inherently libidinous nature of human ambition.

In the *Amores*, Ovid had established love as "a metaphor for the
private life"[21] and situated its erotic subjects literally and specifically in
the real world of contemporary Rome. In the *Ars Amatoria*, he expanded
these ideas, making Rome a mere stage for amorous exploits and treating
Roman history and mythology largely as sources for amorous
precedents.[22] In the *Ars*, historical and mythological heroes contend not
on the battlefield but in the bedroom, and the lover, in Joseph Solodow's
words, becomes the "cultural ideal," a replacement for the warrior, the
orator, and the philosopher.[23] Most significantly, Ovid's *praeceptor
amoris* (as he confidently styled his first-person narrator) easily asserts

the authority hitherto restricted to commemorators of more traditional virtues.

From the outset, as we have seen, amatory poetry sought to exploit the tension between presumably respectable poetic subjects like history, philosophy, and politics and the less reputable "truths" deriving from private desire, the erotic imagination in particular. It is not so surprising, then, that when medieval poets began to challenge institutionalized political and religious pieties, they too turned to the erotic, eschewing the more traditional forms of martial, moralistic, or epideictic verse. Like their classical forebears, they adopted the *recusatio* as an explicit rhetorical tactic learned, most likely, directly from Ovid.[24] Medieval poets, however, were not content merely to use the *recusatio* as a specific rhetorical stratagem; for them it took on broader structural and narrative implications, leading the way to a type of courtly composition characterized by dialectic, irony, and persistent challenge to convention.

Several early troubadour lyrics illustrate the point. The first canso of Guillaume IX of Aquitaine, earliest of the known troubadours, begins:

> Companho, faray un vers . . . covinen:
> et aura. i mais de foudaz no•y a de sen,
> et er totz mesclatz d'amor e de joy e de joven

> (1.1–3)

[My companions, I am going to make a vers that is refined, / and it will have more foolishness than sense, / and it will be mixed with love and joy and youth.][25]

Openly contemptuous of his detractors ("E tenguatz lo per vilan qui no l'enten" [Whoever does not understand it, take him for a peasant]), Guillaume soon abandons any effort at respectability (Is this defection what he means by "foudaz"?) and launches a series of obscene puns, identifying—in a variant of the Ovidian *topos* of the poet-lover as rider—his "good and noble horses" as two women. Thus, this supposedly "refined" poem is something rather different. As in Ovid's *Ars*, the battlefield has been supplanted by another kind of arena or playing field. As Laura Kendrick puts it, "There is virtually no end to the liberties that the playfully facetious interpreter might take with the language of this lyric demanding knightly counsel (*conselh*) on the subject of which *con* to saddle (*selhar*)."[26]

In what is perhaps his best-known poem, Guillaume defiantly asserts, "Farai un vers de dreyt nien" [I will make a *vers* of exactly nothing] to an audience that presumably expected of poetry *sententia* as well as *solas*. Initially claiming to have been inspired while sleeping on his horse ("qu'enans fo trobatz en durmen / sobre chevau"), Guillaume goes on to undermine several kinds of generic expectations—the Macrobian dream vision, the lover-as-rider *topos*, and the *machismo* of the *chansons de geste*—while at the same time challenging his audience's presumed expectations of the discourse available to so powerful an aristocrat. Boasting that he will write a poem without subject or pretense of authority, Guillaume lists a remarkably comprehensive series of negations:

> non er de mi ni d'autra gen,
> non er d'amor ni de joven,
> ni de ren au.
>
> (3.2–4)

[there'll be nothing in it about me or anyone else, / nothing about love or youth / or anything else],[27]

denying (often in the form of paradox) his capacity to understand and evaluate his own experiences or feelings:

> No sai en qual hora•m fuy natz:
> no suy alegres ni iratz,
> no suy estrayns ni sui privatz. . . .
> No sai quora•m fuy endurmitz
> ni quora•m velh, s'om no m'o ditz. . . .
> Malautz suy e tremi murir,
> e ren no sai mas quan n'aug dir.
>
> (3.7–20)

[I do not know the hour of my birth. / I am not cheerful or morose, / I am no stranger here and do not belong in these parts. . . . / I don't know when I slept / or wake, if someone doesn't tell me. . . . / I am sick and shiver at death / and don't know it except when I am told.]

Uncertain of the identity and dwelling of his "amigua" (anticipating the soon common *topos* of *amor de lonh*), uncertain even of his subject and audience, he is confident only of two things: his carnal desire and the role of the poem in helping fulfill that desire:

> Fag ai lo vers, no say de cuy;
> e trametrai lo a selhuy
> que lo•m trametra per autruy

lay vers Anjau,
que•m tramezes del sieu estuy
la contraclau.

(3.43–48)

[I have made this vers, I don't know what about; / and I shall send it to someone / who will send it for me with someone else / to someone in Anjou there; / let him send me from his little box the key / to what we have here.]

Kendrick calls this "a poem that is nearly pure form, an empty figure that we, inevitably, try to fill with a conceptual sense."[28] But we can view it as a provocative adaptation of the Ovidian *recusatio*—a lyric wherein "object" and "incident" are wholly absent ("Anc non la vi et am la fort" [I have never seen her and love her a lot]), with its only real "subject" the libidinous poet himself and his confidence in the power of his language.

Similar to Guillaume's assertion of negation (possibly even an intentional parody) is Raimbaut D'Orange's "Escotatz, mas no say que s'es."[29] Like Guillaume, a member of the high nobility, Raimbaut uses the pretense of self-consciousness to mock his audience's presumed generic and topical expectations. Calling into question the poet's control over his own poetry, each strophe dissolves into several lines of prose, the verse itself essentially indeterminate:

Escotatz, mas no say que s'es
senhor, so que vuelh comensar.
Vers, estribot, ni sirventes
non es, ni nom no•l sai trobar;
ni ges no say co•l mi fezes
s'aytal no•l podi' acabar,
que ia hom mays non vis fag aytal ad home ni a femna en
est segle ni en l'autre qu'es passatz.

(32.1–8)

[Listen Lords ... but I don't know what / to call this thing I'm about to declaim. / *Vers* ? *Estribot* ? *Sirventes*? It's none / of these. I can't think up a name, / and don't know how I'd compose such a thing / if I could not finish it and claim / that no one ever saw the like of it made by any man or woman in our century or in the other which has passed.]

The subversion of expectations extends from rhetoric to religion. Beginning with a pun establishing equivalence between money and spirit ("Car mes amaria seis deniers en mon punh que mil sols el cel" [because I prefer six cents in my fist to a thousand *sols*, (i.e. both "suns" and "sous," "in the sky")]), Raimbaut, invoking the Trinity, facetiously conflates the dual meanings of "dona/ domna":

Dona! Pus mon cor tenetz pres
adossatz me ab dous l'amar.
Dieus, aiuda! *In nomine patris et filii et spiritus sancti* ! Aiso,
que sera domna?

(32.26–29)

[Lady, my heart is your prisoner, / therefore sweeten my bitterness, / Help
me, God, *In nomine patris et filii et spiritus sancti* ! (My lady)[30], how will it
all turn out?]

With customary generic values serving only as inspiration to parody,
Raimbaut, like Guillaume, is sure only of his identity as "joglar" and
poet:

Er fenisc mo no-say-que-s'es,
c'aisi l'ay volgut batejar;
pus mays d'aital non auzi jes
be•l dey enaysi apelar;
e diga•l, can l'aura apres,
qui que s'en vuelha azautar.
E si hom li demanda qui l'a fag, pot dir que sel que sap be far
totas fazendas can se vol.

(32.36–43)

[Now that I conclude my Whatdoyoucall it / for that is how I've had it
baptized; / since I've never heard of a similar thing, / I use the name that I
devised; / whoever likes it, let him sing, / once he has it memorized, / and if
anyone asks him who made it, he can say one who can do / anything and do it
well, when he wants to.]

The poem the only "offspring" of this strange and incorporeal "affair,"
born of the poet alone and baptized by him, Raimbaut underscores the
self-referentiality of the Ovidian mode.

Similar confidence in the poetic authority of amatory verse is
expressed in more courtly terms by the troubadours Arnaut Daniel and
Peire Vidal. In "En cest sonet coind'e leri," Arnaut abjures more
traditional kinds of authorization and status (a *priamel*), expressing his
desire to write only about love:

Non vuoill de Roma l'emperi
ni c'om m'en fassa apostoli . . .
si tot me ten en desert
c'aissi•n fatz los motz en rima.
Pieitz trac aman c'om que laura.

(39.29–40)

[I do not want the empire of Rome, / do not make me pope of it. . . . / for in this desert I cast my words in rhyme. / I labor in loving more than a man who works the earth.]

Yet even while claiming that something as ephemeral and transcendent as love can have poetic validity beyond more prosaic and conventional subjects, Arnaut admits, in the poem's last strophe, that the amorist's role is best expressed in terms of *impossibilia*:

> Ieu sui Arnautz q'amas l'aura,
> e chatz la lebre ab lo bou
> e nadi contra suberna.
>
> (39.43–45)

[I am Arnaut, who hoards the wind, / and chases the hare on an ox, / and swims against the tide.][31]

Peire, in contrast, smoothly equates epic warrior and courtly lover ("Drogoman senher, s'ieu agues bon destrier"):

> D'ardimen vaill Rotlan et Olivier
> e de domnei Berart de Mondesdier . . .
> En totas res sembli ben cavallier;
> si•m sui, e sai d'amor tot son mestier,
>
> (46.13–20)

[For warrior's nerve I am worth Roland and Oliver, / and for making love to these ladies Bérard de Montdidier . . . / No matter what I do, I look like a knight, / for I am a knight, and in love I am master of the craft.][32]

In a second poem, however, Peire calls attention to a consequent enigma:

> Ajostar e lassar
> sai tan gent motz e so,
> que del car ric trobar
> no•m ven hom al talo,
> quant n'ai bona razo.
> Mas auci me aissi
> la bella e cui so.
>
> (48.1–7)

[I can put together and interlace / words and music with such skill, / in the noble art of song / no man comes near my heel, / when I have a good subject. / And yet, behold, she kills me / the beautiful one I belong to.][33]

How can the speaker reconcile the dramatic disjunction between his courtly and poetic skills and the humiliations and debasement he suffers through love? Underscoring the paradox that love simultaneously enfeebles and invigorates (eventually a commonplace of *fin' amors*), he compares the lover-poet to a pilgrim and crusader ("per aital faillizo / fes de mi pelegri" [now through such unkindness / she's made a pilgrim out of me]) who finds his worthiest "field" in the beloved herself:

> am mais un pauc cambo,
> qu'aver sai Lo Daro,
> ni aver Lo Toro
> n'Ibeli.

(48.82–85)

[I love one little field more / Than getting fortresses and cities here, / Le Daron, or Le Toron, / Or Ibelin.][34]

As with Ovid's puns, "cambo" suggests a range of implications from war to procreation.

Other medieval lyric amorists similarly used the principle of *recusatio* to assert the precedence of amatory over military or religious imperatives. The *recusatio* appears not only in the openly Ovidian verse of the English Serlo of Wilton[35] but in the religious lyrics of the Rhinelander Friedric von Hausen, where it mediates between warring erotic and spiritual yearnings.[36] It is evident in the facetiously erotic *Carmina Burana* (for example, "Iam iam rident prata"),[37] and becomes a commonplace of the Petrarchan lyric tradition.[38] But the expedient warrant for a poetics of private life exemplified by the *recusatio* as it appeared in lyric poetry was given yet broader application by the writers of romance. With Vergilian epic still "the primary source of structure—a constant referent of wholeness in an otherwise chaotic world,"[39] the *recusatio*—no longer simply a rhetorical tactic—was integrated by *romanciers* into the narrative structure itself as a stratagem for challenging and parodying prevailing literary expectations.

The earliest medieval narratives to use amatory subjects as alternatives to the episodic battle-centered structure of the *chansons de geste* were the twelfth-century French romances of antiquity.[40] In the Old French *Roman d'Enéas*, for example, the twelfth-century poet often seems to be struggling to keep the narrative focus on the dynastic and imperialistic concerns of his epic source. In both the "Dido" and the "Lavine" episodes, he foregrounds the love story, grafting an amatory imperative onto Vergil's epic framework. In so doing, he frequently compresses or entirely omits important Vergilian narrative elements and, instead, expatiates at length on the psychology and artifices of love, incorporating a full complement of Ovidian rhetorical and amatory commonplaces.[41] Like Vergil, he condemns the passion of Dido and Eneas as personally destructive, politically undesirable, and in violation of divine command ("cele ki mainteneit l'enor / a tot guerpi por soe amor" [she who should protect her domain has abandoned all for her love]; "toz est livrez a male voe, / et terre et femme tient por soe" [he is wholly given over to ruin and holds the country and the woman for his own]).[42] Yet, when he gets to the story of Eneas and Lavine, his perspective changes: love now *legitimizes* the dynastic impulse, making the love affair and the establishment of the new Roman state (in Lee Patterson's words) "not merely simultaneous but synonymous."[43] Clearly dissatisfied with the abrupt Vergilian ending (Aeneas's brutal slaying of Turnus in Pallas's name [*Aeneid* 12.1252–71]), the *Enéas*-poet adds 341 verses wherein the lovers bemoan at length the uncertainty of their still unconsummated relationship, until their marriage assures both personal fulfillment and dynastic succession. In the *Roman d'Enéas*, in short, the love of Eneas and Lavine serves to affirm the moral equivalence of private and public values.

No longer simply a matter of the facetious assertion of the Ovidian *recusatio*, romantic love has become integral to the narrative, its revolutionary effects both rhetorical and ethical. Rhetorically, as Stephen Nichols has pointed out, the dialogic elements necessary to *any* narrative based on romantic love serve to restrain literary monologism, thus subverting "the privileged discourse requisite for unity in the totalizing systems favored by medieval society."[44] Ethically, on the other hand, the linking of *eros* with *epos*, even in the ironical form that constitutes the *recusatio*, offers erotic values (despite traditional taboos) for public approbation. While a full treatment of the use of this enlarged sense of the *recusatio* in medieval romance must be the subject of another paper, I offer here a brief discussion of several prominent examples.

For Chrétien de Troyes, the greatest and most influential of twelfth-century *romanciers*, sexual love (although viewed sometimes as a positive, sometimes as a negative, force) served not only as narrative center but as a crucial instrument of emancipation from religious and political demands on narrative. Like other amatory poets, Chrétien often used the *recusatio* as a means of rhetorical transition.[45] In at least one romance, however, the device fulfills essential structural purposes, helping Chrétien to escape the narrative restrictions imposed by his direct literary progenitors, the *chansons de geste* (possibly even the *Chanson de Roland*) and the Tristan story. That romance is *Cligés*,[46] which, despite

Chrétien's initial mention of his translations of "Ovid's *Commandments* and his *Art of Love*" (both lost), begins heroically: the hero's father, Alexander, travels abroad from his native Greece to seek knightly honor at Arthur's court. However, the nature of the quest changes (as does the tone of the romance) when he meets and falls in love with the beautiful Soredamours, the narrative turning increasingly comic as Alexander's pursuit of martial glory yields to pursuit of erotic pleasure. Chrétien makes the shift in focus explicit some five hundred verses into the romance:

> Del roi Artus parler ne quier
> A ceste foiz plus longuemant,
> Einçois m'orroiz dire comant
> Amors les deus amanz travaille
> Vers cui il a prise bataille.
>
> (vv. 562–66)

[As for the king, it is well known that the Bretons celebrated his arrival and gladly served him as their rightful lord. At this time I do not wish to speak any further of King Arthur; instead you will hear me tell how Love attacked the two lovers against whom he was waging battle.][47]

In the second part of the romance, which focuses entirely on the erotic passion of Cligés and Fenice, the ups-and-downs of their love affair motivate a series of extravagant, often amusing, incidents. Increasingly, however, as the narrative proceeds, both the *chansons de geste* (seen as a specific model of chivalric propriety) and the Tristan story (seen as a specific model of amorous *impropriety*) seem to represent models of excess: the former because the traditional heroic model wholly excludes the private feeling and individualism that, for Chrétien, lies at the heart of the romance genre; the latter because uncontrolled private feelings undermine that *mésure* that Chrétien seems to see as essential not only to *fin 'amor* but to the moral life in general. Throughout *Cligés*, in fact, Chrétien maintains an ironic distance from both the public values represented by knightly enterprise and the private values of *eros*: the first, by repeatedly emphasizing that love is simultaneously an inspiration and an impediment to Cligés's knightly efforts; the second, by suggesting that love is sometimes impossible to distinguish from illusion.[48]

Perhaps the most telling example of the way in which the *recusatio* helped transform epic story into what Derek Pearsall has called "lyric romance"[49] is the literary history of Troy, wherein the two rather graceless late-classical "histories" of Dares and Dictys developed into the great love story of Troilus and Criseyde.[50] Introduced in Benoît de

Sainte-Maure's 30,000-line *Roman de Troie* (where it suffuses approximately one-quarter of the poem), the story of the tragic lovers became the fulcrum of the Trojan narrative for Boccaccio, Chaucer, and subsequent poets from Henryson to Shakespeare.[51]

The first to divorce the love story almost entirely from its Trojan frame, Boccaccio, in the *Filostrato*, focused exclusively on the affair between the lovers Troiolo and Criseida.[52] In both subject and structure, however, and despite its pretensions to epic, the poem has struck many readers as more evocative of lyric than of romance. Its pseudonymous title suggests the autobiographical nature of the poem's overall conception; its *proem* associates the poet-narrator with other desolate lovers. In addition, in adopting a "form traditionally employed to entertain the public with accounts of battles to relate a story of love,"[53] Boccaccio employs a narrative structure based on the principles of *recusatio*. Reversing the emphasis from war to love, he has transposed (in Natali's words) "the epos . . . into a lyrical key" with the result that the Trojan War and the warrior's traditional attributes become a mere background to love:

> L'aspre battaglie e gli stormi angosciosi,
> ch' Ettor e gli altri suoi fratei facieno
> seguiti da' Troian, dagli amorosi
> pensieri però niente il rimovieno;
> come che spesso, ne' piú perigliosi
> assalti, anzi ad ogni altro lui vedieno
> mirabilmente nell' armi operare
> color che stesser ciò forse a mirare.
>
> Né a ciò odio de' Greci il movea,
> né vaghezza ch' avesse di vittoria
> per Troia liberar, la qual vedea
> stretta d'assedio, ma voglia di gloria
> per piú piacer tutto questo facea;
> e per amor, se 'l ver dice la storia,
> divenne in arme si feroce e forte,
> che li Greci il temien come la morte.
>
> (*Fil.* 1.45–46)

[The sharp battles and stern encounters in which Hector and his other brothers, followed by the Trojans, took part, moved him [Troilus] little or not at all from thoughts of love, although often they saw him ahead of others in the most dangerous onsets, performing marvels in arms. So said they who stood and watched him. But it was not hatred of the Greeks which urged him to this, nor desire for victory to free Troy, which he saw hard pressed by siege; but it was the longing for glory, in order that he might the better please, which wrought all this. And through love, if the story speaks truth, he became so fierce and mighty in arms that the Greeks dreaded him like death.][54]

That the war ultimately dooms the love affair (as well as Troilus himself) is an inevitable consequence of Boccaccio's dependence on the antecedent texts that "fixed" the story's outcome.

Even more than Boccaccio, his immediate source,[55] Chaucer subordinates *epos* to *eros* (in other words, Calliope to Venus) throughout the *Troilus*, consciously abjuring the heroic poet's embassy. From the first book to the last, he directs those readers concerned with *epos* to look elsewhere, although his frank acknowledgment of prior authorities reflects his awareness of the powerful historical tradition:[56]

> But how this town com to destruccion
> Ne falleth naught to purpos me to telle;
> ffor it were here a long digression
> ffro my matere and you to long to dwelle;
> But the Troian gestes as they felle,
> In Omer or in Dares or in Dite,
> Who-so that kan may rede hem as they write.
>
> (*Troilus and Criseyde*, 1.141–47)

> And if I hadde ytaken for to write
> The armes of this ilke worthi man,
> Than wolde ich of his batailles endite;
> But for that I to writen first bigan
> Of his loue, I have seyd as I kan—
> His worthi dedes, who-so list hem heere,
> Rede Dares, he kan telle hem alle i-feere—
>
> (5.1765–71)

In the invocation to book 1, Chaucer addresses not Clio, the traditional Muse of History, but Thesiphone, the Fury whose perpetual rage and grief, mirroring love's turbulence, seem appropriate inspiration for the "double sorwe" of Troilus's and Criseyde's unhappy love. When Clio eventually is invoked, in the *proem* to the second book, the invocation is equivocal. Perhaps in recollection of her associations with "eloquentia," she is initially called on as an instrument of imitative versification:[57]

> O lady myn, that called art Cleo,
> Thow be my speed fro this forth, and my Muse,
> To ryme wel this book til I haue do;
> Me nedeth here noon othere art to vse."
>
> (2.8–11)

With an apology to those lovers, who might expect something different from a love story, the narrator claims inspiration not from "sentement" but from his Latin "auctour":

> ffor-whi to euery louere I me excuse
> That of no sentement I this endite,
> But out of Latyn in my tonge it write.
>
> (2.12–14)

Yet Chaucer characteristically undercuts the modest pretense that he is a mere translator (with Clio's aid), first by an explicit excursus on cultural relativity ("Ye knowe ek that in fourme of speche is change / With-inne a thousand yeer" [2.22ff]) that serves to destabilize the notion of a fixed narrative tradition and then by constantly undermining or deconstructing the notion of an authoritative historical record. Like Troilus, in his lover's "disespeir" (2.6), seeking a way "out of thise blake wawes forto saylle" (2.1), the Chaucerian narrator consciously maneuvers the narrative through the shoals of two conflicting literary traditions: one the "public" record established by the prior literary history of Troy; the second the "private" expectations deriving from the long tradition of amatory poetry. Clearly Clio, patroness of the public record, is inadequate to the infinite possibilities of individual experience:

> Ek scarsly ben ther in this place thre
> That haue in loue seid like and don in al,
> ffor to thi purpos this may liken the,
> And the right nought, yet al is seid, or schal;
> Ek som men graue in tree, som in ston wal,
> As it bitit; but syn I haue bigonne,
> Myn auctor shal I folwen if I konne.
>
> (2.43–49)

The authoritative record can, at best, provide only a partial guide ("if I konne") to poetic narrative focused on the private sphere. Although Chaucer, like Boccaccio (although far more reluctantly) is ultimately forced to see lovers' privacy as illusory, with public pressures inevitably coming to bear—Clio, or historical tradition, determining the closure if not the details of the narrative—*Troilus and Criseyde* is unique among the medieval Trojan narratives in the self-consciousness of its scrutiny of the two discordant traditions, historical and amatory, which inform the medieval *roman d'antiquité*.

For Chaucer, as for other classical and medieval amorists, the subject of love served to raise crucial issues of literary and cultural authentication. Medieval poets, much like their Roman predecessors, turned to the subject of love to affirm the legitimacy—sometimes even the supremacy—of private feeling and its discourses. And, as it had done since antiquity, the *recusatio*—with its overt and audacious juxtaposition of sacred and profane values—gave them rhetorical and narrative strategies for expressing their political and moral insurgency.[58]

Notes

An early version of this article (inspired by an NEH Summer Seminar directed by Professor Robert W. Hanning of Columbia) was presented at the Congress for Medieval Studies, Kalamazoo, Michigan, on 10 May 1990. I am grateful to the members of the seminar and of the New York-based medieval group that succeeded it for their many helpful suggestions. I especially want to thank Professors Hanning, Cynthia Gravlee, Anne Schotter, and Robert Stein, as well as Professor Simon Gaunt of St. Catharine's College, Cambridge University.

    1. Dante Alighieri, *De Vulgari Eloquentia*, Ridotto . . . , commentato e tradotto da Aristide Marigo, *Operi di Dante*, 5.6 (Florence: Felice Le Monnier, 1957), 2.2.8. "Wherefore these three things, namely well-being, love, and virtue, appear to be those important matters which ought especially to be investigated [in vernacular poetry], that is, those things which especially pertain to them, such as command of arms, arousal of love, and regulation of the will."

    2. Barry Windeatt suggests that Chaucer may be imitating the opening lines of Dante's *Purgatorio*: "Ma qui la morta poesì resurga, / o sante Muse, poi che vostro sono; / e qui Calïopè alquanto surga, / sequitando il mio canto con quel suono / di qui le Piche misere sentiro / lo colpo tal, che desperar perdono" (1.6–12.) Geoffrey Chaucer, *Troilus and Criseyde: A New Edition of "The Book of Troilus,"* ed. B. A. Windeatt (London and New York: Longman, 1984), 251.

    3. All *Troilus* citations are from Windeatt's edition. For a discussion of Venus's dual aspects, see George D. Economou, "The Two Venuses and Courtly Love," in *In Pursuit of Perfection: Courtly Love in Medieval Literature*, ed. Joan M. Ferrante and George D. Economou (Port Washington, N.Y.: Kennikat, 1975), 17–50.

    4. *House of Fame* [1487], in *The Riverside Chaucer*, ed. Larry D. Benson (Boston: Houghton Mifflin, 1987).

    5. See Moshe Lazar, "Carmina Erotica, Carmina Iocosa: The Body and the Bawdy in Medieval Love Songs," in *Poetics of Love in the Middle Ages: Texts and Contexts*, ed. Moshe Lazar and Norris J. Lacy (Fairfax, Va.: George Mason University Press, 1989), 261.

    6. All citations from Ovid are from E. J. Kenney's edition: P. Ovidi Nasonis, *Amores, et. al* (Oxford: Oxford University Press, 1961). Translations, unless otherwise noted, are my own.

    7. See John M. Fyler, "Omnia Vincit Amor: Incongruity and the Limitations of Structure in Ovid's Elegiac Poetry," *The Classical Journal*, 66.3 (1971): 196–203, as well as the fuller discussion in the first chapter of Fyler's *Chaucer and Ovid* (New Haven and London: Yale University Press, 1979).

8. See Robert W. Hanning's *The Individual in Twelfth-Century Romance* (New Haven and London: Yale University Press, 1977) and his "Courtly Contexts for Urban Cultus: Responses to Ovid in Chrétien's *Cligès* and Marie's *Guigemar*," *Symposium* 35 (1981): 34–56.

9. For a fuller discussion of classical usage of the *recusatio,* see Gordon Williams, *Tradition and Originality in Roman Poetry* (London: Oxford University Press, 1968), 46 *et passim,* to which I am much indebted. Warren Ginsberg surveys classical and medieval examples of the trope in *The Cast of Character: The Representation of Personality in Ancient and Medieval Literature* (Toronto: University of Toronto Press, 1983).

10. Williams, 77.

11. Williams, 80; 83. All texts and translations of Horace are from *The Odes and Epodes*, ed. and trans. C. E. Bennett (Cambridge: Harvard University Press, 1927; rev. and rpt. 1988), 286–87; 20–21.

12. " [T]hese poets adapted the form of the Callimachean refusal to the purpose of making political statements in verse, for this was their particular innovation. Consequently, the hypothesis that they had been urged or merely felt the inspiration to write in epic form about the deeds of Augustus may be treated as an invention; it provided a framework in which they could both praise the regime and express their own views on the themes appropriate to their own poetic ideals and the sources of their inspiration" (102–3).

13. Williams, 243; 247.

14. Williams, 301; *Kenney,* 134–37.

15. Williams, 562; *Kenney,* 58–59.

16. Ginsberg, 31.

17. Ibid.

18. Leslie Cahoon, unlike most readers, sees in the imagery of sexual violence the poet's criticism of Roman militarism. "By weaving together the vocabularies of love and war, the *Amores* suggest that the ambition to conquer is in the process of destroying *socialia iura.* If Rome contains both literally and existentially the kind of *amor* that the *Amores* depict, and if Venus is an internal reflection of the external labors of Mars, then there can be little reciprocal love in Rome, and political and social as well as physical and individual impotence is likely to follow" ("The Bed as Battlefield: Erotic Conquest and Military Metaphor in Ovid's *Amores,*" *TAPA* 118 [1988]: 307).

19. See Paul Veyne, *Roman Erotic Elegy: Love, Poetry and the West,* trans. David Pellauer (Chicago: University of Chicago Press, 1988), 245 n. 12. Veyne describes conventional Roman attitudes towards duty and pleasure in chapter 10: "The Amusing Paradox and the Pleasure Process" (151–68).

20. Williams, 66, and William H. Race, *The Classical Priamel from Homer to Boethius* (Leiden: E. J. Brill, 1982). The *priamel* (L. *praeambulum*) is frequently associated with medieval German aphoristic poetry. For more conventional elegiac use of the trope, see Propertius 2.1.43–45 and Horace, *Odes* 4.3

21. The phrase is Richard Lanham's in *The Motives of Eloquence: Literary Rhetoric in the Renaissance* (New Haven and London: Yale University Press, 1976), 49.

22. The account of the rape of the Sabines, for example, serves primarily to illustrate the sexual spoils of soldiering, 1.102–34.

23. Joseph Solodow, "Ovid's *Ars Amatoria*: The Lover as Cultural Ideal," *Wiener Studien* 11 (1977): 112. Ovid's audacity is especially noteworthy in light of the fact that he, unlike his predecessors, apparently wrote most of his amatory poetry after the promulgation of the moral legislation of 18 B.C.E., which proposed severe penalties (including, in certain circumstances, exile) for the seduction of married women. Williams

(540–42) suggests that this legislation was responsible not only for Ovid's insistence, in the preface to the *Ars*, that his subjects were *meretrices* rather than respectable women, but for the ultimate demise of the erotic elegy itself.

24. Extant manuscripts suggest that the *Amores* could have been known in Western Europe as early as the ninth century, although (unlike the *Ars Amatoria*, the *Tristia*, and the *Metamorphoses*) these Carolingian editions are nowhere cited by name until their inclusion in the French school curriculum in the early eleventh century. E. F. Shannon, *Chaucer and the Roman Poets* (Cambridge: Harvard University Press, 1929; 1957; rpt. New York: Russell & Russell, 1964) identified them with the work often referred to as "sine titulo" in collections of Ovid's works (22ff.), although other scholars have been more skeptical. Ralph Hexter, although admitting that pre-twelfth-century manuscript evidence for Ovid's amatory poetry is scant, notes the proliferation of Ovid manuscripts in the twelfth century. See *Ovid and Medieval Schooling: Studies on Medieval School Commentaries on Ovid's* Ars Amatoria, Epistolae ex Ponto, *and* Epistolae Heroidum (Munich: Arbeo-Gesellschaft, 1986), 4n; 15n. Leslie Cahoon goes further, suggesting that "the early troubadours not only knew Ovid but may have conceivably been part of an Ovidian tradition with roots in the Carolingian Renaissance" ("The Anxieties of Influence: Ovid's Reception by the Early Troubadours," in *Ovid in Medieval Culture: a special issue*, ed. Marilynn R. Desmond, *Medievalia* 13 (1989, for 1987): 119–55). Gerald A. Bond, distinguishing between early and late medieval reception of Ovid, sees the new availability of Ovid's "complete *oeuvre*" as a notable "cultural moment": "A term such as 'New Ovid' would be useful to label the discontinuity in grammarian discourse caused by the introduction of these subversive but authoritative texts" ("Composing Yourself: Ovid's *Heroides*, Baudri of Bourgueil and the Problem of Persona," *Mediaevalia*, 13: 85).

25. Text and translation from Frederick Goldin, ed. and trans., *Lyrics of the Troubadours and Trouvères* (Garden City, N.Y.: Anchor, 1973), 20–21.

26. Laura Kendrick, *The Game of Love: Troubadour Wordplay* (Berkeley and Los Angeles: University of California Press, 1988), 122–23. Simon Gaunt has a valuable discussion of the poem's multiple ironies in *Troubadours and Irony* (Cambridge: Cambridge University Press, 1989), 19–20. Unlike Kendrick, however, Gaunt sees Guillaume as a special case whose apparently subversive posture derives primarily from his uniquely powerful status; i.e. "he can write as he does because he is the Duke of Aquitaine" and is, therefore, "reinforcing institutional authority even though he appears to challenge it" (unpublished letter to me).

27. Goldin, 24–27.

28. Kendrick, 19–20. The poem has elicited numerous readings: biographical, allegorical, burlesque, courtly, metaphysical, and semiotic. A bibliography appears in Gaunt, 206 n.56.

29. Goldin, 178–81.

30. Goldin translates "domna" as "Madam": the translation as "lady" (for which I thank Cynthia Gravlee) reinforces the equivalence with the Virgin.

31. Goldin, 216–19. This form of *adynaton* became a commonplace of Petrarchist love poetry.

32. Goldin, 250–53.

33. Ibid., 254–61.

34. The relationship of the amatory oxymoron of the "strong weakness" to the central Christian paradox is exploited in the strongly sexual imagery of many medieval legends of the Virgin and in the whole tradition of Mariolatry.

35. "Pronus erat Veneri Naso, sed ego mage pronus" ("Ovid was inclined to love, but I am more inclined"). Serlo persistently echoes Ovidian rhetoric and themes and easily adopts the *recusatio*: "Sum tibi non parvi: vix Hector erit mihi par vi, / Vi supero Resum si qua carus tibi re sum— / Quisque mihi dispar, si sis mea, sic ego dis par" [You'll not find me a man of no account: Hector will scarcely be my equal in strength. / I'll be stronger than Rhesus if I am at all dear to you. / No man will be my equal if you are mine—I'll be the equal of the gods]. I am quoting from Peter Dronke, *Medieval Latin and the Rise of the European Love-Lyric* (Oxford: Clarendon Press, 1965), 500–503. Dronke points out "the incongruity between the seeming seriousness of the lover's *planctus* and the outrageous word-play which ends each line" (503).

36. See the first stanza of "Mîn herze und mîn lîp die wellent scheiden": "My heart and my body would like to part / Although they've journeyed together a long time. / My body wants to go fight against the heathens. / My heart has chosen its contest in a girl." The complete poem (in English translation) appears in James J. Wilhelm, ed. and trans., *Lyrics of the Middle Ages: An Anthology* (New York and London: Garland, 1990), 205.

37. "Ergo militemus / Simul Veneri; / Tristia vitemus / Nosque tereri! / Visus et colloquia, / Spes amorque trahant / Nos ad gaudia!" Cited and translated by Wilhelm, 305 (Latin), 37 (trans.).

38. On Petrarch's ambivalent secularism see Hans Baron, "Petrarch: His inner struggles and the humanistic discovery of man's nature," in *Florilegium Historiale: Essays Presented to Wallace K. Ferguson*, ed. J. G. Rowe and W. H. Stockdale (Toronto: University of Toronto Press, 1971), 19–51. I am indebted to George M. Logan for the reference and for the suggestion that Petrarch, too, saw erotic love as an entry into secular experience, which it seems to epitomize in a particularly intense way.

39. Patricia Harris Stäblein, "Sexual Specularity: Multiple Images in the Parodic Dynamics of Twelfth Century Lyrics and Romance," in Lazar and Lacy, 213.

40. Rosemarie Jones, *The Theme of Love in the Romans d'Antiquité* (London: The Modern Humanities Research Association, 1972), has a brief but informative survey of the amatory components of the *romans antique*.

41. For example, he condenses Aeneas's 150-line account of Troy's fall and his own escape into forty verses; he omits all scenes with Anchises and the scene with Creusa's ghost, replacing the 1522 lines of books 2 and 3 of the *Aeneid* with 347 octosyllabic verses. On the other hand, his descriptions of the lovesickness of Dido, Eneas, and Lavine go on for many hundreds of verses. See John A. Yunck, trans., *Eneas: A Twelfth Century Romance* (New York: Columbia University Press, 1974), 79n; 81n *et passim*.

42. Jacques Salverda de Grave,ed., *Eneas* (Paris: Honoré Champion, 1925, 1931; Geneva: Slatkine Rpts., 1975), vv. 1431–32; 1614–15 (translation by Yunck).

43. Patterson views the translation of Roman epic into "romantic comedy" as reflecting Anglo-Norman ideological concerns, particularly regarding the establishment of familial inheritance rights. See *Negotiating the Past: The Historical Understanding of Medieval Literature* (Madison: University of Wisconsin Press, 1987), 179. A similar point is made by Barbara Nolan, who calls *Eneas* "a subtly crafted guidebook for medieval princes and princesses on the nature and art of sound political love and marriage." See "Ovid's *Heroides* Contextualized: Foolish Love and Legitimate Marriage in the *Roman D'Eneas*," *Medievalia* 13: 178. Going even further, Simon Gaunt argues that the *Roman d'Enéas*, "a bridge between epic and romance," actively promotes the ideology of patriarchy. Thus, "the . . . romance enacts not merely the marginalization of war as a transcendental value, but [in its condemnation of the "homosocial" attachment of Turnus and Eneas] the destruction and disintegration of a type of male bonding that could be viewed as closely

associated with the *chansons de geste.*" See "From Epic to Romance: Gender and Sexuality in the *Roman d'Enéas," Romanic Review,* 83 (1992): 9; 24.

44. Stephen G. Nichols, "Amorous Imitation: Bakhtin, Augustine, and *Le Roman d'Eneas,"* in *Romance: Generic Transformation from Chrétien de Troyes to Cervantes,* ed. Kevin Brownlee and Marina Scordilis Brownlee (Hanover, N.H., and London: University Press of New England, 1985), 50–51.

45. For example, in the opening lines (vv. 1–29) of *Le Chevalier de la Charette* (*Lancelot*), where Chrétien disclaims his ability or desire to praise his patroness, Marie de Champagne, preferring, he says, to move directly to his narrative.

46. *Cligés* has a number of possible allusions to the *Chanson de Roland*; its references to *Tristan* are numerous and unmistakable, and it is often referred to as an "anti-Tristan" because of Fenice's attack on the legendary lovers (vv. 3105ff.) and its perversion of the love-potion motif.

47. Alexandre Micha, ed., *Les Romans de Chrétien de Troyes: Cligès.* (Paris: Librairie Ancienne Honoré Champion, 1957). The translation is William W. Kibler's: Chrétien de Troyes, *Arthurian Romances* (New York, London, et al.: Penguin, 1991), 130.

48. In a burlesque of *Tristan,* the Emperor Alis—the soon-to-be-cuckolded husband— drinks a magic potion that gives him the fantasy of Fenice's possession without the reality. Leslie Topsfield tentatively links the repetitions of "neant" in the description of the "unconsummated" wedding night of Alis and Fenice with the "nothingness" (defined as loss of "awareness of his sentient self") of Guillaume IX's "Farai un vers de dreyt nien," seeing both as part of "a controversy about the conflicting roles of feeling and fantasy in love, and in life," with Chrétien's "illusory wedding-night romp" a burlesque of the metaphysical assumptions underlying the controversy. See *Chrétien de Troyes: A Study of the Arthurian Romances* (Cambridge: Cambridge University Press, 1981), 77–78. The paradox of love literature is, of course, that this "nothingness" is precisely what provides the chief poetic impulse.

49. Derek Pearsall, "Development of Middle English Romance," *Studies in Medieval English Romances: Some New Approaches,* ed. Derek Brewer (Cambridge, England: D. S. Brewer, 1988), 16.

50. The romance tradition developed independently of the historical, with Latin and vernacular historians trying to de-emphasize the love story. See C. David Benson, *The History of Troy in Middle English Literature* (Cambridge: Cambridge University Press, 1980), chap. 1.

51. Discussions of the development of the Troy legends in Western tradition are found in R. M. Frazier Jr., *The Trojan War: The Chronicles of Dictys of Crete and Dares the Phrygian* (Bloomington and London: Indiana University Press, 1966); Arthur M. Young, *Troy and Her Legend* (Pittsburgh: University of Pittsburgh Press; rpt. Westport, Conn.: Greenwood, 1971) as well as Benson, *The History of Troy.* For a brief survey of post-Chaucerian treatments of the *Troilus* story, see Benson's "True Troilus and False Cressid: The Descent from Tragedy," in *The European Tragedy of Troilus,* ed. Piero Boitani (Oxford: Clarendon, 1989), 153–70.

52. His probable sources were Benoît and Guido delle Colonne's Latin abridgment, the *Historia Destructiones Troiae.*

53. Giulia Natali, "A Lyrical Version: Boccaccio's *Filostrato,"* in *The European Tragedy of Troilus,* 50–52. Natali, points out, for example, that "the ten-year siege of Troy and [its] causes . . . are summarized in a single introductory stanza, entirely in the imperfect tense" (52). Military actions are dismissed in casual summary ("Le cose andavan sì come di guerra, / tra li Troiani e Greci assai sovente" [1.16.1–2] [Things went on between the Trojans and the Greeks as they very often do in war]), with the only battle

described being Boccaccio's own invention (4.1–3) (53). The focus throughout is on amorous intrigue and lyric monologizing.

54. Ibid. Original from Windeatt's parallel text in *Troilus and Criseyde*, which is based on the edition by V. Pernicone (Bari, 1937).; translation by R. K. Gordon, *The Story of Troilus*, Mediaeval Academy Reprints for Teaching (Toronto: University of Toronto Press, 1978), 36.

55. " [F]or long stretches *Troilus* follows *Filostrato* so closely that Chaucer must have worked with a copy of the Italian in front of him." See Barry A. Windeatt, "Chaucer and the Filostrato," in *Chaucer and the Italian Trecento* (Cambridge: Cambridge University Press, 1983), 164.

56. See Barry A. Windeatt, "Classical and Medieval Elements in Chaucer's *Troilus*," in *The European Tragedy of Troilus*, 118.

57. See Windeatt, *Troilus and Criseyde*, 153 n. 8.

58. Ovidian models continued to inspire literary and political subversion well into the sixteenth century and beyond. See Paul Allen Miller, "Sidney, Petrarch, and Ovid, or Imitation as Subversion," *ELH* 58 (1991), 514: "When Sidney takes [the idealizing Petrarchan tradition] and produces a sonnet sequence in which many of the same rhetorical tropes are used in a fashion which emphasizes their sexual and material aspects, he casts himself not only as an Ovidian poet but also as an ideological rebel." Robert Polhemus discusses the influence of the idea of romantic love on the development of the novel in *Erotic Faith: Being in Love from Jane Austen to D. H. Lawrence* (Chicago: University of Chicago Press, 1990).

Ovidius ethicus?
Ovid and the Medieval Commentary Tradition

WARREN GINSBERG

Ovid is certainly a poet of surprises, but perhaps the most surprising thing about him is his transformation into an ethical pedagogue during the Middle Ages.[1] That a writer whose lascivity gave Augustus an excuse to banish him became a darling of an age of Christian probity is a metamorphosis more wonderful than any he described. Perhaps Ovid's hedonism by itself explains why we have no commentary from late antiquity on any of his works, and why they are cited so infrequently in early-medieval school texts. Indeed, when commentaries do appear, the explanations they give to establish the utility of his poems are clear, if indirect, admissions of how unfit a dispenser of moral precept Ovid is. One text, for instance, in an argument that was common, holds that even the *Ars amatoria* is a species of ethical discourse because Ovid teaches in it;[2] the magister, we may suspect, has his own activity more in mind than Ovid's. Similarly, in another twelfth-century accessus, studied by Ralph Hexter, we discover that Ovid wrote the *Ars* out of compassion for the many distraught Romans who were committing suicide because their love was unrequited.[3]

The strain to give Ovid scruples is evident; the absence of overt moralizing or allegorical reading in these early texts, though, is surprising. One would have thought Heloise's reaction more typical: she wrote to Abelard that even Ovid, the very poet of lust and doctor of immorality ("ipse . . . poeta luxuriae turpidinisque doctor") could give sound advice about avoiding banquets.[4] Her willingness to recognize propriety in Ovid is purchased by her fervent rejection of his eroticism; but in the general cultural economics of the medieval "aetas ovidiana," moral propensities were discovered less grudgingly, indeed in full recognition of the texts' carnality. From the twelfth through the fourteenth century, when the amorous Ovid of the *Amores, Heroides,* the *Ars* and the *Remedia Amoris* exercised enormous influence on the poetic letter, courtly love lyric, and romance, these same poems were routinely classified as ethical in academic commentaries.[5]

Even if we think that the gravity of the commentaries cleared a space for poets' playfulness, the problem of how Ovid became a voice of moral integrity remains.[6] Any ethical rehabilitation of Ovid is doubly astonishing, whatever weight one gives the *Fasti, Metamorphoses,* and poems of exile, not just because it must blink at his insistent advocacy of sexual love, with all its social disruptions, but also because it so misreads his subversiveness.[7] In all Ovid's erotic poems, every principle that literature, philosophy, or politics might offer to guide action is undercut by his skeptical irony and wit, a wit medieval poets definitely acknowledged and responded to.[8] When, for instance, Guillaume de Lorris says the *Roman de la Rose* is a book in which "l'art d'Amors est toute enclose / La maitre en est bele et noive" (38–39) [the art of love is entirely included; the matter is good and new], his terms recall the categories of the academic introduction. At the same time that he secures his poem's status as ethical discourse, however, Guillaume's declaration calls it into doubt. Basing the *Roman*'s claim to goodness and originality on the fact that it is a new "ars amatoria" can only cause the reader to wonder about its truthfulness and what it means by good. If, then, one aspect of Ovid's reception in the Middle Ages entailed embracing this sort of transgressive ambiguity, the designation of poems like the *Ars* as ethical in learned commentary is all the more puzzling. Of course, to the medieval mind, the use of classical Latin texts in medieval education itself established their moral utility. But can anything beyond appeal to such institutional employment, or to pious allegories that transfigured Ovid's texts beyond recognition, account for how this flamboyant, ironic sensualist of pagan Rome became an apologist for Christian conduct?

We should not lose sight of the dimensions of the transformation that the commentators worked. Their object of study, after all, was the Ovid who began his art of how to win a lover by retelling the rape of the Sabine women, and who ended it by giving the following counsel:

> uim licet appelles: grata est uis ista puellis;
> quod iuuat, inuitae saepe dedisse uolunt.
> quaecumque est Veneris subita uiolata rapina,
> guadet, et inprobitas muneris instar habet.
> at quae, cum posset cogi, non tacta recessit,
> ut simulet uultu gaudia, tristis erit.

(1.673–78)[9]

[You certainly can call on force: that kind of force women like. What delights them they often pretend to have given unwillingly. A woman violated by sudden rape feels joy, and holds the wicked deed a form of tribute. But a woman who has retired untouched, though she could have been forced, will be sad, though she pretends to be glad.]

Today, any defense of the brutishness of this passage by pointing to the jocularity of its tone will rightly be rejected as quickly as the woman's protests are brushed aside by the speaker. But Ovid's flippancy here masks an irony that is far more thoroughgoing (and dangerous), because it really does work to prevent taking what he says seriously. To frame instruction on how to win women by describing rapes is to underscore the irrelevance of any formalized *techne*; what need for an art if from start to finish all that winning amounts to is seizure by force?

Similarly, the second book of the *Ars* purports to teach how to hold a lover once she has been won. Yet the initial story of Dedalus and Icarus seems to suggest that one cannot hold what will not be held. That the tale again appears to be at cross-purposes with Ovid's declared intention prompts us to notice that all the instruction of this book is directly opposed to what one learned in the first: if love can be held, how can anyone else, even if instructed by the *Ars*, win it?

Nor are matters clarified when Ovid resolves these conflicts by concluding book 2 of the *Ars* with a description of sexual intercourse:

> conscius, ecce, duos accepit lectus amantes:
> ad thalami clausas, Musa, resiste fores
> sponte sua sine te celeberrima uerba loquentur,
> nec manus in lecto laeua iacebit iners;
> inuenient digiti quod agant in partibus illis,
> in quibus occulte spicula tingit Amor . . .
> crede mihi, non est Veneris properanda voluptas
> sed sensim tarda prolicienda mora.
> cum loca reppereris, quae tangi femina gaudet,
> non obstet, tangas quominus illa, pudor . . .
> sed neque tu dominam uelis maioribus usus
> defice, nec cursus anteeat illa tuos;
> ad metam properate simul: tum plena uoluptas,
> cum pariter uicti femina uirque iacent.
>
> (2.703–8; 717–20; 725–29)

[Now the knowing bed has received the two lovers. Stand by the closed doors of the bedchamber, O Muse. Without you the lovers will spontaneously speak a host of words, nor will the left hand lie idle on the bed. Fingers will discover what to do in those parts whose tips Love bedews in secret. . . .

Believe me, pleasure mustn't be hurried, but gradually slow delay should coax it forth. When you have found where a woman delights to be touched, do not let modesty make you caress her less. . . . [N]either do you want through greater exertion to leave your mistress behind, nor let her run the course before you. Hasten to the goal together; pleasure is complete when both man and woman lie equally overcome.]

In an ironic peripeteia, instead of being at odds with winning love, we now discover that holding it requires winning it, not once, but again and again: the "art" of love turns out to be the act of making love. Forces we thought were in opposition prove to be in collusion: in the parodic dialectic of the *Ars*, thesis and antithesis, instruction and delight, happily collapse into one another, just as its version of men and women does. Ovid only seems to set gaining and holding against one another, since, despite appearances, his purpose is not to achieve a philosophical synthesis but to generate a pleasurable rhetorical friction by continuously arguing for both.

The effects of such a conclusion for ethics are devastating. Desire exists only when it is resisted; by recognizing the autonomy of the object it seeks—its right, as it were, to resist—desire can, on a traditional reading, legitimately call itself moral. If the *Ars* actually recognized the otherness of women, its project to teach men how to love them could truly be an ethical one. But Ovid suggests instead that desire is always resisted from within, and that that resistance is already complicit with the desire that prompts it. For this reason, women in a real sense do not exist in the *Ars*; they have neither the substance nor the presence to obstruct desire or to be its object. Rather, they are only the occasion for desire's fulfillment, and it is fulfillment that the *Ars* actively strives toward and just as actively defers.[10] The final act of holding love does not end Ovid's book so much as it returns to the poem's opening instruction on how to win it. In the same way, the reversals of the third book, which purports to teach women how to win and hold men, reverse nothing. The instruction is the same as in the first two books; to imagine that women would follow it is as much a fantasy as to imagine that men would follow the previous books' advice. Everywhere in the *Ars*, Ovid quite morally shows how desire narcissistically fashions the objects it seeks in its own image in order to extend its existence; desire becomes artful when it resists itself for its own sake.

Of course, one would be right to say that this sort of subordination of women to the perpetuation of desire is peculiarly male, but if in some sense women do not exist in the *Ars*, neither do men. Because Ovid's erotics depends on the deferral of gratification, there is a consistent

elision of *all* bodies in the poem. The most illustrative instance of this
occurs between the end of the first book and the beginning of the second.
During this time, the pupil has won his beloved:

> Dicite 'io Paean' et 'io' bis dicite 'Paean':
> decidit in casses praeda petita meos.
> laetus amans donat uiridi mea carmina palma
> praelata Ascraeo Maeonioque seni.

(2.1–4)

[Cry "Io Paean," and cry it again, the sought-for game has fallen into my
snares. The joyful lover gives green palms to my poem, which he prefers to
old Hesiod and Homer.]

This celebration of the poem's effectiveness is typically broad and self-
congratulatory, but it cannot keep us from noticing that there is no
description here of what the words say the *Ars* has achieved. The record
of going to bed must be postponed until the end of the book, because, as
we have seen, once it has been reported, there is nothing more for an "ars
amatoria" to say.[11] In Ovid, the poem's the thing: its writing displaces
men and women both.

Because Ovid does not present the body and its desires so much as he
represents their textuality, he removes his poems from the orbit of any
ethics that supports or differentiates actions based on gender. Indeed,
Ovid has called into question whether it is possible to decide if the *Ars*
can be ethical in any sense. If intercourse is the point of the *Ars*,
representing it demands graphic explicitness; in fact, once it has been
discovered to be the end that coordinates the set of practices Ovid
describes, pornography becomes the book's "raison d'être." For the *Ars*
to be an "ars," it must be pornographic. But precisely because sex is the
most fleeting, least perdurable aspect of love, Ovid's lubricity is also a
declaration of his morality. Not only does the gaining of love seem,
Icarus-like, simultaneously the occasion of its loss, holding it by
repeatedly retiring to the bedroom is a prescription less apt to lead to a
lasting relationship than to exhaustion: in the *Remedia Amoris*, in fact,
Ovid will counsel repeated indulgence in sex as one way to fall out of
love. From this the moralist can say *The Art of Love* is ethical in that it
demonstrates how desire and fulfillment, by exposing the other's
excesses and deficiencies, are both temptations to be avoided.[12] The
hedonist, on the other hand, can say with equal force that the *Ars*'s worth
is its incitements to sexual consummation. If a principle to guide human
conduct can be recovered under such conditions, Ovid has shown there is
no reason to think reason will discern it.

The art of Ovid's book finally is its writing, which codifies and determines, but resolves nothing, because it enacts and cancels its own program. Of course, when sex is the goal, and still more when rape is sanctioned as a way to achieve it, suggestions that the advice should not be taken does not condone the fact that it has been given. Nevertheless, the *Ars* subverts the pretense that it is educative, or that it mimetically represents the social world, even as it proclaims by its title that it has made love rational and knowable and so can serve as a practical enchiridion of personal relations for Romans. The scandal of Ovid's amatory poems for the exegetical project in general, I would therefore suggest (for in this the *Ars* can stand for the others), lies less in their content than in their manner.[13] If these works were only invitations to sexuality, their provocations could be easily bridled either by rejecting them, as Heloise, or by rewriting their intent: they depict forms of love that should be avoided.[14] Ovid's double-voiced wit, however, which sees physical consummation as the echo of textual deferral, is another matter, since his irony functions as an internal commentary that resists the poem's outward professions of prurience. By anticipating the commentators' moral bias, Ovid preempts their desire to master his text; he has already shown that the ethics of his text, as well as its educative value, depend upon the inclination of the reader. However much interpretation would discipline its meaning, the *Ars* has proleptically assured that we hear a countervoice.

That countervoice, though, does more than preserve the poem's multivalency. It directs our attention to the fact that medieval commentary on Ovid generally, and especially when it is overtly allegorical, is itself a kind of auto-mimesis whose discursive praxis is the mirror image of Ovid's own. If Ovid represents the textualizing of the body and its desires, his works became worthy of imitation in the Middle Ages because monks and schoolmen incorporated them into their project to deny the urgencies of the flesh. If Ovid pretended to make love intelligible, in the exegetes' hands the *Ars* did indeed become rational; by reading their glossed version of it, a man would find a model of that self-control that transforms him into a more perfect image of his Maker. The commentators, however, couldn't maintain that the amatory poems were themselves inducements to such ascetic conduct; when they classified these works as ethical, they were not offering Ovid's poems for the reader's emulation so much as their own textual performance. Certainly the utility of the commentaries derived in part from their ability to serve Ovid's works by making them accessible. Their ultimate value, though, had to reside in the facticity of the commentary itself, since Ovid's poems entered the ambit of ethical discourse only when they were submitted to moral or grammatical explication.

In promoting their ethical Ovid, medieval scholiasts therefore were actually presenting an image of themselves as writers. Indeed, where else but in their own practices could the expositors have discovered ethics for Ovid? Yet it was just this impulse, at once ascetic and narcissistic, to offer themselves as models, that ironically made the exegetes scribes of Ovid's irony, which, as we saw, likewise denies the *Ars*'s "worldliness" by turning to its own writing. In fact, the connection I am suggesting between Ovidian sexuality and the ascetic impulses of the commentaries is less strange than one might think, since Christian self-denial was also an exercise based in textuality. As Geoffrey Harpham has shown, from St. Anthony on, ascetic documents at once equated writing with the body and the fallen world and offered that writing as an object to imitate.[15] The "vita" of the ascetic both substitutes for his acts and extends his life; Athanasius in fact claims that the language of *The Life of St. Anthony*, the inaugural text of Christian asceticism, enables it to be superior as a "picture for ascetic practice" to Anthony himself.[16] Ascetic regimen, whether undertaken alone or in a community withdrawn from society, displaced the body by imitating the text that was its surrogate.

At the same time, however, writing, because it is secondary and belated, was demeaned as the external representation of the heart's inner, immediate truth. "The corporeal form of script," in Harpham's words, "anchored it to the world of death," thereby giving a form to all that the ascetic would abstain from. Yet at the same time the abstractness of writing, its remove from direct contact with the senses, made it a model to be emulated. The scriptural qualities of a text thus enacted a kind of ascesis, a drama of simultaneous temptation and resistance, that provided a paradigm for the ascetic's desire to mortify his flesh.[17]

In the Christian Middle Ages, asceticism undergirds ethics precisely because it read the human body as if it were a text. Once the body was dissociated from complexities of blood and the hour by being equated with the protocols of writing, it became representable and its passions subject to rational government. By bringing to the surface everything that was hidden, by making the difficult plain, the commentators literally generated a chirographic ethics for Ovid by calling attention to how they violated each of his poems in the same way and for the same reason that the ascetic disfigured his body: to make it knowable. And it was just this act of making known that the commentaries would have their readers imitate.

This response to Ovid, I would suggest, marks an important moment in the criticism of the amatory poems, for the medieval academics make us see a fact that Ovid knew but had occluded: desire's true temptation is not gratification but self-denial. The ascetic textuality of the commentary tradition is not alien to Ovid's erotics but its fraternal twin.[18]

On his side, however, Ovid long ago understood what Foucault's *History of Sexuality* has taught us anew: the discourses of knowledge mask less their will to power than their own impulse toward pleasure. Because love in Ovid is always a textual affair, all his amatory poems, but especially the *Ars*, which openly appropriates the forms of didacticism, make us see that ethical abstinence is itself a species of desire. The exegetes could not rewrite Ovid's intent without Ovid in effect underwriting their own. In their zeal, the expositors not only manhandled Ovid's texts the way he advised men to manhandle women, they also opened the door to the possibility that their own critical imperatives would be resisted. The accessus writers themselves implicitly acknowledged that their practice had a material dimension when they gave Ovid back his body in the form of increasingly full biographies of the poet.[19] Perhaps even more telling a demonstration of the erotic propensities of moral interpretation is the long-standing debate about whether Andreas Capellanus is serious or joking, for no matter which side one takes, it is the status of orthodox Ovidian commentary, not the reception of Ovid per se, that the sexuality of the *De Arte* calls into question. Most of all, the full reappearance of fleshly desire in vernacular literary adaptations of Ovid that, like the *Roman de la Rose*, were influenced by the commentaries, shows that carnal cravings haunt all ascetic regimens.

Ovid's hedonism and the ethics of the exegetes: however forced the conjunction seems, because both are textual systems, the inner dynamics of each requires the presence of the other. It seems to me more than a coincidence that the "aetas ovidiana" arose along with the enormous expansion of academic commentary in the High Middle Ages. Then, as now, desire and denial have made us all their scribes.

Notes

1. The bibliography on Ovidian commentary in the Middle Ages is very large. I have found the following especially useful: Don Cameron Allen, *Mysteriously Meant* (Baltimore: Johns Hopkins, 1970), 163–99; E. H. Alton, "Ovid in the Medieval Schoolroom" *Hermathena* 94 (1960): 21–38; 95 (1961): 67–82; Paule Demats, *Fabula* (Geneva: Libraire Droz, 1973); Fausto Ghisalberti, "Arnolfo d'Orléans, un cultore di Ovidio nel secolo XII," Reale Istituto Lombardo di Scienze e Lettere (Milan), *Memorie* 24 (1932): 157–234; Ralph J. Hexter, *Ovid and Medieval Schooling, Münchener Beiträge zür Mediävistik und Renaissance-Forschung* 38 (Munich: Arbeo Gesellechaft, 1986); R. B. C. Huygens, *Accessus ad auctores, Bernard d'Utrecht, Conrad d'Hirsau "Dialogus super Auctores"* (Leiden: Brill, 1970); Wilfried Stroh, ed., *Ovid im Urteil der Nachwelt*

(Darmstadt: Wissenschaftliche Buchgesellschaft, 1969); Edwin A. Quain, "The Medieval Accessus ad Auctores," *Traditio* 3 (1945): 215–64.

2. "Ethicae subponitur, quia de moribus puellarum loquitur" (The *Ars* is classified as ethics because it discourses on the habits of girls). The text (Munich, clm 19475) is printed by Huygens, 33. The utility ("finalis cause") of the work is expressed as follows: "ut perlecto libro in mandatis suis, quid tenendum sit in amore ipsis iuvenibus enucleatum sit" [that once the book and its precepts have been read through, how one should act in love with girls will be made clear]. As Ralph Hexter says, in the monasteries and schools in general, whatever aversion Ovid's eroticism may have aroused "was negated, as the texts themselves indicate, by the value-free function these texts had: instruction" (25).

3. "Siquidem uidens Ouidius iuuenes et puellas quasdam tempore suo ex impericia amoris periculum incurrentes, alios cogi ad laqueum, alios ad suspendium, ne amplius tale quam patiantur, eos in amore peritos reddit." The text (Hafn. 2015 B) is printed by Hexter, 219.

4. "Ipse quoque poeta luxuriae turpidinisque doctor libro Amatoriae Artis intitulato quantum fornicationis occasionem convivia maxime praebeant studiose exequitur, dicens" [That very poet of lust and doctor of immorality also describes assiduously how much banquets especially offer an occasion for fornication, saying]. Heloise here quotes from the *Ars*: 1.233–34, 239–40, 243–44. I quote from Stroh, *Ovid im Urteil*, 16.
Anti-Ovidian comments such as these, which perhaps culminate in the *Antiovidianus*, ed. K. Kienast, in *Aus Petrarcas ältesten deutsche Schülerkreisen*, ed. Karl Burdach (Berlin, 1929), 4:81–111, are found throughout the Middle Ages: they represent another tradition of Ovid's reception. Most condemn Ovid's poems for their moral turpitude, but there are other reasons as well. Petrarch's criticisms are characteristically stylistic. What is of most interest is the fact that these repudiations share the same moral universe as the academic commentaries, yet seem to be at odds with them. This essay offers a tentative explanation why this might be so.

5. For Ovid's influence on the poetic letter in the Middle Ages, see Gerald Bond, "*Iocus amoris*: The Poetry of Baudri of Bougeuil and the Formation of the Ovidian Subculture" *Traditio* 42 (1986): 143–93. Interest in the *Metamorphoses* as a repository of scientific lore also was strong during this time: see Simone Viarre, *La survie d'Ovide dans la littérature scientifique des xiième et xiiième siècles* (Poitiers: CESCM, 1966). Even in the schoolroom, as Hexter notes (17), there was "no sense of incongruousness in approaching love from a scholastic perspective." The first glossed text of any of Ovid's works, found in the ninth-century "Classbook of St. Dunstan," is the *Ars Amatoria*.

6. On the role of the academic commentary tradition in creating a space for vernacular literary production, see Rita Copeland, *Rhetoric, Hermeneutics and Translation in the Middle Ages* (Cambridge: Cambridge University Press, 1991).

7. A telling instance of this misreading is the conventional medieval reception of the *Remedia Amoris*. Although this text contains quite as much explicitly erotic and pornographic material as the *Ars*, because it announced its purpose was to teach how to fall out of love, it became particularly popular as a schooltext. See Hexter, 18–19.

8. I elaborate these ideas in two articles: "Ovid and the Politics of Interpretation," *Classical Journal* 84 (1989): 222–31, and "Ovid and the Problem of Gender," *Mediaevalia* 13 (1989): 9–28.

9. I quote from *P. Ovidi Nasonis Amores . . . Ars Amatoria, Remedia Amoris*, ed. E. J. Kenney, *Oxford Classical Texts* (Oxford: Oxford University Press, 1961). Unless otherwise noted, translations are mine.

10. Medieval commentators also recognized, albeit for different ends, that the *Ars* was not concerned with fulfillment. In an accessus to the *Amores* (Huygens, 37, "Ovidii sine

titulo [II]"), we read that the *Amores* need to be distinguished from the *Ars*: "Ovidius de Amatoria Arte dat precepta amantibus ut sint cauti, hic autem de Amore et in semetipso complet precepta" (In the *Ars* Ovid gives precepts to lovers so that they may take care, here in the *Amores* he fulfills the precepts himself). The same distinction is found in another accessus discussed by Hexter, 18.

11. Perhaps in his own way the author of the accessus in clm 19475 recognized this: he clearly expresses Ovid's aim as if the *Ars* ended with its second book: "Intentio sua est in hoc opere iuvenes ad amorem instruere, quo modo debeant se in amore habere circa ipsas puellas."

12. In this sense, Ovid also authors the moral repudiations of him in the Middle Ages. One striking instance of this is the inclusion of *Ars amatoria* in Jankyn's book of wicked wives in Chaucer's "Wife of Bath's Prologue." See Michael Calabrese, *Chaucer's Ovidian Arts of Love* (Gainesville: University Press of Florida, 1994), 81–109. My point in this essay, however, is to suggest how Ovid authors the commentary tradition as well.

13. On the ironic, rhetorical turn away from the simultaneously advanced claims to mimesis in the *Amores*, see my *The Cast of Character: The Representation of Personality in Ancient and Medieval Literature* (Toronto: University of Toronto Press, 1983), 20–47; in the *Metamorphoses*, 7–14, 56–70. The affinity of the *Heroides* to rhetorical "suasoriae" would have been apparent to any Roman; Ovid, however, has hobbled the letters' rhetorical effectiveness from the start. How can persuasion succeed when it has been deliberately robbed of its immediacy? Once again, irony works against the work's professed intentions. That the same thing occurs in the *Remedia Amoris* would seem to be obvious. Yet this poem was especially prized in the Middle Ages precisely because the commentators said it really does work to undo the effects of carnal love! See the next note.

14. The clearest indication of this is the commentators' attitude toward the *Remedia Amoris*: despite the explicit sexuality of the poem, every bit the equal of the *Ars*, it was held to be highly moral, since it taught men and women alike how to protect themselves against illicit love ("qualiter contra illicitum amorem se armare debeant," in Huygens, 34).

15. Geoffrey Harpham, *The Ascetic Imperative in Culture and Criticism* (Chicago: University of Chicago Press, 1987). Harpham advances the extraordinary claim that *all* ethical criticism is finally ascetic. His reading of Foucault's writings on sexuality are especially suggestive and relevant to my thesis here. See "Saint Foucault," 220–35.

16. Ibid., 5.

17. Ibid., 6.

18. Medieval exegetical practice is the fraternal twin of Ovidian sexuality in another sense as well: it reinscribes gender. Indeed, a feminist reading would rightly point out not only how, by taking the form of inclusive opposites, sex and asceticism become part of the logic of patriarchal logocentrism, but also that desire need not limit its outcome exclusively to gratification or denial. Mutual respect, for instance, is also possible.

19. The best study of these biographies is Fausto Ghisalberti, "Medieval Biographies of Ovid," *Journal of the Warburg and Courtauld Institute* 9 (1946): 10–59.

The Transformation of Ovid
in the Twelfth-Century *Pamphilus*

ANNE HOWLAND SCHOTTER

Although the work of a handful of medieval Latin women writers—
primarily Hroswitha, Heloise, and Hildegard of Bingen—has recently
begun to receive some attention,[1] the fact remains that both the classical
and medieval Latin traditions were overwhelmingly male in perspective
as well as authorship. An outstanding exception is Ovid, who, whether
friendly or unfriendly to women, was certainly interested in their
subjective experience. This essay will explore the use of the Roman
poet's work to construct the female voice in the medieval Latin
Pamphilus, a 780-line poem written in the early twelfth century by an
anonymous author, most likely male, about a seduction that ends in a
rape.[2] I shall argue that although the poet found Ovid the best source
available in the Latin literary tradition for conveying female subjectivity,
he found his female voices in themselves inadequate, and so turned to
Ovid's male-voiced poetry—primarily the amatory works—to
supplement it.

Pamphilus opens with the hero telling Venus of his love for a girl,
Galathea, and the goddess advising him to court her with eloquence but
to be ready to use force. Frustrated by Galathea's clever parrying of his
seduction rhetoric, Pamphilus hires a go-between, an old woman who
arranges a rendezvous for him. When, just as Galathea seems on the
point of yielding, Pamphilus rapes her, she is outraged and protests
eloquently. Upon returning, the old woman feigns ignorance of what has
happened, declares that the couple will get married and live happily ever
after, and demands her payment. Although until recently this poem has
been relatively ignored,[3] opinion of it has begun to change somewhat
with current interest in the female perspective in medieval literature.

Most notably, Allison Goddard Elliott has argued in an introduction to her translation that the sympathetic treatment of Galathea as a rape victim gives the poem a dark cast, as it explores the dangerous consequences of Ovidian seduction games.[4] While her view has been opposed by Ian Thompson and Louis Perraud, recent translators of the poem,[5] it gains support from Jill Mann, who in a volume on Chaucer uses the poem to illustrate the threat of rape lying behind the rhetoric of courtly love.[6] Indeed, Kathryn Gravdal's argument that the representation of rape in medieval literature was both more sustained and more problematical than has been thought[7] encourages us to look at *Pamphilus* in a new light. I believe that the poem condemns rape by dramatizing the woman's point of view and refusing to euphemize the act as a "ravishing." The reader therefore has difficulty accepting either the old woman's pronouncement of a "happy ending" or the standard classification of the poem with the light-hearted and often bawdy medieval Latin narratives known as *comediae*.[8]

Pamphilus is a product of the twelfth-century revival of interest in the trivium, and its dialogue form suggests that it may have been written as a schoolroom exercise in *disputatio* for young men studying dialectic. It is equally part of the twelfth-century rediscovery of Ovid and so closely modeled on his work that it was often attributed to him in medieval manuscripts. But the scholars who have recognized this fact have not examined the dynamics of this intertextuality in the way that Hexter, Bond, and Cahoon have recently done in their studies of the medieval reception of the works of Ovid,[9] and have hence overlooked a particularly complex relation between male and female voices in the poem. The most direct source of male voice is the amatory poetry— particularly the *Amores* and the *Ars Amatoria*. The female voice is most obviously indebted to the *Heroides*, most of which are fictional letters of seduced and abandoned heroines to their faithless lovers, but it also borrows from female-voiced passages in his other works, such as the cries of the rape victims in the *Metamorphoses*. In the speech of Galathea, however, these sources are supplemented with borrowings from the male-voiced utterances in Ovid's poetry. Thus, in expressing her conflicting feelings about Pamphilus, she echoes the male narrator of the *Amores*, besieged by love, while in her outrage after the rape she parodies the language of that narrator, at the same time that she reveals the cruelty of the advice in the *Ars Amatoria*. From all these sources the poet constructs a voice that gives a sense of female subjectivity only suggested in Ovid's amatory poetry and thereby exposes the Roman elegiac *topos* of the helpless lover being forced to commit rape.

In the male-voiced *Ars Amatoria* and *Amores,* the author of *Pamphilus* could have found a model for his major contradiction: the fact that when seduction seems to be successful, the hero resorts to rape. For, despite Ovid's high reputation in the twelfth century as a rhetorical poet, which was at least partly based on the celebration of the artfulness of seduction in both poems, their speakers assume that seduction and rape are closely related. It is true, of course, that the *praeceptor amoris* in the *Ars* emphasizes the importance of eloquence in seduction, pitying the lovesick lawyer who, having previously defended others, is now rendered so speechless that he needs a counselor himself,[10] or urging young men to learn eloquence so that they can win over women as well as judges or senators.[11] Furthermore, in book 2, devoted to maintaining a woman's love, he stresses the superiority of eloquence and patience to good looks and force, citing Ulysses, who, despite his homeliness, was so eloquent ("facundus") that he seduced Calypso by rehearsing the fall of Troy: "non formosus erat, sed erat facundus Vlixes, / et tamen aequoreas torsit amore deas" (2.123–24). Nevertheless, in a well-known passage in the *Ars*, the *praeceptor* recommends rape, insisting that all women want it although they are ashamed to admit it:[12]

> uim licet appelles: grata est uis ista puellis;
> quod iuuat, invitae saepe dedisse uolunt.
> quaecumque est Veneris subita uiolata rapina,
> gaudet, et inprobitas muneris instar habet.
> at quae, cum posset cogi, non tacta recessit,
> ut simulet uultu gaudia, tristis erit.
>
> (*Ars Amatoria* 1.673–78)

[Force is all right to employ, and women like you to use it; / What they enjoy they pretend they were unwilling to give. / One who is overcome, and suddenly, forcefully taken, / Welcomes the wanton assault, takes it as proof of her charm. / But if you let her go untouched when you could have compelled her, / Though she pretends to be glad, she will be gloomy at heart.][13]

As an illustration, he cites Achilles' rape of Deidamia while disguised as a woman in order to avoid the Trojan war, an act that not only vindicated his manhood but also so delighted her that she begged him to stay:

> Haec illum stupro comperit esse uirum.
> uiribus illa quidem uicta est (ita credere oportet),
> sed uoluit uinci uiribus illa tamen.
> Saepe "mane" dixit, cum iam properaret Achilles.
>
> (*Ars Amatoria* 1.698–701)

[She was the one whom rape taught he was really a man. / She was taken by force, by violence—we must believe it— / Still, being taken by force she had achieved her desire. / More than once she would cry, "Stay," when Achilles was leaving.]

The Ovidian topos of the continuum between rhetoric and violence is echoed by Venus at the beginning of *Pamphilus*. For, while she draws generally on the commandment in the *Ars* that the lover devote hard work and artifice to his project (ll. 71–76), she too condones rape if the time is right. First she urges the hero to pay special attention to his speech: "Nec nimium taceas, nec uerba superflua dicas; / Despicit e minimo sepe puella uirum,"[14] and then asserts that "Excitat et nutrit facundia dulcis amorem / Et mulcens animos mitigat ipsa feros" (ll. 107–8; "a sweet eloquence arouses and nourishes love / and flattery softens a wild heart"). Though such praise of "facundia" reflects the admiration of Ovid's rhetorical skill current in the twelfth-century schools, the author of *Pamphilus* seems to have been equally influenced by the Roman poet's acceptance of violence, for Venus immediately goes on to make a pragmatic recommendation of rape:

> Si locus est, illi iocundis uiribus insta,
> Quod uix sperasti, mox dabit ipsa tibi.
> Non sinit interdum pudor illi promere uotum,
> Sed quod habere cupit, hoc magis ipsa negat:
> Pulcrius esse putat ui perdere uirginitatem
> Quam dicat: "de me fac modo uelle tuum."
>
> (*Pamphilus* ll. 109–14)

[If there is an opportunity, urge her with playful violence. / What you scarcely hoped for soon she herself will give. / Sometimes shame may keep her from expressing her desire; / But what she desires to have is what she denies the most, / She thinks it more admirable to lose her virginity by force than that she say, "Do with me as you will."]

Like Ovid's *praeceptor amoris*, Venus argues that women want to be raped because it relieves them of responsibility for their actions. The old woman, a descendant of the cynical go-between Dipsas in *Amores* l. 8,[15] shares this assumption and urges Pamphilus not to be shy but to "be a man" ("esse uirum" [1.546]) when she arranges a rendezvous. Together, she and Venus underscore the powers of verbal and physical coercion arrayed against Galathea.

In the *Amores*, too, the author of *Pamphilus* could have found the threat of rape hidden behind the charm of seduction, although the

rhetorical purpose of those elegies makes it more subtle than in the *Ars*.
As Leslie Cahoon has shown in "The Bed as Battlefield: Erotic Conquest
and Military Metaphor in Ovid's *Amores*," while the *amator* of the
elegies extols the power of eloquence to compensate for his own
powerlessness before the girl's cruelty, he nevertheless betrays thoughts
of sexual violence. She points out that he uses the topos of the lover as
Cupid's captive in *Amores* 1.2 as a pretext for making the girl herself a
captive in *Amores* 1.3, for "by comparing her with Io, Leda, and Europa,
and himself, implicitly, with Jupiter adulter" (1.3.22), he reveals a
fantasy of rape.[16] And again, although in *Amores* 2.12 he celebrates the
peacefulness of his victory over his mistress's husband and guard, he
reveals an interest in rape in his later list of women he blames for causing
war: Helen, Hippodamia, and the Sabines. More overtly, in *Amores* 1.5,
the famous elegy describing the surprise afternoon visit to the lover's
bedroom, the mistress is described as feigning resistance to a rape that
she actually desires.[17] Thus, though Ovid's love of skill and artifice leads
him to prefer rhetoric to force, his narrators in the amatory poetry treat
rape as acceptable if all else fails.[18] That they can sanction rape at the
same time that they praise patience, tact, and eloquence is a sign of that
protean quality that has led Richard Lanham to see Ovid as the paradigm
of the "rhetorical man."[19]

   While the author of *Pamphilus* relies on Ovid's amatory poetry to
construct both his male and female voices, he does so much more
obviously with the former. Specifically, the hero's laments about his
unrequited love draw on the portrayal of the vanquished lover in the
Amores discussed above.[20] In his opening soliloquy he announces, "I am
wounded" ("Vulneror" [1.1]) and later uses military metaphors to
complain to Venus about his prostration at the hands of Galathea:

> Hec mea transiecit certis precordia telis,
> Tela nec inde queo ui remouere mea.
> Vulneris inde mei crescit dolor omnibus horis.
> (*Pamphilus* ll. 41–43)

[She has pierced my heart with well-aimed weapons; / With all my strength I
cannot remove them. / The pain of my wound increases every hour.]

The phrase "certis . . . telis" echoes the complaint of the *amator* in the
Amores that Cupid overcame him with "certas . . . sagittas" [well-aimed
arrows][21]; just as Cahoon[22] and Leo Curran[23] have shown of Ovid's
speaker, Pamphilus presents himself as conquered in order to justify
conquering a woman.

The poem shows a similar indebtedness to the *Ars Amatoria* both in Pamphilus's seduction of Galathea and in his insensitive remarks to her after the rape. When, having been roused from his helplessness by the encouragement of Venus and the old woman, he tells Galathea, "[T]u sola placuisti" (171) [You alone have pleased me], he is directly echoing the *praeceptor amoris*, who urges the lover to tell a girl, "[T]u mihi sola places" (*AA* 1.42) at the beginning of his program to entrap her. Later, asking Galathea why she is crying after the rape, "Curque lauas lacrimis flebilis ora tuis?" (2.700) [And why do you weep and wash your face with tears?], Pamphilus recalls Ovid's account of Romulus's soldier in the *Ars* who, after raping one of the Sabine women, asks, "Quid teneros lacrimis corrumpis occellos?" (*AA* 1.129) [Why are you spoiling your precious eyes with tears? (my translation)].

Unlike Pamphilus's voice, which is derived rather straightforwardly from the male voice in the amatory poetry, Galathea's voice is very complex in its Ovidian intertextuality. It has structural similarities with the voices of the women in the *Heroides* and thematic similarities with the voice of Philomela in *Metamorphoses* 6, but supplements these by transposing male-voiced utterances from the *Amores* and the *Ars Amatoria*. Since Ovid expressed the subjectivity of men more extensively than that of women, the poet turned to the former in order to construct a female voice sufficiently complex for the twelfth century. Galathea's voice appears in four major parts of the narrative: in her clever response to Pamphilus's seduction rhetoric, in her confession to the old woman of the inner struggle between love and fear, in her outcries during the rape, and in her lament about the rape after it is over. The first of these, her response to the rhetoric, owes the least debt to Ovid, for, like the sophisticated rejoinders of the women in Andreas Capellanus's *Ars amandi,* it shows the contemporary influence of the study of dialectic in the schools. Her parrying of her lover's arguments also recalls the medieval shepherdesses of the pastourelles, who often succeed in exposing the sham of the courtly seducer's flattery far better than Ovid's girls are able to do.[24]

The other three narrative occurrences of Galathea's voice, however, are highly indebted to Ovid. The most poignant aspect of the poem—and the one that may have contributed most greatly to its popularity with later vernacular audiences—is its portrayal of Galathea's falling in love with Pamphilus, an event that occurs despite her suspicion of the rhetoric and ceases abruptly with the rape. In portraying her conflicting love and doubt, the poet relies not on the *Heroides* but on the male voice of the *Amores*, most likely because it provides a more serious paradigm of a loving subject.[25] He in fact develops the metaphor of the lover besieged much more explicitly in Galathea's speech than in that of Pamphilus, both in her doubts about love and, as we shall see below, in her sense of violation and helplessness after the rape. She tells the old woman that the violent weapons of Cupid threaten a young girl with serious wounds ("Non leue uulnus habent uiolenta Cupidinis arma," [l. 415]), and later draws out the military metaphors inherent in the topos of love's wound ("uulnus amoris" [l. 624]):

> Me sibi subdit amor, illi licet usque repugnem
> Meque repugnantem forcius urget amor.
>
> (*Pamphilus* ll. 625–26)

[Love overcomes me, although I fight against it, / The more I resist it, the more forcefully love assaults me.]

Galathea's admission of vulnerability establishes a sympathy for her that is not invited for the young women of Ovid's amatory poetry; despite the old woman's charge that Galathea's resistance marks her as prudish (ll. 379–80), we are convinced of the genuineness of her feelings. By transposing Ovid's portrayal of masculine subjectivity to the woman, the poet goes beyond him to create a distinctively medieval psychomachia within a female character, one resembling that in vernacular romances such as *Yvain* and the *Eneas.*

Given this portrayal of Galathea as a loving subject, the ensuing rape scene is particularly abrupt. Although the cynical connoisseur's response invited by Ovid's amatory poetry is impossible for the reader, Galathea's voice is in fact partially constructed out of male-voiced passages found in that poetry. Through her protests alone we learn of the rape:

> Pamphile, tolle manus! . . . te frustra nempe fatigas!
> Nil ualet ille labor! quod petis esse nequit! . . .
> Pamphile tolle manus! . . . male nunc offendis amicam! . . .
> Iamque redibit anus: Pamphile tolle manus! . . .
> Heu michi! quam paruas habet omnis femina uires! . . .
> Quam leuiter nostras uincis utrasque manus! . . .
> Pamphile! nostra tuo cum pectore pectora ledis! . . .
> Quid me sic tractas? est scelus atque nephas! . . .
> Desine! . . . clamabo! . . . quid agis! male detegor a te! . . .
> Perfida, me miseram, quando redibit anus?
> Surge! precor! . . . nostras audit vicinia lites! . . .
> Que tibi me credit non bene fecit anus! . . .
> . . . .
> Hujus uictor eris facti, licet ipsa relucter,
> Sed tamen inter nos rumpitur omnis amor!
>
> (*Pamphilus* ll. 681–92, 695–96)

[Pamphilus, take away your hands! You are exhausting yourself in vain! / This action is useless! What you seek cannot be! / Pamphilus, take your hands away! You are badly offending your friend! / The old woman will shortly return! Pamphilus, take away your hands! / Alas, how little strength a woman has; / How easily you conquer my hands! / Pamphilus, you're hurting my breasts with your breast. / Why are you treating me this way? It is a crime and an unspeakable act! / Stop! I'll cry out! What are you doing? It is wrong to undress me! / Wretched me, when will that treacherous old woman come back? / Get up, I beg you. The neighbors will hear our quarrel! / That old woman did wrong to trust me to you. / . . . / You're the victor in this matter, although I resisted, / but all love between us is destroyed.]

This passage borrows from both male- and female-voiced utterances in Ovid to convey Galathea's sense of outrage. In a far more literal way than the *amator* in the *Amores* or than Pamphilus himself, Galathea uses the military topos of the vanquished lover as she protests that Pamphilus is overcoming ("uincis" [686]) her hands and scornfully points out that, while he is the "uictor " (695) in the encounter, he has destroyed their love. Furthermore, her lament about women's physical weakness (685) makes literal the protest of Ovid's *amator* that Cupid gains no glory in defeating an unarmed victim: "nec tibi laus armis uictus inermis ero."[26]

A second instance of transposition of a male-voiced utterance in Ovid to Galathea during the rape scene is very different, this time originating in a man's expression not of despair but of anger at the thought of a rival. In her repeated demand, "tolle manus" [take away your hands], she echoes a letter from a matched pair in the *Heroides* that recounts an incident of sexual coercion—the epistle of Acontius to Cydippe.[27] The writer tries to force the woman to marry him on the basis of an earlier deception—his tricking her into swearing an unwitting oath as she reads aloud the message, "I will wed Acontius." In the passage echoed by Galathea, Acontius expresses outrage at the thought of an imagined rival's touching Cydippe—his property—while she lies sick. After saying, "iste sinus meus est! mea turpiter oscula sumis!" (20.145) [That bosom is mine! Mine are the kisses that you so basely take!],[28] he goes on to demand,

> a mihi promisso corpore tolle manus!
> improbe, tolle manus!
>
> (*Heroides* 20.146–47)

[Take your hands off the body promised to me! / You depraved one, take your hands off!]

It is surprising that Galathea's expression of outrage at the violation of her body should be borrowed from one of the three male-voiced epistles in the *Heroides* rather than from the more numerous female-voiced ones, which not only generally provide an important source for women's perspective in medieval literature[29] but also specifically give voice to the women victimized by the masculine wiles described in Ovid's amatory poetry.[30] This suggests that the poet found the *Heroides* more useful for the structure of Galathea's voice than for its content.

A more probable source of that voice in the rape scene is Ovid's story of Philomela in *Metamorphoses* 6.424–74, which stands out among the many accounts of rape in that work[31] for the attention it gives the subjective reaction of the female victim. While the rapes of Europa, Leda, and Io are softened and rendered aesthetic by emphasis on the transformations of Jupiter into bull, swan, and cloud,[32] that of Philomela, because of its portrayal of a brutal human rapist and a fiercely resistant victim, is starkly realistic. Ovid tells of how Thracian Tereus persuades the father of his wife, Procne, to allow him to bring her sister Philomela to visit her. Overcome by lust, he rapes Philomela and, fearing her disclosure of the act, cuts out her tongue. Although he imprisons her in the woods, she succeeds in telling her story to her sister by weaving it into a textile and having it conveyed to her. When the horrified Procne finds her sister, they plot together to kill the son of Procne and Tereus and serve his body to his father for dinner. When Tereus asks for the boy, Procne says that he is present already, and Philomela flings the boy's bloody head at him. All three characters are thereupon transformed into birds—the swallow, the nightingale, and the predatory hoopoe, according to the legend.

Though this account of rape and the victim's revenge is far more brutal than anything that occurs in *Pamphilus*, the story's popularity in the same intellectual milieu—for instance, in the Old French adaptation of *Philomena*, often attributed to Chrétien de Troyes[33]—suggests that it could have influenced the poem. In particular, the portrayal of Galathea could be indebted to Ovid's rendering of Philomela's voice. For, despite the fact that she is most often regarded by feminist critics as the paradigm of the woman silenced by patriarchy who nevertheless succeeds in communicating through art,[34] she is in fact quite forthright. Ovid describes her as protesting while being raped: "cum lacrimis, ubi sit germana, rogantem / . . . clamato saepe parente, / saepe sorore sua, magnis super omnia divis" (6.523–26) [calling / For her father, for her sister, but most often, / For the great gods].[35] After the rape, she is even more outspoken, as she beats her breast and cries out, "o diris barbara factis! / o crudelis!'" (533–34) [O wicked deed! O cruel monster, /

Barbarian savage!]. Furthermore, far from being silenced by the rape, Philomela is silenced precisely because of her protest against it. For it is when, believing that she has nothing to lose, she threatens to publicize his deed that Tereus cuts out her tongue ("tua facta loquar: si copia detur, / in populos veniam; ... audiet haec aether" [545–46, 548] [I will proclaim it. / Given the chance, I will go where people are, / Tell everybody; ... / The air of heaven will hear]). The story could have provided the author of *Pamphilus* with a model as well for the contrast between Galathea's bravery and her attacker's cowardice. For, despite her fear for her honor, the young woman urges Pamphilus to tell the go-between what happened ("Pamphile, dic illi" [757]), while he in contrast tries to conceal it.

Although the story of Philomela offers a structural model for Galathea's protests, it has no obvious verbal similarities, and none of the commentators who have so carefully traced Ovidian parallels in the poem has noted it. Nevertheless, *Pamphilus* may contain verbal echoes of Philomela in the references to the outrage of the rape. Galathea refers to it as "scelus atque nephas" (688) [a crime and unspeakable act] and even Pamphilus himself, though blaming his actions on her beauty, refers to "facta nephanda" (712). Ovid describes the rape of Philomela in precisely these terms, saying that Tereus "fassusque nefas" (6.522) [disclosed the unspeakable deed][36] to Philomela before doing it, and having her refer to it as a "nefandos concubitos" (6.540) [unspeakable coupling]. Finally Procne, after receiving the textile recounting the crime ("sceleris" [6.578]), goes into the forest in search of the "domum ... nephandum" (6.601) [unspeakable ... house] in which Philomela is imprisoned.

Whether or not the references in Pamphilus to "scelus" and "nephas" are echoes of the story of Philomela, it is significant that the poet chose to apply them to what Ovid's *praeceptor amoris* would have considered the relatively innocent rape of a young woman by a young man who apparently loves her and whom she is beginning to love—an act he would have seen as no more criminal than Jupiter's poetic "ravishings." If one assumes with the speaker of the *Ars Amatoria* that women really want to be raped, only a rape as brutal and grotesque as that of Philomela, compounded by incest and mutilation, would constitute a "nefas." The medieval poet, in contrast, presents the simple violation of a girl's stated wishes as an outrage.

After the rape, Galathea's final speech contains further Ovidian echoes, again taking the male voice and transposing it. What seems to offend her most is that she was overcome not by Pamphilus's force but by the old woman's fraud, as she blames the latter for the "artibus

innumeris" (761) she had practiced upon her. Recognizing that rhetoric
can be as coercive as rape, Galathea goes on to expand upon an earlier
presentation of herself as a victim of the hunt. She laments "in laqueam
fugiens decidit ecce lepus!" (740) [See how the fleeing hare has fallen
into a trap], and continues,

> Sic piscis curuum iam captus percipit hamum,
> Sic avis humanos capta uidet laqueos.
>
> (*Pamphilus* 764–65)

[Thus the fish, already caught, sees the curved hook, / Thus the bird, caught,
sees the snare of man.]

In comparing the feelings of a woman beguiled to that of a hunted
creature, she exposes the cruelty of Venus's advice that Pamphilus
imitate an artful fisherman ("et piscis liquidis deprenditur arte sub undis"
[85]) and of its source, the *Ars Amatoria*, which urges the lover to set
subtle traps like a hunter (1.45) or fisherman ("qui sustinet hamos, / nouit
quae multo pisce natentur aquae" [1.47–48] [fishermen study the waters /
baiting the hook for the cast just where the fish may be found]). But
though these metaphors point to the suffering of the victim, the fact that
they represent hunting as entrapment rather than depredation, unlike the
metaphors of eagle and wolf bloodying the dove and the lamb with which
Ovid describes the rapes of Philomela and the Sabine women,[37]
emphasizes that the issue is the deceptiveness of seduction rather than the
violence of rape. That Galathea's intellectual pride is hurt, as she sees too
late through the rhetoric of seduction, keeps her from being simply a
pathetic rape victim.

Going on to anticipate her life as a dishonored woman, disowned by
her parents and ostracized by society, Galathea draws out another implication of the metaphor of capture familiar from Ovid's amatory poetry:

> Sed modo quid faciam? fugiam captiua per orbem?
> Hostia iure michi claudet uterque parens.
> Meciar hac illac oculis uigilantibus orbem,
> Leta tamen misere spes michi nulla uenit.
>
> (*Pamphilus* 765–68)

[But now, what shall I do? Shall I flee through the world, already caught? /
My parents will rightly close their doors to me. / I shall search the earth here
and there with watchful eyes, / But find no joyful hope, miserable wretch that
I am.]

Here "captiua" evokes not so much the trapped animal as the military prisoner, a recurrent metaphor in the *Amores*,[38] whose *amator* describes himself as being among the "capti iuuenes" led in Cupid's Roman triumph and as bearing his chains with humbled heart:

> Ducentur capti iuuenes captaeque puellae:
> Haec tibi magnificus pompa triumphus erit.
> ipse ego, praeda recens, factum modo uulnus habebo
> et noua captiua uincula mente feram.
>
> *(Amores* 1.2. 27–30)

[Young men and girls will follow, prisoners in the procession, / Far as the eye can see, adding to pomp and parade, / And I will come dragging along, humbled, my wound fresh upon me, / Bearing my captive chain with what endurance I can.]

But Galathea reverses both the amator's self-serving metaphor and Pamphilus's adaptation of it in presenting himself as wounded and conquered by love (9), as she shows her suffering to be far more real than theirs. Although in the *Amores* Ovid had used "captiua" to hint at the subjectivity of the literally vanquished woman when the *amator*, guilty at having beaten his mistress, ironically presents himself as a conquering hero bringing home a prisoner of war ("ante eat effuso tristis captiua capillo" [1.7.39] [Let her trudge on ahead, hair disheveled, a captive]), such irony did little to undercut the voice of the elegiac male persona. The author of *Pamphilus* does just that, however, in the person of Galathea, who gives the "capta puella" so elegantly referred to in Ovid's *Amores* (e.g., 1.2.27; 2.12.8) a voice. While Ovid's image of male lover as a prisoner of war conquered by a woman is a witty tour de force, the application of the same terminology ("capta," "captiua") to Galathea, conquered by a man physically stronger than herself with the help of a go-between rhetorically more devious, is not.

Thus, while the author of *Pamphilus* shared Ovid's recognition that seduction was an extension of rape, that rhetoric was coercive, he did not share the complacency which Ovid's personae reveal about that fact. And although he found in Ovid's work some important models for conveying woman's point of view in sexual encounters, most notably the female-voiced epistles of the *Heroides* and the protests of Philomela, he did not apparently find it sufficiently complex for his purposes. He consequently turned to Ovid's amatory poetry and the male-voiced epistle of Acontius in order to adequately render female subjectivity. In the voice of Galathea he succeeded in exposing the solipsism of both the newly emergent courtly lover and the earlier Roman elegiac lover on whom he is based.[39]

Broader issues remain about the reception of the poem, both in its own time and in the two centuries following, during which it enjoyed enormous popularity. Was it read as a serious work of amatory instruction (as one of the twelfth-century *Accessus ad auctores* indicates),[40] a celebration of rape (as Gravdal has argued of the pastourelle, a medieval genre with which *Pamphilus* has much in common[41])—or a criticism of rape (as Benkov has argued of the *Philomena*)? Classicists like Cahoon and Hemker who read Ovid's amatory poetry as critiquing sexual opportunism through an ironic persona fail to answer this question, since they do not speak to the medieval reception of his work. Although much remains unanswered about the later reception of the poem, I suspect that a great part of its appeal, at least among later vernacular audiences, came from its skill in playing off Galathea's voice against that of Pamphilus. In this the poem celebrates not rape, but the power of eloquence—its ability not only to coerce the powerless, but to give voice to their subjectivity.

Notes

1. See, e.g., Katharina M. Wilson, *Hrotsvit of Gandersheim: The Ethics of Authorial Stance* (New York: E. J. Brill, 1988); Peter Dronke, *Women Writers of the Middle Ages: A Critical Study of Texts from Perpetua to Marguerite Porete* (Cambridge: Cambridge University Press, 1984); and Barbara Newman, *Sister of Wisdom: St. Hildegarde's Theology of the Feminine* (Berkeley: University of California Press, 1987).

2. Peter Dronke's argument that the poem was written close to 1100 in southwest Germany, at the Bavarian monastery of Tegernsee ("A Note on *Pamphilus*," *Journal of the Warburg and Courtauld Institute* 42 [1979]: 228, 232) has been accepted by the poem's most recent editor, Stefano Pittaluga; see *Commedie latine del XIIe XIII secolo*, ed. Ferruccio Bertini (Genova: Instituto di Filologia classica e medievale, 1980), 13–15.

3. Wilfred Blumenthal's exhaustive study of the poem's Ovidian sources ("Untersuchungen zur pseudo-ovidianischen Komödie *Pamphilus*," *Mittellateinisches Jahrbuch* 11 [1976]: 224–311) and Thomas Jay Garbaty's argument for its influence on Chaucer's *Troilus* ("The *Pamphilus* Tradition in Ruiz and Chaucer," *Philological Quarterly* 96 [1967]: 457–70) are exceptions. Taking a cue from Garbaty, John V. Fleming sees the old woman as "interpres" (go-between) in *Pamphilus* as a paradigm of the mediating quality of literature; see *Classical Imitation and Interpretation in Chaucer's Troilus* (Lincoln: University of Nebraska Press, 1990), 157–83.

4. Allisan Goddard Elliot, "Introduction," in *Seven Medieval Latin Comedies* (New York: Garland, 1984), xxx–xxxii.

5. Ian Thompson and Louis Perraud, *Ten Latin School Texts of the Later Middle Ages* (Lewiston, N.Y.: Mellen Press, 1990), 159–60.

6. *Geoffrey Chaucer* (Atlantic Highlands, N.J.: Humanities Press International, 1991), 98–100.

7. Kathryn Gravdal, *Ravishing Maidens: Writing Rape in Medieval Literature and Law* (Philadelphia: University of Pennsylvania Press, 1991). See also William D. Paden, "Rape in the Pastourelle," *Romanic Review*, 80 (1989): 331–49; Dietmar Rieger, "Le Motif du viol dans la littérature de la France médiévale entre norme courtoise et réalité courtoise" *Cahiers de Civilisation Médiévale* 31 (1988): 241–67; and Robert J. Blanch, "'Al was this land fulfild of fayerye': The Thematic Employment of Force, Willfulness, and Legal Conventions in Chaucer's *Wife of Bath's Tale*," *Studia Neophilologica* 57 (1985): 41–51.

8. See F. J. E. Raby, *A History of Secular Latin Poetry in the Middle Ages* (Oxford: Clarendon Press, 1957), 2.54–69; and Tony Hunt, "Chrétien and the *Comediae*," *MS* 40 (1978), 123.

9. Ralph J. Hexter, *Ovid and Medieval Schooling. Studies in Medieval School Commentaries on Ovid's "Ars Amatoria," "Epistulae ex Ponto," and "Epistulae Heroidum"*, Münchener Beiträge zur Mediävistik und Renaissance-Forschung, 38 (Munich: Arbeo-Gesellschaft, 1986); Gerald A. Bond, "Composing yourself: Ovid's *Heroides*, Baudri of Bourgueil, and the Problem of Persona," *Mediaevalia* 13 (1987): 83–117; and Leslie Cahoon, "The Anxieties of Influence: Ovid's Reception by the Early Troubadours," *Mediaevalia* 13 (1987): 119–55.

10. "Quique aliis cauet, non cauet ipse sibi; / illo saepe loco desunt sua uerba diserto, / resque nouae veniunt, causaque agenda sua est" (E. J. Kenney, ed., Ovid's *Amores, Faciei Femineae, Ars Amatoria, Remedia Amoris* [Oxford: Clarendon Press, 1961], 1.84–86). Subsequent references will be to this edition.

11. "Quam populus iudexque grauis lectusque senatus, / tam dabit eloquio uicta puella manus" (ibid., 1.459–72 ff.).

12. Elliott makes the connection between the following passage and the rape in *Pamphilus* (xxviii). (See n.14, below.)

13. Rolfe Humphries, trans., Ovid's *The Art of Love* (Bloomington: Indiana University Press, 1955), 125–26. Subsequent references will be to this translation.

14. *Pamphilus*, ed. E. Évesque, in *La "Comédie" latine en France au XIIe siècle*, ed. Gustave Cohen (Paris: Société d'Edition "Les belles lettres," 1931, vol. 2, ll. 105–6. "Neither be too silent, nor speak unnecessary words; / from the slightest thing a girl often despises a man"; Allison Goddard Elliot, trans., *Pamphilus, Seven Medieval Latin Comedies* (New York: Garland, 1984). Subsequent citations and translations, unless otherwise indicated, will be from these two volumes.

15. Garbaty, 458–59.

16. *TAPA*, 118 (1988): 293–307.

17. Elliott contrasts Galathea's genuine resistance to the coyness of Ovid's experienced Corinna (xxx–xxxiii).

18. Although Cahoon ("A Program for Betrayal: Ovidian *Nequitia* in *Amores* 1.11, 2.1, and 3.1," *Helios* 12 [1985]: 33) and Hemker argue that Ovid is subverting patriarchal attitudes through an ironic persona in his amatory poetry, it is unlikely that either a Roman or a medieval audience would have read his poetry that way.

19. *Motives of Eloquence: Literary Rhetoric in the Renaissance* (New Haven: Yale University Press, 1976), 48–64.

20. Blumenthal, 230–31.

21. "Me miserum! certas habuit puer ille sagittas. / uror, et in vacuo pectore regnat Amor" (*Amores*, 1.1.25–26). References are to Kenney. This translation is mine, but subsequent ones will be from Humphries, *The Art of Love*.

22. Cahoon, "Bed," 295.

23. "*Desultores Amoris*: Ovid *Amores* I.3." *CP* 61 (1966): 47–49.

24. Cahoon, "Anxieties," 146–48.

25. Blumenthal notes the use of male voiced-passages (234). Bond points out that the *Heroides* have a far more patronizing attitude toward the abandoned women than Baudri of Bourgeuil's twelfth-century adaptation of them (90–91).

26. *Amores* 1.2.2; in Kenney.

27. Cited by Blumenthal as source in rape scene.

28. Ovid, *Heroides* 20.145; in Grant Showerman, ed. and trans., *Heroides and Amores*, 2nd ed., rev. G. P. Goold (Cambridge: Harvard University Press, 1977); translation is mine.

29. See Dronke, *Women Writers*, 84–106, and Marina Scordilis Brownlee, *The Severed Word: Ovid's Heroides and the Novela Sentimental* (Princeton: Princeton University Press, 1990), 5–9. Bond sees the epistles as a source of a new subjective voice in twelfth-century literature generally.

30. Cahoon, "Anxieties," 147.

31. See Leo Curran ("Rape and Rape Victims in the *Metamporphoses*," *Arethusa* 11 [1978]: 211–41) and Joann Dellaneva ("Ravishing Beauties in the *Amours* of Ronsard: Rape, Mythology, and the Petrarchist Tradition," *Neophilologus* 73 [1989], 23–35) for the prominence of rape in the work.

32. Leonard Barkan points out that these are the only Ovidian rapes that Renaissance artists felt it was acceptable to depict; see *The Gods Made Flesh: Metamorphosis and the Pursuit of Paganism* (New Haven: Yale University Press, 1986), 218.

33. See Edith Joyce Benkov, "*Philomena*: Chrétien de Troyes' Reinterpretation of the Ovidian Myth," *Classical and Modern Literature* 3 (1983): 201–9, and E. Jane Burns, *Bodytalk: When Women Speak in Old French Literature* (Philadelphia: University of Pennsylvania Press, 1993).

34. See Patricia Klindienst Joplin, "The Voice of the Shuttle is Ours," *Stanford Literature Review* 1 (1984): 26–27, and Christine Froula, "The Daughter's Seduction: Sexual Violence and Literary History," *Signs* 11 (1986): 621–64, for a psychoanalytic interpretation of the myth.

35. Ovid, *Metamorphosen*, ed. V. A. Van Proosdij (Leiden: Brill, 1968), 6.523–26; Ovid, *Metamorphoses*, trans. Rolfe Humphries (Bloomington: Indiana University Press, 1955), 146.

36. This and the remaining translations from the *Metamorphoses* in this paragraph are my own.

37. Philomela trembles after the rape "velut agna pavens" mangled in the jaws of a wolf and "ut . . . columba" fears the talons of the bird of prey that bloodied her feathers (ll. 527 and 529). The Sabine women flee their pursuers "ut fugiunt aquilas, timidissima turba, columbae / utque fugit uisos agna nouella lupos" (Kenney, 1.117–18). See Hemker, 45.

38. Cahoon, "Bed," 297.

39. Cahoon, "Anxieties," 147–48.

40. See Hunt 129–30; Dronke, "A Note" 225; and Thompson and Perraud 160–61.

41. Gravdal,, 16–17, 104–21; based on her article, "Camouflaging Rape: The Rhetoric of Sexual Violence in the Medieval Pastourelle" *Romanic Review* 76 (1985): 360–73.

2
Desiring through the Troubadours, Desiring through the *Lais* of Marie de France

Discourse Desired: Desire, Subjectivity, and *Mouvance* in *Can vei la lauzeta mover*

SIMON GAUNT

Can vei la lauzeta mover is a *locus classicus* of desire in medieval literature. As one of the two most famous poems in the troubadour corpus (the other I have in mind is Jaufré Rudel's *Lancan li jorn*), *Can vei* is cited and anthologized not only as an exceptionally accomplished but also a paradigmatic love lyric, standing near the beginning of a vernacular tradition that culminates in Dante and Petrarch. In *Can vei*, the poet portrays his complete powerlessness in the face of desire, his loss of identity through love and his metaphoric death and exile, which he attributes to his lady's cruelty. Bernart de Ventadorn's modern reputation as the archetypal "courtly lover" rests to a large extent on this poem and, for generations of modern readers (including myself and my students), it is one of the first Occitan lyrics encountered in the classroom: the exquisite opening image of the falling lark and the famous stanza that contains an allusion to Narcissus are enticing points of entry into the tradition. The centrality of *Can vei* in modern reception of the troubadours is further guaranteed by a number of influential readings and by the fact that it was so widely disseminated in the Middle Ages, surviving as it does in twenty manuscripts with citations in a number of romances and didactic texts.

Modern readings of *Can vei* focus on desire and identity: in love poetry, the two can hardly be considered separately. Trained in the techniques of close reading or "explication de texte," critics have elaborated their interpretations on the basis of a progression of ideas from stanza to stanza: their view of the first-person subject of the text and of his desire is produced from this progression. And yet the critical text of *Can vei* that has been disseminated in the twentieth century follows a stanza order only found in two manuscripts, and other versions of the poem were far more widely diffused in the Middle Ages; a rather different view of "Bernart," of the "subject" of *Can vei,* emerges from these versions, and a rather different view of his desire.

In this essay I hope to illustrate, through an examination of *Can vei,* the difficulties of charting the relationship between the desiring subject and the text in medieval love poetry when the text in question, if it survives in more than one manuscript, may be subject to *mouvance.*[1] I will begin with a brief account of *Can vei* in its modern incarnation, followed by a selective outline of its critical reception, before looking more closely at the status of the text that modern critics have used. Taking my cue from Amelia E. Van Vleck's work on the textuality of troubadour lyric, I shall then turn to the poem's medieval manifestations and offer a reading of just one "alternative" version.[2] My reading of this version will of course be grounded in a particular sequence of stanzas and in the progression of ideas that it produces: when a poem is read or performed, a linear sequence of stanzas is inevitably imposed. However, what I hope to show is that if the text and structure of a poem are unstable, the status of the subject and of his desire is in consequence problematic. I would thereby like to reiterate a cautionary truism of medieval studies that medievalists nonetheless frequently forget: namely, that our view of any medieval text is shaped by its medieval transmitters and by its modern editor(s). Since transmitters, medieval and modern, have determined the form of the texts that we know, the desires of readers are always already inscribed in medieval texts. The "desiring subject" of a medieval love lyric is consequently inherently plural, the text always already invested with subjectivities and desires other than the author's. If, in my own comments on *Can vei,* and in my accounts of other critics' readings, I have recourse to terms such as "the poet" or "Bernart" to designate the text's first-person subject, this is simply because they are difficult to avoid and because the consistent use of "scare quotes" is cumbersome. But I hope that the extent to which the subjectivity of "the poet" or "Bernart" is occluded and problematized by a complex manuscript tradition will emerge from my discussion.

There are three principal editions of Bernart de Ventadorn's *cansos:* Carl Appel's in German (1915), Stephen Nichols et al.'s in English (1962), and Moshé Lazar's in French (1966). For *Can vei,* as with many of the poems, Nichols and Lazar follow Appel closely; neither notes that the manuscripts offer divergent stanza orders. Appel's edition has been reproduced (directly or indirectly) in all the main scholarly anthologies that contain the poem. Here is his text.[3]

I   Can vei la lauzeta mover
      de joi sas alas contral rai,
      que s'oblid' e•s laissa chazer
      per la doussor c'al cor li vai,
5   ai! tan grans enveya m'en ve
      de cui qu'eu veya jauzion,
      meravilhas ai, car desse
      lo cor de dezirer no•m fon.

II   Ai las! tan cuidava saber
10 d'amor, e tan petit en sai!
      car eu d'amar no•m posc tener
      celeis don ja pro non aurai.
      tout m'a mo cor, et tout m'a me,
      e se mezeis et tot lo mon;
15 e can se•m tolc, no•m laisset re
      mas dezirer e cor volon.

III   Anc non agui de me poder
      ni no fui meus de l'or' en sai
      que•m laisset en sos olhs vezer
20 en un miralh que mout me plai.
      miralhs, pus me mirei en te,
      m'an mort li sospir de preon,
      c'aissi•m perdei com perdet se
      lo bels Narcisus en la fon.

IV 25 De las domnas me dezesper;
      ja mais en lor no•m fiarai;
      c'aissi com las solh chaptener,
      enaissi las deschaptenrai.
      pois vei c'una pro no m'en te
30 vas leis que•m destrui e•m cofon,
      totas las dopt' e las mecre,
      car be sai c'atretals se son.

V   D'aisso•s fa be femna parer
      ma domna, per qu'e•lh o retrai,
35 car no vol so c'om deu voler,
      e so c'om li deveda, fai.
      chazutz sui en mala merce,
      et ai be faih co•l fols en pon;
      e no sai per que m'esdeve,
40 mas car trop puyei contra mon.

VI   Merces es perduda, per ver,
          (et eu non o saubi anc mai),
          car cilh qui plus en degr' aver,
          no•n a ges, et on la querrai?
45   a! can mal sembla, qui la ve,
          que*d* aquest chaitiu deziron
          que ja ses leis non aura be,
          laisse morir, que no l'aon!

VII   Pus ab midons no•m pot valer
50   precs ni merces ni•l dreihz qu'eu ai,
          ni a leis no ven a plazer
          qu'eu l'am, ja mais no•lh o dirai.
          aissi•m part de leis e•m recre;
          mort m'a, e per mort li respon,
55   e vau m'en, pus ilh no•m rete,
          chaitius, en issilh, no sai on.

VIII   Tristans, ges no•n auretz de me,
          qu'eu m'en vau, chaitius, no sai on.
          de chantar me gic e•m recre
60   e de joi e d'amor m'escon.

I When I see the lark beat its wings against the sun's ray, and when it forgets itself and lets itself fall because of the sweetness that invades its heart, ah, such an intense longing takes hold of me that no matter whom I see joyful, I am amazed that my heart does not at once melt from desire.

II Alas, I thought I knew so much about love, and I know so little, for I cannot stop loving the woman from whom I will have no favor. She has taken from me my heart and my very being, and herself and the whole world, and when she took herself away from me, she left me nothing but desire and a longing heart.

III I never had any power over myself, nor was I my own from the moment she allowed me to look into her eyes, into a mirror that pleases me greatly. Mirror, since I gazed upon you deep sighs have killed me, for I lost myself just as the fair Narcissus lost himself in the fountain.

IV I despair of ladies; never more will I trust them; for just as I used to respect them, now I will despise them. Since I know that not one of them helps my case with the woman who destroys and confounds me, I fear and mistrust them all for I know they are all the same.

V Thus my lady seems just like a woman, which is why I reproach her with it, for she does not want what one must want and she does what is forbidden her. I get no mercy, and have behaved like the fool on the bridge and I do not understand what is happening to me except that my aspirations were too high [literally: "I went too far uphill"].

VI There is truly no mercy and I knew nothing of this, for the one who ought to be most merciful is not at all, and where then should I seek it? Ah! How bad it looks to whoever sees her, that she lets this desiring wretch, who will have nothing good without her, die without helping him.

VII Since neither beseeching nor begging for mercy, nor any right that I have, get me anywhere and since she does not like my being in love with her, I will not tell her this any more. Thus I leave her and give up. She has killed me and I reply as if dead, and I go away, since she will not retain me, wretched, in exile, I know not where.

VIII Tristan, you will have nothing from me, for I go away wretched, I know not where. I give up and stop singing and remove myself from joy and loving.

This version of *Can vei* offers a well-crafted and coherent sequence of themes and metaphors. The poem opens with the lark flying up a ray of sunlight towards the dazzling vision that is the object of its desire: its ecstasy as it flies towards the sun is so intense that it loses all sense of itself and falls backwards. As with the lark, the poet's desire deprives him of self-control (5–8), a theme that is continued in stanza 2, where the poet becomes pure desire (15–16), and further developed in stanza 3 with the comparison to Narcissus. Stanzas 4, 5, and 6 then express despair at the lady's frosty responses, and stanza 7 rounds the main body of the poem off with the image of exile as metaphoric death, echoing "m'an mort li sospir" in stanza 3 as well as the end of stanza 6 where the poet says his lady is killing him. The *tornada* concludes the poem with an address to "Tristan" (who was of course exiled and who died for love) and with the poet saying he will abandon song.[4] The progression of the poem is evident: the first three stanzas equate desire with powerlessness and loss of selfhood, the poem then shifts to a sustained sequence of stanzas voicing despair, and finally the poet claims that his lack of satisfaction in love is the equivalent of death and exile. If he criticizes his lady (25–40), the prevailing mood is nonetheless one of submission to her will (49–56).

The poem is further bound together by a pattern of images of rising and falling: the lark (1–4), Narcissus falling into the fountain (23–24), the fool falling off the bridge (38),[5] who is evoked after the poet has "chazutz en male merce" (37), and the poet rising too much "contra mon" (40). The poet's disappearance into exile in stanza 7 is thus underscored by a pervasive metaphor of falling and consequently marks all the more vividly the poet's sense of loss of identity, a notion introduced in stanza 2 ("tout m'a me") and further developed with the comparison to Narcissus. Like the lark and Narcissus, the poet is in love with an unobtainable image, and this supplies a further pattern to the metaphors, which help construct the first-person subject. As Sarah Kay has shown, the Narcissus simile in stanza 3 need not necessarily evoke self-love: Narcissus, in the Middle Ages, was an *exemplum* of unrequited love, not of self-love, and the image he saw in the fountain was not himself but an image of perfection, so Narcissus may be evoked here to figure the self's relation to the other, rather than the self's relation to the self.[6] The poet loves and needs his *domna* as other, but he is careful to distinguish between this ideal image, a figure within his own discourse, and real women, who are denigrated (25–40).

If the poem movingly evokes the loss of self through love and the pain caused by desire when union with the beloved is not achieved, the final stanzas seem to shift the realm of love from the private into the public. Whereas the poet's loss of control over himself has been apparent throughout, stanza 7 introduces a new sense of loss: the loss of social identity. As an exile, he is removed from the world that gives him his identity, and in the *tornada* this is equated with ceasing to sing. The complete despair of the lover unloved climaxes with his falling silent: in the courtly world of poetry, he ceases to exist. This is clearly a conceit, in that all troubadours fall silent at the end of their songs, but the effect here is powerful: the lady's unwillingness to gratify the poet's desire leads to his obliteration from the poetic universe.

Perhaps the most influential reading of this rich poem is Erich Köhler's in an article published in 1964 in which he argues that the troubadour lyric represents "la projection sublimée de la situation matérielle et sociale de la basse noblesse."[7] Köhler's thesis has been refined or contested by a number of critics, and I do not intend to defend or criticize his approach here, only to set his reading of *Can vei* in context.[8] For Köhler, the frustration of the "courtly lover" is a sublimated expression of the frustration of the lower nobility, more particularly of the *iuvenes* (landless young nobles) who are thought to have populated twelfth-century courts.[9] The *domna* of the *canso* represents less a real object of erotic desire than the power and social position she stands for metonymically through her connection with her husband, the *senher* of the court. Köhler's aim is to show the relationship between "superstructure poétique" and "infrastructure sociale": amorous desire mediates frustrated social ambition, and love service is equivalent to feudal service.[10] In Köhler's view, courtly literature enables the creation of a shared ideology for a class otherwise in danger of disintegration. His choice of *Can vei* as a vehicle to illustrate his argument is iconoclastic: he chooses the most lyrical and enchanting of troubadour songs in order to show the ideological underpinning of even the most haunting of personal poetry. In a *tour de force* of close reading and critical demystification, Köhler turns the metaphors of the poem inside out to argue that, rather than articulating a sense of isolation and lonely individuation through disempowerment, *Can vei* expresses a sublimated desire for social integration. The Narcissus simile enables the poet to glimpse "celui qu'il voudrait être," and the structure of the poem as a whole is governed by a shift from personal to social concerns, culminating in the image of exile and in the use of the verb *retener* (line 55), a feudal term.[11] The use of a feudal term to describe the bond between poet and lady is symptomatic of the "real" theme of the poem. The poet fears less rejection by his "lady" (a construct of his own discursive framework) than his putative failure to find a place within the courtly social order. Köhler is critical of modern ideas of the individual: "la pensée romantique et post-romantique part de la disjonction fondamentale de la société et de l'individu, et elle finit nécessairement par croire que tout sentiment sincère doit s'exprimer contre la société." For Köhler, "toute *canso* réussie formellement est un gage d'intégration de l'individu à son univers."[12] The desire expressed in *Can vei* is consequently the desire of a group, and the "subject," if not a collective subject, is certainly a subject with whom a group of men identify.

Other important readings of *Can vei* have been more oriented towards the idea of the individual, sometimes as a reaction to Köhler's thesis. For many critics, *Can vei* is a *cri de coeur*, expressing deep personal feeling, articulating sometimes a desire for, sometimes a fear of, loss of identity. Thus, in Frederick Goldin's powerful reading, Bernart seeks the fulfillment of oblivion (stanza 1) through union with an image of perfection of his own creation (stanza 3), which is figured through the Narcissus simile; whereas for Leslie Topsfield, Bernart eschews the escapism of the imagination, since his "*Jois* is here in this world, visible, tangible, to be known through his senses and expressed through the living image."[13] Sarah Kay's judicious account of the mirror image and of the Narcissus simile is more concerned with emotion as an effect of the rhetoric of the poem, rather than as its source, but like Goldin and Topsfield she prefers to see "social vocabulary" as illustrative of "an individual relationship" rather than as a sign of any (perhaps unconscious) engagement with class tensions.[14] Another feature of the text that has elicited critical interest in relation to the poet's sense of self is paradox. Thus, for Jean-Charles Huchet, the song records "un moment où le monde vacille pour le sujet qui se sent appelé à disparaître afin que règne ce qui fait sa joie et son malheur."[15] Paradoxically, the subject can only register his existence by enacting his obliteration. As R. Howard Bloch puts it, "Bernart uses his voice to renounce song": *Can vei* thus seems to show that the *canso* is always predicated on unrequited desire, which in turn leads to what Bloch calls a "despoliation of the self."[16]

The readings I have just schematically outlined are all generated by reading the poem as a sequence of ideas. For example, Köhler insists on the absolute logic of the *enchaînement des idées*, and particularly on the structural importance of the position of stanza 4, which marks the transition from the personal to the social, while Goldin talks about the "clear progression" of the poem.[17] Whereas none of the other critics I have mentioned acknowledges that alternative stanza orders for *Can vei* exist, Kay and Huchet draw the mobility of stanza order in transmission into their discussion, but only to make a plea in favor of what Kay calls "the stanza-ordering traditionally adopted," Kay to stress the structural importance of stanzas 3 and 4 at the center of the poem, and Huchet to argue that "la troisième strophe constitue bien le coeur de la *canso*"; both suggest that Bernart's songs frequently turn around what Kay calls a "central image" and Huchet "un noyau central."[18] Like Köhler, Kay argues for a "greater 'objectivity' in the latter part of the poem," but whereas Kay correctly observes in a note that "the ordering i–ii–iii–iv is found in three MSS, the ordering i–ii–iv–iii in seven, of which two do not contain stanza vi and six omit stanza vii," Huchet erroneously asserts that the stanza order of the edition he uses (Lazar's) is that of the majority of manuscripts.[19] Neither critic lists or considers alternative stanza orders.

Before turning specifically to the question of stanza order, it is worth highlighting a few of Appel's editorial decisions at crucial points in the poem with a view to illustrating the extent to which modern readings depend on his value judgments about Bernart's poetic practice. For all critics, the nub of the poem is Appel's stanza 3 with the Narcissus simile. It is therefore noteworthy that the scribes of five manuscripts apparently failed to recognize the reference to Narcissus, offering the following readings: *C* "marcesis," *E* "marsilis," *N* "marselius" (with "Narcisus" added by a later hand in the margin), *R* "marsili," *a* "narcilis." In addition, *MPSU* read "narcius," *Q* "narcis," and in *V* the last part of the line is missing. The original reading was in all likelihood "Narcissus," which is attested in the other nine manuscripts that transmit the stanza, but these variants may well indicate that the reference to Narcissus was not as crucial to an understanding of the poem for medieval transmitters as it has been for modern critics.

A striking feature of Appel's text, related to the Narcissus simile, is that the lady's eyes are the mirror in which the poet sees the perfect vision that is the object of his desire: in other words, the lady is the mirror of perfection, not the image of perfection. The subtlety of this in Appel's text depends upon the wording of lines 19–20. These lines create an equivalence between the lady's eyes and the mirror, which is subsequently transformed through the simile into the mirror of Narcissus. But Appel's text here derives from a small number of manuscripts. *AGLPSV* read "de mos holhs," *C* "a mos holhs," *M* "Qe li plac qem laisset vezer," *N* "Ca sos bels oils mi fes vezer," *R* "pus elam mostret son voler." Furthermore, the preposition *en* is missing in *EQU*, with the missing syllable supplied by a scanning first-person object pronoun before the verb in *QU* (*Q* "Qant me laisset sos oils veder"), giving the completely different sense that the poet sees his lady's eyes in a mirror. The precise wording that elicits modern readings of stanza 3 is thus only found in *DIKOa*, of which only *DIKO* appear to have registered a reference to Narcissus. The image in Appel's text is arresting, but its basis in the manuscript tradition is far from secure, and in many medieval versions of *Can vei* the equivalence between the lady's eyes and Narcissus's mirror is not suggested.

Apart from the Narcissus simile and the mirror image, another key element in the poem for modern readers is the ending, and critics comment admiringly upon the verbal echo between lines 55–56 and line 58 in the *tornada*.[20] This type of verbal echo is common in troubadour lyric and would seem to be a compelling reason for adopting at least the 7–8 sequence of Appel's edition. However, a study of the manuscript variants reveals that the "echo" is weaker in medieval versions of *Can vei* than in Appel's, even in the two manuscripts that place Appel's stanza 7 immediately before the tornada (*QU*). There are three elements in the echo: "e vau m'en . . . no sai on" / "qu'eu m'en vau . . . no sai on" (lines 55–56 and 58), the repetition of "recre" (lines 53 and 59), and the repetition of "chaitius" (lines 56 and 58). Whereas the first two elements are common to almost all versions that have the *tornada* (*U* reads "rete" in line 59), the repetition of "chaitius" only occurs in one (*E*), which does not place the *tornada* after stanza 7 but after stanza 3 (see below). Otherwise, "chaitius" is found in the last line of stanza 7 in *ADEFGIKLMPQS* (*CRU* "faiditz"; *N* "Marrig"; *V* "E mexil e res"; *O* "Cais en exil"; *a* "chazutz"), but in the second line of the *tornada* we read "marritz" in AGLPQSU ("chaitius" in *CO*, though this produces no echo; no *tornada* in *DIKMNRVa*; Appel omits the variants for *U* in these lines). There clearly is an echo between the *tornada* and the text, but it is debatable whether this is as strong as Appel's text suggests and whether the echo is with a stanza fixed in the preceding position or with a stanza in the middle of the poem.[21] My point in dwelling on these seemingly trivial details is that Appel offers us a finely wrought, seamless poem, but that some of the elements that modern readers have most admired are to a certain extent of his confection and are not found in many medieval redactions, if at all.

Appel seems to have had a clear idea of what constituted a good poem and then to have set out to create one from a complex manuscript transmission. He saw the possible subtleties of one way of presenting the Narcissus simile and mirror image, so he edited accordingly; he thought there should be a verbal echo between the final stanza and the *tornada*, so he made sure there was one; he structured the poem around an aesthetically pleasing shift from desire to despair. I have no doubt that these operations were deliberate. A fine latter-day troubadour, Appel was in many respects a more meticulous transmitter of *Can vei* than the medieval scribes who copied it. After all, did any of them scour Europe to transcribe and collate twenty different versions of the poem? But behind his work—veiled rather than concealed—lie a number of competing versions of *Can vei* that actually circulated in the Middle Ages.

The stanza orders found in the manuscripts are as follows:

12345678	*QU*
12347568	*C*
12435768	*0*
1243576	*MR*
124357	*Na*
143675	*I*
1243675	*K*
1243756	*V*
12456738	*E*
12467358	*AGLPS*
124673	*D*
12	*WX*

In addition, stanza 7 is in *F,* and extracts from *Can vei* are cited in a number of didactic and narrative texts.[22]

The two manuscripts that transmit the stanza order Appel adopts are both relatively late (fourteenth-century) Italian manuscripts that frequently display similarities, as they do for this poem. Indeed, for *Can vei,* the fact that both manuscripts intervert lines 37–40 and 45–48, garbling in a similar fashion lines 46 and 48 in the process (Appel's line numbering: 46 *Q* "asses oils chattiu desiron," *U* "Ai sos oils chaitiu desiron;" 48 *Q* "Lais mor sem no ma bon," *U* "Las morz serai si non maon," *Q* being hypometric in 48), and have a garbled first half of line 44, suggests that they derive ultimately from a common source (44 *Q* "et ieu ola qerrai," *U* "E ren mais on lai qerai," both hypometric). Neither is a "good" manuscript that any editor would choose as a base manuscript, and a perusal of the texts they offer of *Can vei* makes it clear why. Both are riddled with linguistic peculiarities (for example, intervocalic [z] written "d" in both, thus in line 1 *Q* "laudetta," *U* "lauderta," line 3 *QU* "chader"), and with errors. Apart from the mistakes already listed, and giving the scribes the benefit of the doubt for "variant" readings that make sense, a number of other "variants" in both manuscripts suggest faulty transmission. These are as follows.

Q: 1 "ueu" (for "vei"); 7 "mai" (producing a pronoun with no apparent grammatical function); 24 "lo bel narcis en la fon" (hypometric); 27 "char tener"; 28 "deschar tenrai"; 38 (line 46 in this manuscript) "E ai far ben de fols un pon"; 49 "En uer midon" (which garbles the syntax of the stanza); 52 "Qe mam"; 57 "Tristezi" (*GLPS* read "Tristeza" here).

U: 6 "ia usion" (suggesting the scribe misunderstood "iausion" in his source); 12 "ias" (producing a reflexive pronoun with no grammatical function); 13 "Tot mal cor et tolt ma se" (hypometric); 22 "isospirs"; 55 "E uau men sil nom rete" (hypometric); 58 "Qe uau men maritz e non sai on" (hypermetric); 59 "rete" (for "recre").

To give credence to the stanza order transmitted by these two manuscripts when they are otherwise defective transmitters of the poem, possibly deriving from a common source, is not the soundest of editorial practices.

The mobility of stanza order in transmission is common in the troubadour and *trouvère* love lyric. This led Paul Zumthor to argue that the stanza was an autonomous unit in the *trouvère chanson*, that its internal structure was more susceptible to fruitful analysis than its position in a song, and that "rarement, l'ordre de succession des éléments est significatif comme tel."[23] Recently, Amelia Van Vleck has refined Zumthor's argument. She suggests that some troubadours used complex, patterned rhyme schemes that require a particular stanza sequence in order to fix this sequence in transmission and thereby to safeguard a linear argument.[24] For example, Bernart de Ventadorn's *Tant ai mo cor* (Appel and Nichols 44, Lazar 4) uses a form called *coblas capcaudadas*. It has the rhyme scheme ababababacccb with "c^1" as a constant rhyme word (*amor*): the "ab" rhyme sounds change each stanza, but the "b" rhyme of stanza 1 becomes the "a" rhyme of stanza 2, which introduces a new "b" rhyme, which in turn become the "a" rhyme of stanza 3 and so on. Only one sequence for the stanzas is possible if the rhyme scheme is to be observed. Although there are textual variants within lines, the rhyme words are relatively stable, and there is no transposition of stanza order, even though the poem is transmitted in eleven manuscripts: the poem has a clear logical progression and structure.[25] On the other hand, Van Vleck argues that when troubadours use stanzaic forms that do not impose a particular sequence on the poem, such as the *coblas unissonans* of *Can vei* (stanzas that have the same rhyme scheme with the same rhyme sounds), transposition in transmission is the norm and that even when a rhyming device that ought to impose a particular sequence is used, transposition still occurs for some songs.[26] Agreeing with Zumthor that the stanza is the important structural unit in a courtly lyric, Van Vleck nonetheless argues that sequence *is* important to any given reading or performance, provided we recognize that the sequence in question could be the work of a performer or scribe.[27] She notes briefly that the stanza order of modern editions of *Can vei* is found only in two manuscripts and comments "one cannot safely perform the kind of literary analysis that relies on linear development without first ascertaining that a particular linear development is part of what constitutes 'the text'."[28]

Highlighting the role of the scribe or performer in the transmission of a troubadour poem, and consequently in the production of the texts we know, renders the status of the subject of any poem, and of his desire, problematic. Whose desire then is articulated in *Can vei*? And in which poem? I do not seek to deny the existence of an "author" for *Can vei*. Somebody composed it and I have no objection to calling him "Bernart de Ventadorn," but we can only speculate as to the form of the original text, since the texts we read have undergone transformation at the hands of at least one scribe, probably more, and this in addition to any modifications that took place in performance. And yet it is striking that the manuscripts themselves often seek to portray troubadour songs as "subjective," as autobiographical, as recording lived experience and feelings.[29] On the one hand texts change, on the other their transmitters claim their authenticity as witness to the troubadours' lives. This apparent paradox is eliminated, however, when we remember that troubadour *cansos* are fictional representations of someone's desire, not spontaneous articulations of desire. "Real feelings" give *Can vei* its power to move, but they are the object of representation in the poem as well as its inspiration: they have been appropriated by listeners, transmitters, editors, and readers, to be then invested with their own desires. Within the fictional frame desire produces the text, but if we take a step outside that frame, we realize that desire is also an effect of the text's rhetoric. When the rhetoric is differently organized, a different image of the subject and of his desire emerges. The "Bernart de Ventadorn" of any one manuscript is different from that of any other. The "Bernart de Ventadorn" of a modern critical edition is different from that of any medieval manuscript.[30] Thus, as Jean-Charles Huchet has suggested (and this despite his apparent defense of the authenticity of a modern edition of *Can vei*), every act of transmission is also an act of appropriation of the subject of the poem: "Chaque version manuscrite sera trace d'un sujet évanoui. La transmission constitue un temps indispensable dans la constitution du sujet."[31]

Reading Appel's edition of *Can vei* as an expression of someone's desire, whether this is understood as desire for social integration, identity, or a woman, is to read the poem as if it were a modern poem, signed by its author in a printed book, where the identity of the author is controlled and produced by an institutional and legal framework of publishers, birth certificates, and copyright. If the poem that modern critics have read reflects any one person's desire with any certainty, it is Carl Appel's, since his edition is not a medieval redaction. The astute readings of modern critics are a tribute to his work, and it is not surprising if they share his view of what constitutes a good poem, since they are, broadly speaking, part of the same culture. However, the dangers of reading only the modern critical edition are that our interaction with the medieval versions of *Can vei* will be completely filtered through the modern sensibilities that governed the editorial process and that we will consequently miss the dissonances between modern sensibilities and medieval texts that can make reading medieval texts such an exciting experience.

Although I am insisting on the validity of multiple versions of *Can vei*, the poem is not subject to infinite variation through *mouvance*. Key thematic features and links seem to have determined the poem's transformation into different forms, and, despite the high degree of variation in stanza order, in other respects the text shows a degree of stability. There are no "apocryphal" stanzas, clearly added during transmission: every stanza is attested in almost all the manuscripts, and even the *tornada* is in ten. Furthermore, there are few variants that produce different versions of complete stanzas.[32] This suggests that the text of the poem was well known, but the transposition of stanzas is in consequence all the more striking since the same textual material is deployed to produce different poems. Thus, just as the versions of *Can vei* that have survived have been subject to the desires of transmitters, so the articulations of desire they transmitted through the poem were

determined by the substance of the poem they read in their sources. Does
the poem then invite some forms of transformation yet resist others? And
to what extent is the mobility of stanzas part of the aesthetics of the
culture that produced the poem?[33]

If the stanzas are autonomous units, it is nonetheless apparent that
certain sequences of stanzas recur in a number of different versions. For
example, putting stanzas 1 and 2 aside since they always open the poem,
the most common sequence is 1–2–4 (fourteen manuscripts, as opposed
to 1–2–3 in only three). This means that despair—and also hostility to
women—is introduced earlier in the poem and that the line "De las
domnas me dezesper" glosses not the Narcissus image but the stanza on
the poet's powerlessness. This is perfectly logical, but it produces a
different progression from that discerned by modern critics. Other
common sequences are 6–7 (as in Appel, eleven manuscripts, linked by
allusions to death) and 3–5 (ten manuscripts). This last pairing is
interesting on two counts. First, it brings together two stanzas with
images of falling; secondly, in five manuscripts (*AGLPS*), it brings them
together at the end, thereby displacing the Narcissus image from the
center or *noyau* of the song. Indeed, in a further two manuscripts (*DE*),
stanza 3 comes at the end of the poem, though in both of these after
stanza 7, so that the image of exile (a social state) is displaced by the
more personal meditation on identity. My point is not that the
transposition of stanzas prevents logical progression in the poem but that
it produces a different logic. That the pieces of the jigsaw seem able so
successfully to make different pictures may suggest the stanzas were
composed with some degree of mobility in mind, though perhaps with
ideal pairings suggested by content (such as 6–7 and 3–5). At the very
least, the series of metaphors of falling, the references to death, and the
syntactic autonomy of the stanzas mean that logical connections emerge
when the stanzas are transposed. Even when a stanza appears to be
syntactically linked to what has gone before (such as stanza 5 which
opens "D'aisso"), the referent is vague enough to allow for mobility.

As autonomous syntactic units, all the stanzas have a finely wrought
internal structure. All exploit the conventional division of the *cobla* into
frons and *cauda*, with the rhyme scheme abab/cdcd marking a shift
between the two halves that is often reflected in the content. Thus, for
example, in stanza 1 there is a shift from metaphor (the lark) to
exposition, whereas in stanza 3 the shift is from exposition to *exemplum*
(Narcissus). Rhyme is exploited to highlight key ideas. Thus, the "a"
rhyme position is occupied predominantly by infinitives that stand
metonymically for the content of the stanza:[34] for example, "mover"/
"chazer" in stanza 1, "poder" (which is used as a noun here)/"vezer" in

stanza 3. The "b" and "c" rhymes, are on the other hand, often used to mark subject/object relations, the "b" rhyme because many of the rhyme words are first person verb forms (10 "sai," 12 "aurai," 26 "fiarai," and so on), the "c" rhyme because some of the rhyme words are pronouns (13 "me," 21 "te," 23 "se").[35] The stanzas are carefully executed, formally balanced units, and their internal coherence seems to be recognized in relatively stable transmission.

The most widely diffused medieval version of *Can vei* is in *AGLPS*; the stanza order they transmit is supported by *D* (which is identical but lacks this version's final stanza and the *tornada*) and to a certain extent by *E*, which has the sequences 1–2–4 and 6–7–3 as in *AGLPS*. Here is a version of *Can vei* based on *A*. I have resolved common abbreviations but followed *A*'s practice of writing elided vowels in full. I have allowed "i" for [j] to stand but written [v] as "v," rather than "u," for legibility. The modifications I have made are otherwise all to correct what are almost certainly copying errors.[36]

I	Qan vei la lauzeta mover	
	de ioi sas alas contra•l rai	
	que s'oblida e•is laissa cazer	
	per la doussor c'al cor li vai.	
5	Ai! Tant grans enveia m'en ve	
	de cui que veia iauzion,	
	meravillas ai car desse	
	lo cors de desirier no•m fon.	
II	A las! Tant cui[a]va saber	MS: "cuiua"
10	d'amor e qant petit en sai,	
	car ieu d'amar no•m puosc tener	
	cell*ei* don ia pro non aurai.	MS: "Cellui"
	Tolt m'a mon cor e tolt m'a se,	
	e mi meteus et tot lo mon,	
15	e qan si•m tolc no•m laiset re	
	mas desirier e cor volon.	
III	De las dompnas mi desesper:	
	jamais en lor no•m fiarai,	
	e aissi cum las suoil captener,	
20	enaissi las descaptenrai.	
	Pois [vei] c'una pro no m'en te	MS: no "vei"
	vas lieis qe•m destrui e•m cofon,	
	totas las dopti e las mescre,	
	car ben sai c'atretals si son.	

IV 25 Amors es perduda per ver,
et ieu non o saubi anc mai,
que cil que plus en degra aver,
non a ies, et on la qerrai?
Ai! Cum mal sembla qui la ve,
30 E az aqest caitiu desiron,
qe ia ses lieis non aura be,
laisse morir, qe no•il aon.

V Puois ab midonz no m•pot valer
Dieus, ni merces, ni•l dreitz q'ieu ai,
35 ni a lieis no ven a plazer
Qu il m'am, ia mais no lo dirai.
E si•m part de lieis e•m recre:
mort m'a e per mort li respon,
e vau m'en s'ella no•m rete,
40 caitius, en issill, no sai on.

VI Anc non agui de mi poder,
ni non fui meus de lor en sai
qe m laisset de mos huoills vezer
en un miraill qe mout mi plai
45 Miraills, pois me miriei en te,
m'ant mort li sospir de prion,
E aissi•m perdiei cum perdet se
lo bels Narcisus en la fon.

VII D'aisso fai ben femna parer
50 ma dompna, per q'ieu lo retrai,
e ar non vol so qe deu voler,
e so c'om li deveda fai.
Cazutz sui e mala merce,
et ai be faich co•l fols e•l pon,
55 e non sai per que m'esdeve,
mas car poiei trop contra amon.

VIII Tristan, non avetz ies de me,
qe vau m'en marritz, no sai on,
de chantar mi lais e•m recre,
60 e de ioi e d'amar m'escon.

Whereas Appel's version produces a progression from desire to despair, from the personal to the social, the progression here is quite different. In Appel's text, death, exile, and silence are brought together in stanzas 7 and 8 to produce a powerful image of a solitary and unhappy poet that concords well with the post-romantic notion of the alienated artist: he fades into a dignified despair that deprives him of his social identity and ultimately prevents him even from speaking. Here the poet goes on speaking after he has evoked exile. The Narcissus stanza that immediately follows becomes an exposition of past feelings rather than an explanation of present mood. If Narcissus is taken as an evocation of oblivion and loss of selfhood, then the last line of stanza 7 (my numbering) offers a sharply individuated image of the poet battling against the world: this would seem to support Köhler's view of the troubadour as socially frustrated, but perhaps not his ideas on integration. However, if Narcissus is also taken as an *exemplum* of unrequited love (as he surely should be), then the end of the poem expresses intense misogyny since "D'aisso fai ben femna parer" (line 49) becomes a gloss on the Narcissus simile.[37] This picks up on the central *noyau* of this version: here, Appel's stanzas 4 and 6 are brought together as stanzas 3 and 4 to produce a sustained attack on women and on the poet's lady in particular. The whole poem is less focused on the lover, more focused on the inadequacies of women. Whereas Appel's "Bernart" falls silent in a moment of moving pathos, receding gracefully into metaphoric exile, manuscript *A*'s "Bernart" stomps off angrily, and his renunciation of singing is determined by his anger. Even the address to Tristan fits this mood with an assertive present tense "avetz" rather than a plaintive future "auretz."

This version fits the conventional stereotype of a "courtly" poem a good deal less well than Appel's. It is, however, in its misogyny, a perfect example of the reflexes that feminist scholarship has imputed to the troubadour lyric.[38] If desire is initially the dominant theme, misogyny and anger dominate the end. Both versions might in fact reflect something of the subjectivity of someone we might call "Bernart," but we might also consider the import of the fact that the less "courtly" version had more currency in the Middle Ages and that circulation in this form was no impediment to the song's popularity. Medieval tastes were clearly somewhat different from Appel's.

I am not proposing that modern readers simply replace Appel's *Can vei* with my "alternative" version from *A*. I am suggesting rather that multiple versions of *Can vei* need to be considered differentially in order to assess the poem's production, transmission, and reception, and that an understanding of the text's mobility is crucial to a sense of how subjectivity and desire are inscribed in and constructed by it. But the return to manuscript redactions that this entails has methodological ramifications that perhaps exceed my consideration of subjectivity and desire in this one poem. That I have chosen to offer an "alternative" version of *Can vei* that lends itself to a reading informed by a feminist epistemology is, of course, an act of appropriation reflecting my own desire to read and present medieval texts in a particular light. And yet, if I have reinvented *A*'s text for this article, I have not invented it. Appel made his version of *Can vei* conform to his view of "courtly" poetry and he thereby occluded (no doubt unintentionally) a number of ideological and formal features of the poem that are of interest to modern scholars. Medieval texts can, of course, be recuperated for feminist readers (or queer or postcolonial readers for that matter) without their being re-edited, but who knows what new texts, or new versions of old texts, await rediscovery? Scholars seeking to revise or challenge conventional views of the Middle Ages cannot afford to rely on existing editions: they need philology as much as they need theory.

To return to *Can vei*, it is clear that the expectations of modern readers and the form of the text that they have used have conspired to render the poem more "courtly" in its modern reception than it was in its medieval transmission. The different text of *Can vei* produces a different image of the poem's desiring subject and of his desire, a different view of courtliness. *Can vei* has acted as a mirror for modern concerns and sensibilities from Carl Appel onwards. It offered in the Middle Ages and offers now a discursive mold into which readers can pour their own ideas about desire. A desire for a discourse of desire has determined its reception and transmission.[39]

Notes

1. The term "mouvance" was coined by Paul Zumthor to denote how medieval texts are transformed in transmission; for a definition, see *Essai de poétique médiévale* (Paris: Seuil, 1972), 507. See also Rupert T. Pickens, "Jaufré Rudel et la poétique de la mouvance," *Cahiers de Civilisation Médiévale* 20 (1977): 323–37, and *The Songs of Jaufré Rudel* (Toronto: Pontifical Institute, 1978); and Amelia E. Van Vleck, *Memory and Re-creation in Troubadour Lyric* (Berkeley: University of California Press, 1991), 71–90, on *mouvance* in troubadour poetry. Pickens argues that troubadours composed knowing that their work would be transformed by performers and transmitters. For Pickens, different manuscript versions of the same lyric constitute separate poems. His approach is exemplified by his own edition of Jaufré Rudel, which offers multiple versions of poems that survive in more than one manuscript. For Pickens, it is pointless to try to distinguish authorial redactions from later *remaniements*; for a critique of this position, see Sarah Kay, "Continuation as Criticism: the Case of Jaufré Rudel," *Medium Aevum* 56 (1987): 46–64. Pickens's approach represents a strong challenge to the two traditional methods of editing troubadour lyrics: the so-called Lachmannian method, which aims to reconstruct a single original, and the so-called Bédieriste, which aims to reproduce as closely as possible one "good" version. According equal value to all

versions, however, is a questionable procedure. Some manuscript versions of some songs (such as *QU*'s of *Can vei*) are clearly faulty.

2. See Van Vleck. I am not, however, entirely in agreement with Van Vleck's thesis: for example, she attributes *mouvance* largely to oral transmission and to changes made for performances, but I would attribute a greater role to written transmission and prefer to look at the composition of the *chansonniers*, rather than imagine oral performances that may have preceded them. However, Van Vleck's work has obviously shaped my thinking in this essay. I am indebted in a more general way to the work of other scholars, for example "new philologists" such as Cerquiglini, Hult, and Masters as well as "old philologists," not least Carl Appel, whose edition of Bernart de Ventadorn is monumental and remains unsurpassed, and also John Marshall. See Bernard Cerquiglini, *Eloqe de la variante: histoire critique de la philoloqie* (Paris: Seuil, 1989); David Hult, "Reading It Right: The Ideology of Text Editing," *Romanic Review* 79 (1988): 74–88; Bernadette A. Masters, "The Distribution, Destruction and Dislocation of Authority in Medieval Literature and its Modern Derivatives," *Romanic Review* 82 (1991): 270–85, and *Esthétique et manuscripture: le << Moulin à paroles >> au moyen âge* (Heidelberg: Winter, 1992); and John H. Marshall, *The Transmission of Troubadour Poetry* (London: Westfield College, 1975). As Marshall writes: "Editors of medieval texts are, as a race, not to be trusted" (11).

3. See Carl Appel, ed., *Bernart von Ventadorn: seine Lieder* (Halle: Max Niemeyer, 1915), poem 43; Moshé Lazar, ed., *Bernard de Ventadour: troubadour du XIIème siècle: chansons d' amour* (Paris: Klincksieck, 1966), poem 31; and Stephen G. Nichols Jr., et al., eds., *The Songs of Bernart de Ventadorn* (Chapel Hill: University of North Carolina Press, 1962), poem 43. Lazar and Nichols only modify minor details of Appel's text. It is hard to work out exactly how Appel produced his text, but having adopted the stanza order of *QU*, he appears to have worked from a number of manuscripts for the text (at least *ACEI*). His earlier edition of *Can vei* is similar to his 1915 version but has a slightly different orthography; see Carl Appel, *Provenzalische Chrestomathie* (Leipzig: Reisland, 1895), 56–57. I can locate no justification of his choice of stanza order. Appel comments of *Can vei* (Appel, *Bernart*, 250) that although the complexity of the manuscript tradition makes the construction of a stemma unthinkable, the text can nonetheless be established with a degree of certainty because of the agreement of large numbers of manuscripts. This is a view that is broadly endorsed by Michael Kaehne, *Studien zur Dichtung Bernarts von Ventadorn*, 2 vols. (Munich: Wilhelm Fink Verlag, 1983), 2:235–37, who proposes one correction to Appel's text, suggesting that line 50 should read: "Deus ni merces ni•l dreihz qu'eu ai." While acknowledging that the stanza orders in the manuscripts make it difficult to recreate the logic of Bernart's poem, Kaehne goes on to endorse Appel's choice of stanza order (ibid., 2:236–37). Anthologies that include *Can vei* are too numerous to detail, but see for example Martin de Riquer, *Los trovadores*, 3 vols. (Barcelona: Ariel, 1975), 1:384–87, who also offers a convenient list of the sigla that are conventionally used to designate Occitan *chansonniers* (1:12–13), together with a brief, tabulated description. The translation of *Can vei* in this essay is my own. I have consulted microfilms of *AQU* and otherwise worked from Appel's variants (1895 and 1915).

4. "Tristans" in line 57 is thought to be *senhal* (a code name for a real person) and not simply a reference to the literary character. A substantial amount of scholarship has been devoted to identifying the person concerned. Whereas Lazar (274 n.11) thinks the *senhal* designates the poet's lady, there is a general consensus that it designates the contemporary troubadour Raimbaut d'Aurenga and that *Can vei* is part of a poetic exchange with Raimbaut and with Chretien de Troyes. See Maurice Delbouille, "Les

senhals littéraires désignant Raimbaut d'Orange et la chronologie de ces témoignages,"
Cultura Neolatina 17 (1957): 64–72; Costanzo di Girolamo, *I trovatori* (Turin: Bollati
Boringhieri, 1989), 120–41; Kaehne, 2:243–50; Maria Luisa Meneghetti, *Il pubblico dei
trovatori: ricezione e riuso dei testi lirici cortesi fino al XIV secolo*, 2nd ed. (Turin:
Einaudi, 1992), 101–6; Don A. Monson, "Bernart de Ventadorn et Tristan," in *Il Miglior
fabbro: Mélanges Pierre Bec* (Poitiers: CESCM, 1991): 385–400; and Aurelio Roncaglia,
"*Carestia*," *Cultura Neolatina* 18 (1958): 121–37.

5. The "fool falling off the bridge" is generally taken to be proverbial: see Appel,
Bernart, 156. But for a different interpretation, see Thomas D. Hill, "The Fool on the
Bridge: *Can vei la lauzeta mover* Stanza 5," *Medium Aevum* 48 (1979): 198–200.

6. Sarah Kay, "Love in a Mirror: An Aspect of the Imagery of Bernart de Ventadorn,"
Medium Aevum 52 (1982): 272–77; see also Frederick Goldin, *The Mirror of Narcissus in
the Courtly Love Lyric* (Ithaca: Cornell University Press, 1967), 27, and, on the self-self
and self-other configurations in medieval treatments of Narcissus, Jane Gilbert,
"Comparing Like with Like: Identity, Identicalness and Difference in Selected Medieval
French and English Narratives" (unpublished Ph.D. dissertation, Cambridge, 1993), 87–
130.

7. "Observations historiques et sociologiques sur la poésie des troubadours," *Cahiers
de Civilisation Médiévale* 7 (1964): 27–51.

8. See Simon Gaunt, "Marginal Men, Marcabru and Orthodoxy: the Early
Troubadours and Adultery," *Medium Aevum* 59 (1990): 55–72; Ingrid Kasten,
Frauendienst bei Trobadors und Minnesängern im 12. Jahrhundert (Heidelberg: Winter,
1986), 130–41: Sarah Kay, *Subjectivity in Troubadour Poetry* (Cambridge: Cambridge
University Press, 1990), 40–41 and 112–31; Ursula Liebertz-Grün, *Zur Soziologie des
"amour courtois"* (Heidelberg: Winter, 1977), 97–108; Linda M. Paterson, *The World of
the Troubadours: Medieval Occitan Society, c.1100–1300* (Cambridge: Cambridge
University Press, 1993), 28–36; and Aurelio Roncaglia, "*Trobar clus*: discussione
aperta," *Cultura Neolatina* 29 (1969): 5–55. Specifically on Köhler's reading of *Can vei*
(although he makes reference to a German version, rather than the article in French that I
have used), see Kaehne, 2:237–41.

9. Köhler's 1964 article needs to be read in conjunction with Georges Duby, "Dans la
France du Nord au XIIᵉ siècle: les 'jeunes' dans la société aristocratique," *Annales* 19
(1964): 835–64, and Erich Köhler, "Sens et fonction du terme 'jeunesse' dans la poésie
des troubadours," in *Mélanges Crozet*, 2 vols. (Poitiers: CESCM, 1966): 1:569–83, as
well as the critics cited in the previous note.

10. Köhler, "Observations," 29 and 40.

11. Ibid., 47–51, quotation on 49.

12. Ibid., 41.

13. Goldin, 96–101; Leslie T. Topsfield, *Troubadours and Love* (Cambridge:
Cambridge University Press, 1975), 129–30.

14. Kay, "Love," 285 n.38.

15. Jean-Charles Huchet, *L'Amour discourtois: la "Fin'amors" chez les premiers
troubadours* (Toulouse: Privat, 1987), 197.

16. R. Howard Bloch, *Medieval Misogyny and the Invention of Western Romantic Love*
(Chicago: Chicago University Press, 1991), 146–47 and 145.

17. Köhler, "Observations," 51; see also 42–43 on the importance of stanza order in
troubadour lyric qenerally; Goldin, 97.

18. Kay, "Love," 278–79; Huchet, 195–96.

19. Kay, "Love," 281 and 284 n.32; Huchet, 195. See also Kaehne, 2:236–37, for
further justification of the order Appel adopts. A number of critics suggest stanza order is

crucial in *Can vei*; for example, see Peter E. Bondanella, "The Theory of the Gothic Lyric and the Case of Bernart de Ventadorn," *Neuphilologishe Mitteilungen* 74 (1973): 369–81, and Nathaniel B. Smith, "*Can vei la lauzeta mover*: poet vs. lark," *South Atlantic Bulletin* 40 (1975): 15–22.

20. For example, see Goldin, 101; Huchet, 196; Kaehne, 2:236–37; Kay, "Love," 278; and Köhler, "Observations," 50. For other examples of such echoes, see Jean-Marie-Lucien Dejeanne, ed., *Poésies complètes du troubadour Marcabru* (Toulouse: Privat, 1909), poem 17; Pickens, *Songs*, 5:1.

21. Echoes between the *tornada* and the text need not be with the last stanza. For example, see Appell, *Bernart,*, poem 44, ll. 45–48 and 73–76; this in a poem where the stanza order is fixed by the verse form.

22. For details, see Appel, *Bernart*, 249, and Lazar, *Bernard*, 273.

23. Zumthor, 193.

24. Van Vleck, 117–26.

25. See Simon Gaunt, *Gender and Genre in Medieval French Literature* (Cambridge: Cambridge University Press, 1995), 152–58, and Van Vleck, 119–21.

26. Van Vleck, 91–121.

27. Ibid., 128.

28. Ibid., 97.

29. See Kay, *Subjectivity*, 2–3. This conflicts with Zumthor's view of medieval lyrics: "l'aspect subjectif de la chanson (le sens du *je* qui la chante) n'a pour nous d'existence que grammaticale" (192), on which see Kay, *Subjectivity*, 5–6.

30. The view of a troubadour in a manuscript is shaped by the songs that are anthologized in it, by the texts of these songs in it, by any *vidas* or *razos* (short prose narrative texts that frame the lyrics in a biography), and by the other troubadours anthologized in the manuscript. The comprehensiveness of modern editions and the fact that they devote a single volume to the work of just one troubadour produce a different view. My view then of the "identity" of troubadour poets differs from many scholars in that I think that taking any given text to be exclusively the work of a named poet, and consequently drawing conclusions about that poet, is highly problematic. My position is also different from Zumthor's (cited in the previous note) in that I think that the view of the poet's identity that emerges from the manuscripts is important to the aesthetic of the medieval lyric. Along with Kay, *Subjectivity*, 1, I take subjectivity to mean "above all the elaboration of a first-person (subject) position in the rhetoric of courtly poetry."

31. Huchet, 44.

32. On "apocryphal" stanzas in Jaufré Rudel's lyrics, see Kay, "Continuation." For an example of substantially "rewritten" stanzas see Dejeanne, *Marcabru,* iv.

33. This is (at least by implication) the view of Pickens, Van Vleck and Zumthor.

34. I take the idea of rhyme as metonymy from Sarah Kay, "Derivation, Derived Rhyme and the Trobairitz," in *The Voice of the Trobairitz: Perspectives on the Women Troubadours*, ed. William D. Paden Jr. (Philadelphia: Pennsylvania University Press, 1989), 158.

35. Interestingly, in line 13 of *ACMU*, read "se" rather than "me" with a consequent change of "se" to "mi," in the following line. See the text of *A*, above.

36. Lines 19, 30, 47, and 51 appear hypermetric, but *A* writes "et" when the conjunction is to be scanned as a separate syllable; see lines 26 and 54. *A*, a thirteenth-century Italian manuscript, is thought to be a "good," even a "hypercorrect" manuscript, that is a manuscript in which the scribe has corrected mistakes in his sources and regularized the texts: the assignation of the letter "A" to this manuscript is in itself a recognition of its relative freedom from error (see Marshall, 9), though not of course a

guarantee of the authenticity of its texts, if by "authenticity" is meant "proximity to that the original author wrote." I have not translated A's text as, despite the different stanza order, the reader can use my translation of Appel's version in conjunction with my discussion of the variants (above).

37. As Kaehne, 2:239, notes, this is the only instance of *femna* in Bernart's surviving corpus. The word may in itself have misogynist overtones. The misogynist gloss to Narcissus here suggests an intriguing parallel to the *Romance of the Rose*, where Guillaume de Lorris famously turns the Narcissus story against women; see Guillaume de Lorris and Jean de Meun, *Le Roman de la Rose*, ed. Armand Strubel (Paris: Livre de Poche, 1992), lines 1504–7.

38. See E. Jane Burns, "The Man Behind the Lady in Troubadour Lyric," *Romance Notes* 25 (1985): 254–70; Gaunt, *Gender*, 122–79; and Kay, *Subjectivity*, 95–101.

39. I would like to thank Joan Haahr, Ruth Harvey, Sarah Kay, and Linda Paterson for their helpful comments on a first draft of this article.

Loc Aizi/Anima Mundi: Being, Time, and Desire in the Troubadour Love Lyric

CHARLOTTE GROSS

The earliest use of the Old Occitan expression *loc aizi* occurs in Jaufre Rudel's famous song of distant love, where the lyric "I" wishes that he might see his beloved "truly, in pleasant places ["en locs aizis"] so that the chamber and garden might seem [to him] forever a palace" ("Veraiamen, en locs aizis, / Si qe la cambra e•l jardis / Mi resembles totz temps palatz!").[1] This wish may strike us as extravagant. Seemingly not satisfied with the conventional erotic setting of "cambra" or "jardis"—chamber or garden—the troubadour immediately superimposes a second and metaphorical vision ("totz temps palatz") upon the original true sight ("veraiamen") of the first. In so doing, he ensures the integrity of his distant love, who is removed from the poetic present to the subjunctive similitude of reverie. Equally importantly, having constructed his "pleasant place" from a real garden transfigured as everlasting palace, Jaufre well expresses what I take to be the fundamental nature of the troubadour *loc aizi*. In this unstable threshold place of mutual love, a fragile construct of desire, opposites meet and are for an instant reconciled—near and far, temporal and eternal, self and other, aspirant and ideal, becoming and Being. "Life is not possible without an opening into the transcendent," writes Mircea Eliade:[2] the *loc aizi* of the troubadour love lyric, a vernacular *locus amoenus* accessible only in dream, vision, or memory, transforms ordinary time and space to connect *sai* and *lai*, abolishing the distance and disproportion separating the lover and the idealized lady of the *canso*.

My discussion of the *loc aizi* in the poetry of three troubadours— Jaufre Rudel (fl. 1125–48), Bernart de Ventadorn (fl. 1150–80), and Raimbaut d'Aurenga (fl. 1144–73)—takes as its starting point Peter

Dronke's observation that for the writers of the twelfth century "the opposition between this-worldly and otherworldly can never be absolute, and is . . . [indeed] surmountable."[3] In turning first to two twelfth-century accounts of the Platonic world soul, I will examine as preface a paradigmatic philosophical model of the meeting and fusion of ontological opposites. This is Plato's *anima mundi*, at once immanent and transcendent, an intermediary between the sense-perceptible and the intelligible worlds. But this is not a study of "influence." Rather, both the *loc aizi* of troubadour poetry and the *anima mundi* of twelfth-century philosophy may be viewed as analogous constructs, rhetorical and cosmological, as expressions in disparate forms of discourse of corresponding impulses to unite two worlds. Each is thus an aspect of a larger cultural and intellectual change of the twelfth-century renaissance, a modification of Christian-Platonic ontology away from binary oppositions and towards intermediary constructs—a rapprochement of becoming and Being that has also been described as an impulse towards "the relativization of this-worldly and otherworldly."[4] These corresponding and parallel efforts to bring together distinct and heterogeneous ontological orders share an inherent instability— characteristic of all such intermediary constructs—that is itself an essential feature of twelfth-century thought.[5] For both the poets and the philosophers, the pervasive search for courtly and cosmological order coexists with a fascination with indeterminate boundaries and heterogeneous constructs. The troubadours' *loc aizi* is a hypothetical and designedly unstable moment of desire fulfilled; the world soul, from the first metaphysically and theologically problematic, proves at once attractive and profoundly threatening to Christian thinkers.

Plato's notion of an *anima mundi*—the rational and immortal soul that perfects and gives life to the cosmos (*Tim.* 33b)—poses for twelfth-century thinkers what R. W. Southern has called "the most intractable problem of the *Timaeus*."[6] As an intermediary between the intelligible archetype and the sensible universe, the world soul effects and guarantees cosmic order; for twelfth-century thinkers, the *anima mundi* moreover links Creator and creation in a bond expressive of divine love. Yet Christian theologians can scarcely account for Plato's mixture and fusion of heterogeneous ontological modes: the world soul is at once eternal and temporal, one and many, transcendent and inherently operative in the physical universe. Writing in 1138, two years before the Council of Sens, William of St. Thierry attacks those reported to identify Plato's world soul with the Holy Spirit, vilifying William of Conches as "the basilisk mounted on the coils of Abelard the serpent."[7] In fact, in their treatment of Plato's *anima mundi*, Abelard and William have distinct purposes and take distinct approaches, together representative of twelfth-century thought.

Abelard's approach is theological. In his three treatises on Christian doctrine, written in the second and third decades of the twelfth century, Abelard looks to Old Testament prophets and pagan philosophers for divinely inspired testimony to the Christian conception of the Trinity, finding in the Timaean world soul "a most beautiful figure" of the Holy Spirit.[8] Despite the condemnation at Sens, then, Abelard does not literally identify the world soul with the Holy Spirit. "The things said by the philosopher must be taken metaphorically [*per involucrum*]," he writes; for example, that the Soul is located in the middle of the world symbolizes that "divine grace is offered to all in general."[9] But *involucrum* or not, Abelard must confront the problem of the soul's heterogeneous ontology, its simultaneous transcendence and immanence. To this end he distinguishes between *spiritus*, the name of an eternal nature, and *anima*, the name of a vivifying function (*officium*) that has its beginning with the creation of the world.[10] Elsewhere, sidestepping this ontological issue altogether, Abelard finds in Plato's account of the soul's undivided and divided substance an allegory of the unity and manifoldness of the Trinity.[11] Thus his "solution" to the ontological problem of the world soul is in effect a theological focus on the transcendent. As D. E. Luscombe notes, "[Abelard's] interpretation is mystical in the sense that he does not attribute to the *anima mundi* the physical, cosmological activities which were described by some of his contemporaries."[12]

Among these contemporaries is William of Conches, who at the beginning of his career affirms both the cosmological and theological aspects of Plato's world soul. According to William's early Boethian gloss (c. 1120), "[T]he world soul is a natural vigor by which certain things have movement, others growth, others feeling, and others discernment. . . . But it seems to me that this natural vigor is the Holy Spirit, divine and benevolent concord."[13] A similar theological identification with the Holy Spirit remains implicit in the later Timaean gloss (c. 1130), where the world soul is defined theologically and also cosmologically as the universal source of life and motion.[14] But in his repeated efforts to explain the soul's simultaneous transcendence and immanence, William betrays a certain uneasiness: according to one account, the indivisible substance of the World Soul is the intelligible archetype, the divisible substance *hyle* (unformed matter); according to another, "[The *anima mundi*] is indivisible in essence but divisible in its powers," since the soul functions differently in plants, animals, and people (*Glosae* 76).[15] At the same time, no reader of the Timaean gloss

can fail to notice the similarity between William's definition of the world
soul—a life-giving *spirit* inherent in things ("spiritus rebus insitus")—
and his concept of nature, a life-giving *force* inherent in things ("vis
rebus insita").[16] Indeed, according to the classic argument of Tullio
Gregory, William's cosmological treatment of the world soul leads
directly to the twelfth-century idea of an autonomous nature, a complex
of secondary causes that assists the Creator.[17] Thus William abandons his
identification of the world soul with the Holy Spirit not merely through
prudence or in reaction to the Council of Sens. Like Abelard unable to
hold together the soul's metaphysical and physical halves—unable to
work with so heterogeneous a construct—William nevertheless finds the
anima mundi profoundly attractive as a unifying cosmic structure. When
in 1144 he abandons the doctrine of the world soul altogether, he
continues his cosmological approach, positing nature itself as an
intermediary between Creator and creation.[18]

If the philosophers persistently try to bridge the gap between Being
and becoming, the troubadour poets—as I will suggest in my discussion
of the *loc aizi*—similarly seek an intermediate way between imperfection
and perfection. If one considers the troubadour love-lyric as a courtly
cosmos, the *canso* is structured by an ontology analogous to the
Christian-Neoplatonic distinction between temporal becoming and
eternal Being: the lover aspires towards an idealized lady who, conceived
as a source of being and perfection, is separated from him by an
inviolable metaphysical distance. Insofar as he is represented as suffering
continuous emotional vicissitude—balanced like a ship on the wave,
trembling like the hawthorn branch—the lyric lover is associated with the
mutable, imperfect, and temporal. And insofar as she embodies a
projected ideal of social and personal worth, the lady or *domna* is
identified with the perfect, immutable, and eternal; as Joan Ferrante
writes, she is conceived as "source and repository of all good
qualities."[19] This ontological paradigm, introduced by the first known
troubadour, Guilhem IX of Aquitaine, is illustrated most clearly in the
grammatical structure of his finest *canso*, "Mout jauzens me prenc en
amar."[20] Here the desiring lover is suspended in time by negative
modals—I dare not, I ought not, I know not how to, I can't—while the
idealized lady, represented as an eternal force or pure being, is removed
from time altogether by a series of infinitive end-rhymes that designate
her omnipotence: her love can heal, renew, prolong life, make courtly—
guerir (48), *renouvellar* (35), *sanar* (25), *encortezir* (30).[21] The first
troubadour's ontological paradigm is equally illustrated in its negative
form. When the figure of the ideal lady is absent from the world of the

canso, as in Guilhem's "Pos vezem de novel florir" (#7), courtly being is reduced to nothingness—as the lyric speaker laments, "Tot es nïens" ("All is nothing," 18)—and temporal becoming degenerates to stasis, a *durée nulle* of past, present, and future privation: "A totz jorns m'es pres enaisi / C'anc d'aquo c'amei no•m jauzi, / Ni o farai, ni anc non ho fi" ("It has always happened to me thus, that what I loved I never enjoyed, nor shall I [enjoy it], nor ever did I," #7.13–15). As developed by Jaufre, Bernart, and Raimbaut, the *loc aizi* of mutual love is an effort to reform the basic ontology of the *canso*, to bridge the infinite gulf separating the lyric lover and lady by reshaping being and time with desire.

In the *cansos* of Jaufre Rudel, who uses both spatial and temporal distance to symbolize metaphysical superiority, the far-off love is always absent from the poetic present, accessible only in dream or reverie. "Et es ben paisutz de manna / qui ren de s'amor gazaigna" ("He who gains anything of her love is indeed fed with manna," #4.20–21), writes Jaufre, suggesting that imagined moments of meeting provide entry to paradise.[22] But of even greater interest to the modern reader are the unstable preliminary forms and manifestations of the *loc aizi* that emerge from Jaufre's experiments with the surreal time of dreams and visions. Unlike consciously willed reverie—the controlled work of waking imagination, as in "Lanqand li jorn"—dreams and visions for Jaufre may unpredictably result in either joyous union or nightmare separation. In "Quan lo rossinhols el follos," for example, the speaker-lover transcends space and time while "sompnhan dormen" ("dreaming asleep," #5.16) to find desire abundantly fulfilled: "la jau joyos jauzen" ("there I enjoy her joyously joyful," #5.18). Yet in a second nightmare vision of the same *canso*, running towards the object of desire only increases the distance between the lover and his *amor*:

> D'aquest amor suy tan cochos
> que quant ieu vau ves lieys corren,
> vejaire m'es qu'a reüsos
> m'en torn e que lay•s n'an fugen;
> e mos cavals y cor tan len
> a greu cug mais que•y attenha,
> s'amors no la•m fay remaner.
>
> (#5.22–27)

[I am so anxious for/desirous of this love, that when I go running towards her/it, it seems to me that I turn around backwards and that she goes off fleeing there; and my horse goes there so slowly that I hardly think I will ever get there, if love does not make her stop for me.]

This disorienting confusion of motion and direction, near and far, fast and slow, backward and forward—and is the dreamer riding or on foot?—suggests that the attempt to collapse the distinction between *sai* and *lai* is not without difficulty or danger. Here, for example, the participles "corren" and "fugen" denote motions in opposite directions, and thus an ever-increasing distance between the lyric lover and his *amor:* space and time have ceased to be consistent and predictable.

For Jaufre, in fact, any attempt by ungoverned desire (e.g., "enveyos," "cossiros," "cochos," #5.8, 15, 22) to abolish distance in dream or vision is invariably marked by instability, turmoil, and a confusion or blurring of the boundaries that usually delineate the world and the self. In "Quan lo rossinhols," for example, Jaufre elides the distinction between vision and reality: the dream-sequences of the *canso* are both recounted in the present indicative, grammatically marked as "real events," while the "reality" of waking moments is consistently undercut by Jaufre's use of negative and subjunctive verbs.[23] In "Pro ai del chan essenhadors," to take another example, the speaker's heart, spirit, and will ("voluntatz," #1.41) desert his sleeping body to travel to the lady's castle, fragmenting the lyric self but ultimately failing to abolish the distance between the lover and his *amor*. It seems likely, as Sarah Kay writes, "that for the medieval lover bilocation is just a fact of life."[24] But in "Pro ai del chan," the speaker both encloses his love in his heart (#1.30–32) and proclaims that his heart dwells wholly *lai*, there with her: "Lai es mos cors, si totz c'aillors / non a ni sima ni raïtz" ("My heart/body is there so entirely that elsewhere it has neither top nor root," #1.33–34).[25] The dream-sequence of Jaufre's *canso* therefore suggests not simply the fragmentation of self but also a confusion of boundaries—inside and outside, self and other— that points to the instability of all poetic constructs that attempt to abolish distance or absence in the *canso*. Unlike the controlled and conscious desire of reverie, which draws a distant love into the garden or under the curtains in purely hypothetical time, Jaufre's dreams and visions, at their most violent and destabilizing, set in relief precisely what will prove problematic about the *loc aizi* in later troubadour poets.

As developed by Bernart, the *loc aizi* is additionally identified with origins, becoming an *illud tempus,* or eternal present, of mutual love in which the lover may return to the source of his being, the lady. Twice said to have created the lover from nothing, "de nien," the *domna,* or lady, is for Bernart strongly associated with first beginnings.[26] Her gaze creates a day of nativity (#2.46–49), her welcome fixes the "bels comensamens" or "beautiful beginning" of time (#14.6), her love makes one day worth more than a hundred (#44.41–42). Most succinctly designated as "paradis" (#37.29), Bernart's *loc aizi* of reverie enables the lover, if only in imagination, to transcend hope and despair, to return to the perfection of origins, and—most importantly—to collapse the metaphysical distance separating him from the lady. As the troubadour writes: "[A]l prim de nostr' enamorar / feiram chambis del esperitz / . . . / . . . tot par a par, / e foram de dos cors unitz!" ("[A]t the first hour of our love, we would exchange spirits; completely equal and alike, we would unite two hearts" (#42.59–64). No longer having need of language, the lyric "I"—earlier fragmented into a silenced mouth and clamoring heart—is now reintegrated and renewed. At the same time, this moment of unity is highly unstable, for as a fusion and *con*fusion of self and other, this-worldly and otherworldly, materiality and ideality, the *loc aizi* violates courtly ontology—that is, the paradigm instituted by Guilhem and developed by Jaufre, which decrees that the third in the courtly triangle be distance. When Bernart's lyric lover seeks a perfected self in the imagination of origins, he inevitably finds himself mortal. His necessary fall from the *loc aizi* threatens him with imminent death, leading to motifs of ending. As the speaker of another song laments: "Si no•m aizis lai on ilh jai / . . . / doncs, per que m'a faih de nien? / Ai las, com mor" (my emphasis; "If she does not shelter me there where she lies, then why did she create me from nothing? Alas, I am dying!" #19.46–49).

As a structural feature of about one-fourth of Bernart's *cansos*, the *loc aizi* brings together lover and lady in carefully staged scenes of creation and dissolution. By thus displacing beginnings and endings to the middle strophes of the love song, Bernart both contains the instabilities inherent in the *canso*'s economy of desire and delineates a process of courtly self-construction. In "Lonc tems a q'eu no chantei mai," for example, the lover fallen from the *loc aizi* recovers his identity by reinstating the lyric ontology, redefining himself to the courtly audience as both singer and lover: "Ve•us me del chantar garnit, / pois sa fin'amors m'o assol" ("You see me prepared to sing, since her noble love allows me," #19.65–66). On the other hand, Bernart's most famous *canso* offers a negative vision of the *loc aizi*, strongly recalling the dangers adumbrated by Jaufre. In "Can vei la lauzeta mover," the *loc aizi* of love-union is metonymically represented by a "miralh," or moment of perception so intensely focused that subject and object fuse too completely to admit of separation. With distance entirely abolished in the mirror, all boundaries are effaced and the distinction between self and other is rendered meaningless. All that remains of the lyric self is the destabilizing force of (disembodied) desire: "Tout m'a mo cor, e tout m'a me, / e se mezeis e tot lo mon; / e can se•m tolc, no•m laisset re / mas dezirer e cor volon" ("She has taken my heart, myself, herself, and the whole world; and when she took

herself from me, she left me nothing but desire and a desiring heart,"
#31.13–16). Explicitly renouncing song and love, the embittered speaker
of "Can vei la lauzeta" ends by entirely negating the courtly paradigm,
denigrating all *domnas* and deserting his own métier.[27]

In conclusion, I turn briefly to the *cansos* of Raimbaut d'Aurenga, for
whom the lady is often explicitly associated with divinity.[28] Her laughter,
writes the poet, is like the laughter of God or four hundred angels
(#35.31–35); God gives her sovereignty over the whole world (#30.53–
56) and shows restraint in not raising her up to him with kisses (#22.25–
26). When entirely possessed by such nearly divine love (as in "Ara•m so
del tot conquis"), the lyric "I" discovers a *loc aizi* where time, change,
and antitheses are transcended and the self lost in unity: "C'oblidat n'ai
gaug e ris / E plor e dol e feunia / . . . / Ni crei . . . / Que res, mas Deus,
me capdel" ("I have forgotten joy and laughter, and tears and grief and
sadness . . . nor do I believe that anything but God governs me"; #29.3–
7). But while this extraordinary *canso* overcomes the opposition between
Being and becoming, for Raimbaut the *loc aizi* is more frequently
mediated by language and associated with the art of poetic
composition.[29] When someone speaks of his *domna*, for example, the
lover imagines himself in paradise (#29.45–49); listening to others
perform his songs—thus praising the lady he cannot name—he thinks he
possesses God (#22.12–16). When fully developed, Raimbaut's *loc aizi*
resolves the polarities of speech and silence, creating a hypothetical
moment where both lover and lady, discourse and desire are one. As he
suggests in a closing petition, there is little difference between making
verses and making love: "Domna, no•us quier ab la lengua / Mas qu'en
baisan vos estrenga" ("Lady, I ask you nothing with my tongue but that
in kissing I may embrace you," #38.57–58). Elsewhere the lover
imagines embracing the lady's "nou cors" ("fresh body," #35.45–49)
within the same "nou cor" ("new heart," #35.1) with which he composed
his *vers*, creating an interior *loc aizi* that fuses self, other, and song.

Finally, in reinventing and reordering the world of contraries—ice and
flowers, songs and thunderclaps, valleys and hills—Raimbaut directly
addresses the paradigm of binary oppositions that, as I have suggested,
preoccupies both philosophers and poets in the twelfth century. In "Ar
resplan la flors enversa," the troubadour unites, transforms, and
transcends opposites to create a vision of mutual love and joy attained:
"Mas ar, Dieu lau, m'alberga Joys" ("Now, I praise God, Joy shelters
me," #39.39). When, in the envoy, he sends his verse to be sung *lai*, there
where neither frost nor cold has power to hurt, and where its shoots will
enter his lady's heart, he reshapes the troubadour *loc aizi* to an enclosed
garden celebrating both love and poetic performance.[30] On the one hand,

Raimbaut's "flors enversa" ("inverted flower")—the song itself, sent to the lady—is a purely rhetorical means of bridging the distance between lover and *domna, sai* and *lai,* for the singer's plea to let Love unite him with the lady remains a hypothetical moment of the *tornada*: "Doussa dona, Amors e Joys / Nos ajostan" ("Sweet lady, may Joy and Love unite us," #39.50). Yet if Plato's *anima mundi,* intermediary between the intelligible and sensible realms, was only a "likely story" for the auditors of the *Timaeus,* and if the world soul was similarly construed as fable or allegory by twelfth-century philosophers, then we may read Raimbaut's "flors enversa"—and the troubadour *loc aizi*—as yet another metaphor for the uncertain effort to join two worlds.

Notes

1. For Jaufre's "Lanqand li jorn son lonc en mai," I follow the edition of Rita Lejeune, in *Studi in onore di Angelo Monteverdi* (Modena: Società tip editrice, 1959), 1:403–42; all translations are mine. See also Rupert T. Pickens, ed., *The Songs of Jaufre Rudel* (Toronto: Pontifical Institute of Medieval Studies, 1978), 150–213. On the Old Occitan *aizi,* see Roger Dragonetti, "*Aizi* et *aizimen* chez les plus anciens troubadours," in *Mélanges de linguistic romane et de philologie médiévale offerts à M. Maurice Delbouille* (Gembloux: Duculot, 1964), 2:127–53.

2. Mircea Eliade, *The Sacred and the Profane* (New York: Harcourt, Brace & World, 1959), 34.

3. Peter Dronke, "Profane Elements in Literature," in *Renaissance and Renewal in the Twelfth Century,* ed. Robert L. Benson and Giles Constable (Toronto: University of Toronto Press, 1991), 590. Dronke here refers generally to twelfth-century intellectual trends, and specifically to the metaphysics of David of Dinant (c. 1200).

4. Ibid. The clearest example of this impulse is the increasing emphasis (originating in the late eleventh century) upon the humanity of Christ. For a related example of the rapprochement between heaven and earth, see Caroline Walker Bynum's recent study of the relation of body and soul (esp. in the thirteenth century) in *The Resurrection of the Body in Western Christianity, 200–1336* (New York: Columbia University Press, 1995), 318–43.

5. For a discussion of intermediary constructs in the thirteenth century (e.g., the idea of Purgatory), see Jacques LeGoff, *The Medieval Imagination,* trans. Arthur Goldhammer (Chicago: University of Chicago Press, 1988), 70–71. LeGoff attributes the thirteenth-century impulse toward the formation of intermediaries to an increased interest in "earthly life." In the twelfth century, I would suggest, a new interest in the earthly or physical coexists with a search for intelligible or spiritual causes. See also LeGoff, *The Birth of Purgatory,* trans. Arthur Goldhammer (Chicago: University of Chicago Press, 1984).

6. R. W. Southern, *Platonism, Scholastic Method, and the School of Chartres* (Reading: University of Reading, 1979), 21. For an overview of twelfth-century treatments of the Platonic world soul, see Winthrop Wetherbee, *Platonism and Poetry in the Twelfth Century* (Princeton: Princeton University Press, 1972), 32–36; and Tullio

Gregory, "The Platonic Inheritance," in *A History of Western Philosophy*, ed. Peter Dronke (Cambridge: Cambridge University Press, 1988), 68–70.

7. William of Saint-Thierry, "De Erroribus Guillelmi de Conchis," P.L. 180, 333A, cited in Peter Dronke, *Fabula: Explorations into the Uses of Myth in Medieval Platonism* (Leiden: E. J. Brill, 1974), 60. Despite this contemporary charge, Dronke finds no evidence for a "direct link" between the writings of Abelard and William of Conches: "[I]f there was any direct influence, I think it was informal and reciprocal" (ibid.).

8. *Theologica "Summi boni"* (c. 1118–20), cited in Dronke, *Fabula*, 61: "De hac autem anima, si diligentius discutiantur ea, quae dicuntur tam ab hoc philosopho quam a ceteris, nulli rei poterunt aptari, nisi spiritui sancto *per pulcherrimam involucri figuram* assignentur" (my emphasis). See also Gregory, 60. On Abelard's conviction that divine inspiration is proper to both (pagan) philosophy and (Scriptural) prophecy, see *Fabula*, 58–67.

9. "Clarum est ea, quae a philosophis de anima mundi dicuntur, per involucrum accipienda esse"; moreover, Abelard continues, "Alioquin summum philosophorum Platonem, summum stultorum esse deprehenderemus" (*Theologica Christiana* 1.106, cited by Gregory, 60; see also Dronke, *Fabula*, 63). On the interpretation of the soul as "set in the centre of the universe, that is, of divine grace offered to all in general," see *Theologia Scholarium*, cited by Dronke, *Fabula*, 62–63.

10. "Philosophus eundem [Spiritum Sanctum] qui in essentia propria aeternaliter subsistit, incoepisse quantum ad effecta sua voluit, ex quibus eum animam magis quam Spiritum appellavit. Spiritus quippe nomen est naturae, anima vero officii" (*Intro. ad theol.*, 2.17, cited in Tullio Gregory, *Anima Mundi: La filosofia di Guglielmo di Conches e la Scuola di Chartres* [Florence: Sansoni, 1955], 147). See also Gregory's discussion of Abelard in his *Anima Mundi*, 133–54; and the clear summation of D. E. Luscombe, *The School of Peter Abelard* (Cambridge: Cambridge University Press, 1969), 125.

11. Luscombe, 125.

12. Ibid. As Luscombe points out, unlike the cosmologists, Abelard never claims the reverse position, that the Holy Spirit is the world soul.

13. "Anima mundi est naturalis vigor quo habent quedam res tantum moveri, quedam crescere, quedam sentire, quedam discernere. Sed quid sit ille vigor queritur. Sed, ut mihi videtur, ille vigor naturalis est Spiritus Sanctus, id est divina et benigna concordia, que est id a quo omnia habent esse, moveri, crescere, sentire, vivere, discernere. Qui bene dicitur naturalis vigor, quia divino amore omnia crescent et vigent. Qui bene dicitur anima mundi, quia solo divino amore et caritate omnia quae in mundo sunt, vivunt et habent vivere" (cited in Gregory, *Anima Mundi*, 15–16).

14. See William of Conches, *Glosae Super Platonem*, ed. Edouard Jeauneau (Paris: Vrin, 1965), 71: "Et est anima mundi spiritus quidam rebus insitus, motum et vitam illis conferens. . . . Hunc spiritum dicunt quidam esse Spiritum Sanctum, quod nec negamus nec affirmamus." William adds, however: "Et bene [Plato] dicit 'excogitavit' et non 'creavit' secundum quod anima dicitur Spiritus Sanctus. Non enim a Deo factus est nec creatus nec genitus sed procedens est Spiritus Sanctus" (*Glosae* 74). All citations will be to this edition of the *Glosae* and noted parenthetically according to *capitula*; all translations are mine.

15. "Est enim individua in essentia—spiritus enim est carens partibus—sed dividua est per potentias. Aliam enim potentiam exercet in herbis et arboribus, aliam in brutis animalibus, aliam in hominibus" (*Glosae* 76).

16. "Et est natura vis rebus insita similia de similibus operans" (*Glosae* 37); "Et est anima mundi spiritus quidam rebus insitus, motum et vitam illis conferens" (*Glosae* 71).

17. For Gregory's argument, see *Anima Mundi*, 184–88; and especially Tullio Gregory, *Platonismo medievale: studi e richerche* (Rome: Instituto storico italiano, 1958), 135–50.

18. Dorothy Elford, "William of Conches," in Dronke, ed., *History,* 308–27, persuasively argues that "William's confidence in the consistency and dynamic order of the natural world . . . increased to the point where he longer needed the doctrine of the world soul; the *natura rerum* itself constituted a sufficient guarantee of the unity of the cosmos."

19. Joan M. Ferrante, *Woman as Image in Medieval Literature* (New York: Columbia University Press, 1975), 66–67; see also Frederick Goldin, *The Mirror of Narcissus in the Courtly Love Lyric* (Ithaca: Cornell University Press, 1967), 70–77, who argues that the *domna* is a reflecting mirror in which the lover envisions a perfected self. As recent studies have made clear, this courtly ontology is the product of a patriarchal society; see, e.g., E. J. Burns, "The Man Behind the Lady in Troubadour Lyric," *Romance Notes* 35 (1985): 254–70. As a projected ideal of male aspiration, the *domna* represents the eternal and unchanging; but as a reflection of misogynist anxiety, she is depicted as temporal and changeable, a "cor volatge" ("fleeting heart") dangerously exempt from male control. On courtly ontology, see also C. Gross, "The Cosmology of Rhetoric," *Rhetorica* 9.1 (1991): 39–53.

20. *The Poetry of William VI, Count of Poitiers, IX Duke of Aquitaine*, ed. Gerald Bond (New York: Garland, 1982), 32–35. All citations will be to this edition and will be noted parenthetically; all translations are mine.

21. For the lover's suspension in time, see (e.g.) "no•m dey" (7), "no•m say," (8), "no poc hom" (13), "no•y poiri'" (18), and "no l'aus" (46) in Bond #9. For the lady's power and transcendence of time, see st. 5: "Per son joy pot malautz sanar / E per sa ira sas morir / . . . / E•l plus cortes vilaneiar / E•l totz vilas encortezir" (#9.25–30).

22. *The Poetry of Cercamon and Jaufre Rudel*, ed. George Wolf and Roy Rosenstein (New York: Garland, 1983), 138–39 (#4.20–21). All further citations (except from "Lanqand li jorn") will be to this edition and will be noted parenthetically; all translations are mine. For various manuscript versions of Jaufre's songs, see the indispensable edition of Pickens.

23. Thus, e.g., the dream-sequence of ll. 15–19 is conveyed in the indicative, the "waking reality" of ll. 20–21 in the subjunctive mood; this procedure is followed throughout the *canso*.

24. Sarah Kay, *Subjectivity in Troubadour Poetry* (Cambridge, England: Cambridge University Press, 1990), 67.

25. As Pickens points out, "in the nominative singular it is impossible to distinguish *cors* ("body") and *cors* ("heart")" (141). "Heart," however, is the more frequently adopted reading. I note that the dream-sequence of "Pro ai" (sts. 5–6) is fragmented in manuscript tradition; st. 5 appears only in MS. e^3, st. 6 only in C. See Pickens, 136–37.

26. *Bernard de Ventadour: Chansons d'amour*, ed. Moshé Lazar (Paris: Klincksieck, 1966). All further citations will be to this edition and will be noted parenthetically; all translations are mine. For the lady as creator, see #2.42 and #19.48; for her control of origins/time, see, e.g., #2.46–49.

27. The readers who have commented on this famous *canso* are many: for an argument that the "miralh" of "lo bels Narcisus" (24) does not refer to self-love, see Sarah Kay, "Love in a Mirror: An Aspect of the Imagery of Bernart de Ventadorn," *Medium Aevum* 52 (1983): 272–85.

28. *The Life and Works of the Troubadour Raimbaut d'Orange*, ed. W. T. Pattison (Minneapolis: University of Minnesota Press, 1952). All further citations will be to this

edition and noted parenthetically; all translations are mine, with indebtedness acknowledged to Pattison.

29. As Simon Gaunt observes in *Troubadours and Irony* (Cambridge: Cambridge University Press, 1989), 121, Raimbaut's work "resists systematization." By turns serious or parodic—in one song, for example, desire makes the lover lose in one day the fat he gains in a month (#15)—Raimbaut seems most committed to his own poetic craft.

30. Raimbaut writes: "Mos vers an—qu'aissi l'enverse, / Que no•l tenhon bosc ni tertre— / Lai on hom non sen conglapi, / Ni a freitz poder que y trenque. / A midons lo chant e•l siscle, / Clar, qu'el cor l'en intro•l giscle, / Selh que sap gen chantar ab joy / Que no tanh a chantador croy" ("May my verse go—for thus I invert it, so that neither wood nor hill might hold it [back]—there where one does not feel the frost and cold has no power to cut. May it be sung and whistled clearly to my lady, so that its shoots enter her heart, by a singer who can sing nobly with joy, for it is not fitting for a base singer"; #39.41–48). For a textual antecedent to this "*loc aizi*" of *fin'amors*, see Marcabru, "Al son desviat, chantaire": "L'amors don ieu sui mostraire / Nasquet en un gentil aire, / E•l luoc[s] on ill es creguda / Es claus de rama branchuda / E de chaut e de gelada, / Qu'estrains no l'en puosca traire" ("The love of which I am teacher was born in a noble family, and the place where she flourished is enclosed with branching boughs, and [protected] from heat and ice, so that no stranger can take her from there"; #5.49–54; J.-M.-L. Dejeanne, *Poésies complètes du troubadour Marcabru* [Toulouse: Privat, 1909], 21).

"Kar des dames est avenu / L'aventure": Displacing the Chivalric Hero in Marie de France's *Eliduc*

SANDRA PIERSON PRIOR

Like most of Marie de France's *lais*, *Eliduc* contains an explicit discussion of the *lai*'s name:

> D'eles deus ad li lais a nun
> *Guildeluëc ha Guilliadun.*
> *Elidus* fu primes nomez,
> Mes ore est li nuns remuez.
>
> (*Eliduc*, 21–24)[1]

[From these two the *lai* is named / *Guildeluec and Gualadun.* / At first the *lai* was called *Eliduc*, / But now the name has been changed. (21–24)][2]

As Matilda Tomaryn Bruckner points out, the concern with what a *lai* is called is part of Marie de France's general interest in naming—whether of the *lais* themselves, of their characters, or of their poet.[3] Naming a *lai* is one way of labeling its significance, but it is most commonly and simply a way of telling what, or more often whom, the *lai* is about—and thus a *lai*'s name serves the role of modern titles[4] and in fact was used that way in the only surviving complete manuscript of Marie's *Lais*.[5]

The naming of *Eliduc* involves a choice between two names.[6] In this particular case, we are told that the *lai* had been called *Elidus*, but since it is really about the women, its name has been changed to *Guildeluëc ha Guialliadun.*

Closer examination reveals that the discussion of the title in this *lai* is unusual in several respects. First, there is the naming's placement,

123

neither at the end nor at the very beginning but almost two dozen lines into the poem; second, there is the name's inaccuracy, for the change of title announced in this passage apparently never "took," at least not in the surviving manuscript, not in modern editions, and not even, judging from the last lines of the *lai*, with the poet herself.[7]

The unusual features of this *lai*'s naming reflect both a central issue— who or what the story is about—and a central strategy—displacement— that characterize the *lai* as a whole. For, as I hope to show, in *Eliduc* Marie has displaced the chivalric hero of her story, and with this displacement and its accompanying change in discourse, there is a strong, if implicit, questioning of the values of the *lai*'s courtly world, a world that reflects both the social-political situation of Marie's time and place and also the imaginative world found in other twelfth-century literature. Marie effects this questioning and readjustment through a series of complex moves in the narrative, some of them fairly typical and some of them highly unusual. Beginning with the most literal displacement—a spatial and physical one—that takes her chivalric hero away from his home and following with a gradual displacement in language—from the discourse of warfare and chivalry to that of desire, Marie then completes the displacement of chivalric values with some unusual plot motifs: the shipboard incident and the weasel episode. The *lai* concludes in the mode and world of Christian monastic service—a radical shift from the chivalric world of war and love service.

This last displacement, in mode and values, is signaled by a little-noted, but I believe highly significant, characteristic of the *lai*'s naming in the prologue—the switch in syntactical subject from chivalric hero to *l'aventure*—a displacement that provides a clue to the whole process of naming a *lai* and to Marie's project in telling this one. For, in those early lines we are told the reason for the change in title: it is because "des dames est avenu / L'aventure dunt li *lais* fu" [to the ladies happened the adventure from which the *lai* was made] (25–26; my translation).[8] To say that the adventure happened to the ladies is to imply that *lais* are told about *aventures*, not about people. A startling aesthetic for many of us today, this insistence on a plot-driven, not character-driven, narrative undermines a formalist or a structuralist approach to the *lai*'s subject matter. Taking narrative as analogous to the deep structures of grammar and syntax, the structuralist analysis would posit the romance hero as subject, with the lady as the object of his deeds and desires.[9] However, if *l'aventure* becomes the grammatical subject, as it does in the renaming of *Eliduc*, then we ought perhaps to take *l'aventure* as the topical and thematic subject and read the characters as the objects of the story and its events, thereby removing all three of them from the center of the poem's imaginative world.

I would like now to trace the series of narrative moves that displace the hero geographically, linguistically and culturally, and finally thematically and topically. Turning to the opening lines of the *lai*, even before the discussion of its name, we find, unusually for Marie's *lais*, a fifteen-line plot summary:

> En Bretaine ot un chevalier
> Pruz e curteis, hardi et fier;
> Elidus ot nun, ceo m'est vis.
> N'ot si vaillant hume el païs!
> Femme ot espuse, noble e sage,
> De haute gent, de grant parage.
> Ensemble furent lungement,
> Mut s'entreamerent lëaument.
> Mes puis avint par une guere
> Que il alat soudees quere;
> Iloc ama une meschine,
> Fille ert a rei e a reïne.
> Guilliadun ot nun la pucele,
> El rëaume nen ot plus bele!
> La femme resteit apelee
> Guildeluëc en sa cuntree.
>
> (5–20)

[In Brittany there was a knight, / brave and courtly, bold and proud; / Eliduc was his name, it seems to me, / no man in the country was more valiant. / He had a wife, noble and wise, / of high birth, of good family. / They lived together a long time / and loved each other loyally; / but then, because of a war, he went to seek service elsewhere. / There, he fell in love with a girl, / the daughter of a king and a queen. / Guilliadun was her name, / no girl in the kingdom was more beautiful. / Eliduc's wife was called / Guildeluec in her country. (5–20)]

Everything about these seven couplets suggests that we are about to get a chivalric romance, maybe not in length (chivalric romances tend to run to thousands of lines, not hundreds), but certainly in subject matter and world view.[10] The language of this passage reflects the values of an idealized warrior culture: a knight who possesses a warrior's virtues of bravery and skill, combined with a nobleman's good breeding and manners and a lady of noble birth, who is wise and faithful.[11]

At the same time, the *lai*'s preliminary plot summary hints at a darker and cruder reality behind the idealized chivalric values. Through the term *soudees*, which is nothing more nor less than fighting for hire,[12] and through the indication that Eliduc is forced to leave his own land to find work, the poem comes close to describing the actual conditions of a working knight in twelfth-century France. On the other hand, these references to fighting are balanced by the promise of a love story that will come with Eliduc's journey to another land. That promise shifts the emphasis in this introductory plot summary from the problems of war and vassalage to the conflicts in a love triangle.

Moreover, this early reference to the love story actually names the two women in Eliduc's life, and that naming of the women, unusual for Marie's *lais*,[13] opens the door to a very different kind of story, different both from the chivalric romance seemingly promised and from the *lais* that precede *Eliduc* in the collection. Further, it is immediately after the naming of the women that Marie goes on to claim that the *lai*'s name has been changed from *Eliduc* to *Guildeluëc ha Guilliadun*, a change that switches protagonists—from a knight to his two ladies. The name change also switches the language, and by implication the culture—from Anglo-Norman to Celtic, since two words in this revised title are Breton forms: the coordinating conjunction Breton *ha* for French *et*; and a Breton name, *Guildeluëc*, for the first of the ladies named.

The plot préçis in the beginning of this *lai* thus not only summarizes the deeds of Eliduc but also outlines the metanarrative: the story of the change in this *lai*'s name and the corresponding displacement of the Anglo-Norman warrior culture. Since this introductory summary breaks off with Eliduc's falling in love with the king's daughter, both stories—Eliduc's and that of the narrative's naming—are left unresolved, natural enough for the basic narrative but a bit strange for the question of naming. The strong suggestion is thus that this story is being told as much as to work out its title and its values as to bring Eliduc's adventures to closure.

Following the prologue, with its plot summary and naming, the *lai* returns to its story of Eliduc, who "aveit un seignur, / Rei de Brutaine la Meinur" [had a lord, / a king of Brittany] (29–30). Blessed with a good wife and loyal to his lord, Eliduc appears to be in an excellent situation for a chivalric knight. Unlike the half-formed Guigemar, for example, Eliduc lacks nothing in himself—he is completely successful, but therein lies his problem. For it is Eliduc's success that inspires envy and slander, which in turn ruin his relationship with his king. What seems to be an ideal state of affairs turns out to be a fragile one, since all rests upon the king's goodwill. In this, Eliduc seems to typify the *iuvenes*, who according to Duby, were in tenuous situations: awaiting an inheritance or marriage to a wealthy woman; or looking to a reward for military service—needing, in other words, anything that would give their position some permanence and place them less at the mercy of a ruler's patronage.[14] As Marie tells us through the wisdom of the *vileins*, Eliduc is vulnerable to the ill will of his peers precisely because "[l']amur de seignur n'est pas fiez" [the love of a lord is not a fief] (63).

It is a bit startling to have a *vileins* [peasant] pronounce this aphorism to a plowman, both of whom are presumably outside the feudal relationship of lord to vassal with its rewards for loyal service, its fief-granting, and its oaths of loyalty.[15] The effect of Marie's attribution of this comment to a peasant is to remove us from a courtly and chivalric worldview, or at the very least from the perspective of the upper classes. Indeed, the employment of mercenary soldiers and of unmarried, landless knights was common enough in twelfth-century Anglo-Norman society[16] and was often a business arrangement closer to the relationship between a landholder and farmworkers than to the idealized bond between lord and vassal so often praised by clerks and chroniclers.[17] Eliduc thus seems reduced from a *chevalier* to an out-of-work soldier who is forced to leave home to look for a job. At the same time, Eliduc is also portrayed as a member of the leisure class, or at least as a knight in a romance, one who seeks *aventure*, since, after all this job-searching rationalization for his departure, we are told that he is going to Logres, where "une piece se deduira" [he will enjoy himself for a while] (70).[18]

Benefiting from the political instability of Logres, where there are several kings (89) and not one central sovereign, Eliduc finds a king in need of his services. The arrangement between Eliduc and his new lord, although couched in the language of courtliness, is clearly a contract for military service, "soudees" (110), which is accepted for a limited period of time, since the king provides for "as much as [Eliduc and his men] might want to spend in a month" (128). This arrangement is then extended when Eliduc forms a similar bond of temporary loyalty and service with the knights languishing in the besieged town (185–200).[19]

In both of these contracts, the one between Eliduc and his lord and the one between Eliduc and the local knights, all the stress is upon success in defeating the oppressors, not upon shows of martial skill or the winning of honor and fame, which Eliduc says "n'ateint a nul espleit" [serves no purpose] (171). A very business-like military move this is then, one that Hanning and Ferrante find somewhat less than noble.[20] Certainly, Eliduc's way of defeating Totnes's enemy adds to the suggestions that Eliduc is basically involved in the practical, hardheaded business of war.

Up until this point in the *lai*, we have an uncharacteristic story for Marie, precisely because it reads like a tale of chivalric prowess, although here there is even more emphasis on war (as opposed to tournaments) than is usually found in the more courtly and love-centered of the chivalric romances. The focus of Marie's story so far is upon social/political relationships and military strategy, so much so that the world described comes close to the actual one of Western Europe in the mid- to late-twelfth century. Even the apparent discrepancy between Marie's warring Logres and the stable and central government of late twelfth-century England is perhaps not an inaccurate reflection of the civil and dynastic wars between Stephen and the Empress Matilda, which were in recent memory, or the more nearly contemporaneous efforts Henry II had to make to pacify England and its Celtic borderlands (although admittedly the battles between Stephen and Matilda took place in the west and central shires, and it was Scotland, Wales, and Ireland that were causing the problems for Henry II, while, on the other hand, the war Eliduc finds is in Devon, as is made clear by the place names of Totnes and Exeter, both in Devon).[21]

All in all then, the first 270 lines of *Eliduc* are atypical of the Breton *lai* genre (or at least the genre as adapted by Marie), for normally Marie's *lais* contain little or nothing of war and not much about feudal relationships. At the same time, what we most often associate with Breton *lais*—magic, love, and fairy stories—is wholly absent from this first part of *Eliduc*, which by itself is longer than Marie's shortest *lais*.[22] Indeed, so far this *lai* tells a story more concerned with the grubby underside of chivalry—the actual work of fighting—than one expects to find even in those narratives, such as chivalric romances and chansons de geste, that are primarily concerned with the deeds of the idealized warrior class.

Moreover, judging from the plot summary given in the prologue, this first section tells almost the entire story, omitting only the hero's love for the daughter of a king and queen. But it is that one last bit of the tale that radically changes this tale of soldiers and war into something very different. Just as in the prologue's summary the mention of Eliduc's love for Guilliadun signals the discussion of the change in the *lai*'s title, so the entrance of Guilliadun into the fuller narrative, after the first 270 lines, displaces the soldier-hero and his absorption in the business of fighting. With this new beginning, it is as though everything that we have heard of Eliduc and his *aventure* is but the occasion for the meeting of Eliduc and Guilliadun.

When this new subject, love, displaces the story of a knight looking for a war, it changes the import of Eliduc's prowess and martial feats. It is not only that Eliduc's chivalric adventures now serve as a means for the two lovers to meet (which, after all, is the way it often works in chivalric romance, when Yvain meets Laudine in Chrétien de Troyes's *Yvain*, for example), but also that these exploits provide a way of objectifying and evaluating Eliduc. Eliduc's military success is just one of his many qualifications as an object of Guilliadun's fantasy and desire:

> Elidus fu curteis e sage,
> Beaus chevaliers e pruz e large.
> La fille al rei l'oï numer
> E les biens de lui recunter.
>
> (271–74)

[Eliduc was courtly and wise, / a handsome knight, brave and generous. / The king's daughter heard him spoken of, / his virtues described. (271–74)]

It is as though we are meeting Eliduc for the first time, at the beginning of a story. Indeed we are in a new story with a new subject, for we have moved from the public, twelfth-century, Anglo-Norman world of men to the private desires of a Cornish girl, and while we never really return to the former, neither do we linger long with the latter. Eliduc's complicated relationships with his lords are reduced to plot devices for moving Eliduc back and forth between the two women and their respective lands. The point when Guillaudun enters the narrative thus marks the beginning of a critical transition, a transition in which we move from chivalric romance to *lai*, from political and military action to love and desire.

The language also changes, but more slowly. At first the language of feudal vassalage remains, but it is joined by the discourse of Ovidian love, and together they create a story about both the private feelings of love and the public events in a formal relationship. Such a conflation, not uncommon in courtly literature, whether narrative or lyric, is here clearly an uneasy union. Guilliadun becomes the servant of love personified as a feudal lord, who "lance sun message / Ki la somunt de lui amer, / Palir la fist e suspirer" [sent her a message, commanding her to love him, that made her go pale and sigh] (304–6). Sleepless and torn by the fears common to those overtaken by desire, Guilliadun says she will die "s'il ne m'aime par amur" [if he does not love me with real love] (349). In these passages, Guilliadun has become the desiring Ovidian female,[23] and Eliduc is simply her desired lover, with no characteristics other than those that recommend him to her desire (and notably no mention of a wife—a central attribute of Eliduc's in the first description of him, the one that opens the *lai* [5–10]).

In turn, Eliduc's feelings have become typical of the desired object rather than of the desiring subject. He is concerned about this beautiful princess because she "tant ducement l'apela / E de ceo k'ele suspira" [summoned him so sweetly, / because she had sighed] (317–18). Yet for a while at least, Eliduc remains conscious of his obligations to his wife and to his new lord. Superficially he is a bit like a romance heroine who worries about her honor, but Eliduc's position here is actually quite different from a desired woman's, for he is still working within the world of military vassalage. Moreover, Eliduc deals with the problem of one too many women in the same way that he handled the problem of one too many lords, by putting a time constraint on the service to the newer of the two obligations. He tells Guilliadun:

> Un an sui remés od le rei,
> La fiancë ad de mei prise.
> N'en partirai en nule guise
> De si que sa guere ait finee,
> Puis m'en irai en ma cuntree,
> Kar ne voil mie remaneir,
> Si cungié puis de vus aveir.
>
> (524–30)

[I've been retained by the king for one year; / he has accepted my pledge, / I shall not leave him under any condition / until the war is over. / Then I shall return to my country / if I can get your leave, / because I don't want to remain. (524–30)]

Eliduc fails to see that love is not the same as military service and cannot be pledged for limited amounts of time. Immersed in the rhetoric and values of chivalry, he can only think of desire as another kind of military strategy; indeed he has conflated and apparently confused his obligation to the King of Totnes (whom he has promised to serve for a year) with his commitment to the King's daughter (from whom he requires leave in order to depart). The conflation of love service with war service is mirrored in the language. We are told, for example, that Eliduc has been "*suspris*" by Love (712), conquered as in battle. While this kind of imagery is conventional in much courtly literature, it is unusual for Marie and for the women in this *lai*, who avoid chivalric discourse and are not given to speaking either of love as a battle or of lovers as warriors. The implication for the reader is that these topoi of love as war are not that useful, that love is not like a battle, and that the strategies a warrior uses are inappropriate for satisfying desire.

In the remainder of the *lai*, even Eliduc will eventually learn to think of love as something quite different from warfare or vassalage. Not for Marie or her chivalric hero is the conflation found in other twelfth-century courtly narratives of prowess with courtesy and of war with love.

For in *Eliduc*, the values of chivalry, as mirrored in the language of warfare and vassalage, are not simply readjusted but, along with the chivalric hero himself, are fully displaced. In effecting these radical displacements, Marie gives the critical role of resolution to Guildeluëc, the wife back in Brittany.

Guildeluëc reenters the story, for the first time with a voice and a central place in the action, only after the conflict has reached a point of extreme desperation. Eliduc, having languished with frustrated longing back at home, returns to Totnes to sneak Guilliadun out of her father's home and carry her back to Brittany. When a storm arises and threatens their ship, a sailor cries out that Eliduc is the cause of their impending deaths, since, in bringing home another woman when he already has a wife, Eliduc has acted "Cuntre Deu e cuntre la lei, / Cuntre dreiture e cuntre fei" [in defiance of God and the law, of right and of faith] (837–38). One solution, articulated by the sailor, is direct, if cruel: eliminate the extra woman by throwing her overboard. Eliduc's reaction is equally brutal: screaming insults like "Fiz a putain" [son of a bitch] (843), Eliduc throws the sailor overboard. This violent, vengeful action helps neither Guilliadun nor Eliduc, in part, of course, because the sailor is right: Eliduc has acted unlawfully and disloyally.

Beginning with his decision to return to Logres to get Guilliadun and ending in Guilliadun's apparent death, Eliduc's actions have become increasingly violent. His fetching of Guilliadun has all the marks of an abduction, clearly not a chivalric act, while his behavior on shipboard is even worse, since it marks him as an angry bully instead of a prudent, wise leader. In fact, it is no doubt significant that, despite his explicit role as an active warrior, the only physically aggressive act we see Eliduc perform is the one against his own man. At the same time, Eliduc's moving outside the code of chivalry eventually provides the opportunity for his wife to effect a resolution to the conflict, not by violence or violation of chivalric codes, not by Ovidian seduction or persuasion, but by compassion and alertness to opportunity, and by moving into the mode of Christian myth and sacrifice.

Arriving in Brittany, with Guilliadun unconscious and to all appearances dead, Eliduc is left with the task of trying to dispose of her body and plan her funeral rites. It is at this point in the story that Guildeluëc is finally allowed to act, and it is she who saves Guilliadun and restores all to happiness. In effecting the resolution, Guildeluëc does more than bring about the happy ending to a love story. She, in fact, changes that love story to a different kind of a love story: from a tale of chivalric prowess, Ovidian desire, and a love triangle to a tale of *caritas* and the love shared in a Christian community. This change is made possible through substituting one kind of sacrifice—the sacrifice of death that would have repressed and silenced forever the desiring woman—to a sacrifice by the undesired woman, who, unlike her husband, does not force laws, customs, or *aventure* to bend to her desires. Rather, Guildeluëc observes action as much as she initiates it, and she responds to *aventure* more thoughtfully.

Guildeluëc's markedly different way of acting is clearest in the chapel scene, which climaxes the *lai*. Having learned with the aid of her chamberlain where Eliduc has been sneaking off to each day, Guildeluëc goes to the chapel and discovers Guilliadun lying apparently dead. Guildeluëc's reaction is telling: devoid of anger and jealousy, she feels only sorrow and grief. As she laments over the lifeless "bele femme" [lovely woman] (1026), the chamberlain kills a weasel that has run over Guilliadun's body. At this point the weasel's companion comes up and, in a strangely detailed scene, circles the dead animal's head, prods it with its foot, "semblant feseit de doel mener" [gave signs of grieving] (1044), and then races out of the chapel. The weasel returns with a red flower and places it in the mouth of the dead animal, which promptly revives. Observing all this and reacting quickly, Guildeluëc has her chamberlain get the flower from the weasel so that it can be used to revive Guilliadun.

Guildeluëc's actions in the remainder of the *lai* continue as decisive and as self-sacrificing and charitable as her quick-witted move to save Guilliadun. Reuniting Guilliadun with Eliduc, Guildeluëc then renounces her place as Eliduc's wife and enters a convent, which she asks Eliduc to endow for her. All is done according to her request, and then some, for the *lai* concludes with Eliduc's and Guilliadun's joint decision (or maybe it is not so "joint") also to embrace the monastic life—Guilliadun joining Guildeluëc in her convent and Eliduc entering a new monastery, which he endows for himself and his men (Eliduc's straitened circumstances, those that initiated his departure from Brittany, having vanished without explanation). And so all live happily ever after, presumably well into the true "ever-after."

In some respects, Guildeluëc's motivations, which bring about the happy ending, conform to the values of the courtly, chivalric world, and yet they certainly contrast with Eliduc's way of playing his role as chivalric knight in a love story. One could perhaps explain the differences as a case of a poorly understood and inadequately embraced set of ideals and a nobler, more sincere fulfillment of those same ideals. Or the differences might be seen as simply those of gender—the active knight versus the passive lady. I think, however, Marie has made a more complicated case than either an old-fashioned, moralizing reading of sincerity versus hypocrisy or even a more up-to-date gendered interpretation. The different ways Guildeluëc and Eliduc deal respectively with the chivalric virtue of loyalty provide an especially revealing commentary. Early in the *lai*, when we are told that Eliduc and his wife "mut s'entreamerent lëaument" [loved each other loyally] (12), loyalty is simply a central value of marriage, a value not too highly placed apparently, since it is not long before we see Eliduc break his parting promise to stay loyal to his wife. Admittedly he is somewhat troubled at first by this marital disloyalty, for the narrator claims that Eliduc "sa lëauté voleit garder" [wanted to keep his faith] (467), but he couldn't stop himself from loving Guilliadun (468–69).

Eliduc seems to honor feudal vassalage more than marital fidelity, or at least he invokes his oaths of loyalty to both kings more often than he thinks of his wife. He gives his Breton lord's "busuin" [need] (611) and Eliduc's own oath of fealty ("serement conjuré" [596]) as the compelling reasons for leaving Totnes before the end of the time of his promised service, although he also tacks on a reference to his wife's claims, a reference so thrown aside that it is hard to tell what it means.[24] Similarly, Eliduc appeals to his oath to the King of Totnes when he tells his Breton wife that he must return to the country where he had been. Eliduc emphasizes the demands of his loyalty of vassalage, for he says to Guildeluëc: "ne voil ma fei trespasser" [I don't want to betray my faith] (739). Strictly speaking, Eliduc is not telling the truth here, since the faith he wishes not to betray is his pledge to Guilliadun, not his pledge to Guilliadun's father, the king. What is even more telling about Eliduc's explanation is its demonstration of his continued immersion in a world of competing loyalties, where vows of vassalage are invoked only in order to satisfy one's desires and where lovers are interchangeable with feudal lords, so much so that, as I have noted, editors and readers have trouble keeping the two straight.

Guildeluëc, on the other hand, suffers from no such confusion of loyalties. While noteworthy for her own faithfulness, she does not manipulate her ties in order to please herself. She, in fact, renounces her marriage bonds in order to respond appropriately to the *aventures* that have come her way. Using legal language, Guildeluëc breaks her vows openly and formally by declaring to Guilliadun: "Del tut le voil quite clamer / E si ferai mun chief veler" [I want to leave him completely free, and I shall take the veil] (1101–2). The phrase "clamer quite"—from the legal Latin term *quietum*, and found in English as well (it survives today as "quit-claim")—signals Guildeluëc's legal breaking of a legal obligation. She does this to preserve the principle of the marriage bond, since, as she points out to Eliduc, it is not good ["bien"] for a man to have more than one wife (1128–30), a principle Guildeluëc takes as a reason for leaving her husband.

Guildeluëc's decision to enter a convent is proof that her role is not merely a passive one, but it is not quite the bold and decisive action of a central hero or heroine. It is more accurate to say that Guildeluëc acts in response to *aventure* and in the mode of sacrifice. Eliduc, on the other hand, tends to act precipitously and violently. Plotting an ambush as a way of winning a war, abducting a princess from her homeland, and killing a follower who has dared to challenge one's actions are hardly the idealized deeds of chivalry. Such acts were, however, not unknown in Marie's world of twelfth-century France and England; they are also found in courtly romances, where, depending upon the poet, they are presented with a greater or lesser degree of criticism.

Eliduc's final deeds—endowing and founding two monasteries—not only contrast with his earlier violent, even bullying, behavior, but they also demonstrate a newly gained power and a capability previously lacking in him. In the end of the tale, there is no mention of Eliduc's once all-powerful king, for Eliduc's dependence on mercenary warfare and on the favors of a lord has inexplicably evaporated. The tale's resolution has been made possible only by letting the *aventure* happen to the ladies, so they in turn can move it out of the chivalric world of warfare into one of love and Christian sacrifice.

That Marie is adducing Christian values in *Eliduc* and thereby recentering the chivalric world is not just demonstrated by the *lai*'s conclusion, with the foundation of the two monasteries, but is, in fact, signaled much earlier by the turn from deeds of war and feelings of desire to modes of Christian myth and sacrifice. For, in fact, the resurrection of Guilliadun is but the delayed conclusion to the shipboard incident, and together the two scenes work typologically in evoking the Sign of Jonah. Like Jonah, Guilliadun and Eliduc bring the threat of disaster upon their ship because they are violating the laws of God. Like Jonah, Guilliadun undergoes an experience analogous to death, and like Jonah, she is eventually restored to life. Of course, the variations in this version of the Jonah story are important: it is a nameless sailor who is thrown overboard, not the person running away; it is Guilliadun who is restored, not the sailor; and there is no prophetic mission and no divine call, indeed no divine voice. Instead, Guilliadun is restored to her place as Eliduc's beloved, the very role that got her into trouble in the first place.

These variations, in themselves displacements of a typological story, raise the possibility of near-blasphemy (the Sign of Jonah, is, after all, the preeminent Christological sign),[25] since Marie has put a woman and animal magic in place of divine power and the romantic reunion of an adulterous couple in place of a prophetic mission. In fact, however, the episode results in a very Christian, even orthodox, conclusion: the foundation of monasteries and the transformation of connubial and sexual love to Christian *caritas*. The adaptation of the smaller narrative, the Sign of Jonah refigured as the near-death and resurrection of Guilliadun, in turn completes the revision and displacement of the larger story, from the tale of Eliduc to the *aventure* of the two *dames*, and finally to simply an *aventure* to be remembered.

The mode of Christian sacrifice and of the *caritas* that accompanies it characterize the conclusion of the *lai*, which shows all three of the story's protagonists working together in neighboring Christian communities. Sending messages back and forth, they are even syntactically joined, acting upon each other and with each other, in full and equal love:

> Deu priouent pur lur ami
> Qu'il li feïst bone merci,
> E il pur eles repreiot.
> Ses messages lur enveiot
> Pur saveir cument lur estot,
> Cum chescune se cunfortot.
> Mut se pena chescuns pur sei
> De Deu amer par bone fei
> E mut par firent bele fin.
>
> (1171–79)

[They prayed to God for their friend— / that He would have mercy on him— / and he prayed for them. / He sent messages to them / to find out how they were, / how each was doing. / Each one took great pains / to love God in good faith / and they made a very good end. (1171–79)]

In these lines, no one is named or singled out, so completely have they been united in the larger community of prayer, so fully have they set aside individual heroism and worldly position.

The implication that all of the major characters have been displaced from the center of the action and that the *lai* is no longer the story of Eliduc nor even that of the two ladies is confirmed in the closing couplets:

> De l'aventure de ces treis
> Li auncïen Bretun curteis
> Firent le *lai* pur remembrer,
> Qu'hum nel deüst pas oblier.
>
> (1181–84)

[From the adventure of these three, / the ancient courtly Bretons / composed the *lai*, to remember it, / so that no one would forget it. (1181–84)]

Thus Eliduc, the *chevalier*, has not so much been displaced by the *dames* as by the *aventure*. The *lai*, which serves as a memory of that *aventure* and of all three adventurers—notably here unnamed—should rightly no longer bear the name of either *Eliduc* or *Guildeluëc ha Guilliadun*. Neither name is inclusive enough nor general enough to serve as an indication of the Christian social union and harmony Marie evokes in the end.

But medieval scribes and modern editors are apparently not as open to this lesson in *caritas* as Marie would have us be, for this, her longest and fullest Breton *lai*, has resisted all attempts to change its name. *Eliduc* it remains—in manuscript, in modern editions, in translations. At least outside the fiction, the chivalric hero and lover maintains his place, however tenuously, and presumably with some, if not all, of the values of chivalric romance intact.

Notes

1. Marie de France, *Les Lais de Marie de France*, ed. Jean Rychner (Paris: Honoré Champion, 1978). All subsequent quotations are taken from this edition. In this particular passage Rychner has emended the spelling of the second lady's name from Gualadun to Guillidun in order to make it accord with that of its other appearances in the text. Unlike other editors and translators, Rychner believes there is no reason to maintain the spelling of the manuscript here (281).

2. Marie de France, *The Lais of Marie de France*, trans. Robert Hanning and Joan Ferrante (New York: Dutton, 1978; rpt. Durham, N.C.: Labyrinth, 1982), 196. Note that, unlike Rychner, Hanning and Ferrante emend the spelling of Guilliadun's name (cf. note 1). Except when otherwise noted, all subsequent translations of Marie's poem are from this text; note that, unless there is some special need for them, I omit the line markings from translations, although Hanning and Ferrante's translation is in verse form, usually in line-by-line correspondence to the original.

3. Matilda Tomaryn Bruckner, "Strategies of Naming in Marie de France's *Lais*: At the Crossroads of Gender and Genre," *Neophilologus* 75 (1991): 31–40, esp. 32.

4. Ibid., 33.

5. Although there exist five manuscripts containing one or more of the *lais*, only one of them, BL MS Harley 978, contains *Eliduc* (Rychner, xix–xx). This manuscript also is the unique text for other parts of the *Lais*—namely, the Prologue, *Laüstic*, and *Chaitivel*. Dated to the mid-thirteenth century, Harley 978 is a compendium of various genres, including religious tracts, hunting treatises, lyric poems, and other miscellanea in prose and verse. Worthy of note in regard to the names of the *lais* is the fact that in this manuscript each *lai* is headed by its name, written in red ink in the top margin and marked with a paragraph marker—all very much in the style of modern titles, even

though the common view is that medieval manuscripts do not have titles but rather incipits and explicits and other kinds of rubrics describing their contents.

6. Of Marie's *Lais*, only *Chaitivel* involves a choice of two distinctly different names. In *Chaitivel*, as the narrator explains, the *lai* bears two names—some know it by one, some by the other. This is somewhat different from the claim in *Eliduc* that the name has been definitively changed. Other *lais*, *Laüstic* and *Bisclavret* for example, are given alternate names, but these are simply the same name in different languages: Breton, French, and English for *Laüstic*; Breton and French for *Bisclavret*.

7. In BL MS Harley 978, the name or title for the last *lai*, written, as with the other *lais*, in the top margin of the page on which it begins, is "Eliduc" (f. 172v). And "Eliduc" is the title that modern editors give in their editions and translations.

8. I am following Rychner, who takes *avenir* as both the object of "cunterai" and the subject of "est avenu"; previous scholars and editors have divided equally between these two alternatives (see Rychner's note, 281). *Avenir* is sometimes used as an impersonal construction (as in "lur est avenu" [it happened to them]), but, as Rychner points out, there is no example of this in the *Lais*; so if a choice has to be made as to whether *aventure* is the object of the "telling" or the subject of the "happening," then the latter is the right choice. Still, the best solution seems to be Rychner's—allowing the substantive, *aventure*, to work as both the object of the verb that follows in the next line and the subject of the verb that immediately precedes. Furthermore, chiasmic syntax stresses the importance of *aventure*—it is what happened to the characters, what the Breton harpers record and remember, and what the poet Marie tells.

9. On structuralist analyses of romance, see Terence Hawkes, *Structuralism and Semiotics* (Berkeley and Los Angeles: University of California Press, 1977), 91–92. Compare also Erich Auerbach, "The Knight Sets Forth," in *Mimesis*, trans. Willard R. Trask (Princeton: Princeton University Press, 1953), 123–42. Auerbach's claim that "a self-portrayal of feudal knighthood with its mores and ideals is the fundamental purpose of the courtly romance" assumes that the idealized knight is the subject of the courtly romance, although Auerbach also stresses the importance of *avanture* [sic] as "a very characteristic form of activity developed by courtly culture" (134).

10. I am using "chivalric romance" in the simplest and loosest sense possible: as a romance about the adventures of a knight. For an excellent discussion of the problems of defining chivalric romance and the way it has been understood by critics and scholars of this century, see Robert W. Hanning, "The Criticism of Chivalric Epic and Romance," in *The Study of Chivalry: Resources and Approaches*, ed. Howell Chickering and Thomas H. Seiler (Kalamazoo, Mich.: Medieval Institute Publications, 1988), 91–113.

11. On the aristocratic values of chivalry in Marie's *lais*, see Jean Flori, "Seigneurie, Noblesse et Chevalerie dans les *Lais* de Marie de France," *Romania* 1987 (108): 183–206; and his later article "Aristocratie et valeurs 'chevaleresques' dans la seconde moitié du XIIème siècle: L'exemple des *lais* de Marie de France," *Le Moyen Age, Revue d'histoire et de philologie* 96 (1990): 35–65. For an account of the historical development of these values and their association with the warrior class, see Maurice Keen, "The Secular Origins of Chivalry," in *Chivalry* (New Haven: Yale University Press, 1984), 18–43.

12. Rychner translates the term "soudee" as "service de guerre" [war service] (314). The term appears three times in *Eliduc* (ll. 14, 110, and 118) and once in *Milun* (l. 122). Compare the related term *soudeier* (*Eliduc*, 339), which Rychner translates "homme de guerre, capitaine" [warrior] (314); and also *soudeür* (*Eliduc*, 246; this latter may be a scribal error or probably an alternate spelling for *soudeier*—see Rychner's note, 283). See also the note on *soudees quere* in Hanning and Ferrante, 196.

13. Bruckner, 38.

14. Georges Duby, "Youth in aristocratic society: Northwestern France in the twelfth century," in *The Chivalrous Society*, trans. Cynthia Postan (Berkeley and Los Angeles: University of California Press, 1980), 120. See also Keen, 29–30.

15. There has been a long-lasting debate among medieval historians as to the precise nature of vassalage and feudal ties: what might be the connection between vassalage and fief-granting, and whether "feudalism" is even a viable term. For a full discussion arguing for the links between vassalage and fiefs, see F. L. Ganshof, *Feudalism*, trans. Philip Grierson (Toronto: University of Toronto Press, 1996), esp. 150–55. For the leading objection to such links and to the relevance of the term "feudalism," see E. A. R. Brown, "The Tyranny of a Construct: Feudalism and Historians of Medieval Europe," *American Historical Review* 79 (1974): 1063–88. For a recent, full reexamination of the issues, see Susan Reynolds, *Fiefs and Vassals: The Medieval Evidence Reinterpreted* (Oxford, N.Y.: Oxford University Press, 1994). In *Eliduc* at least, there is some indication that Eliduc's problem stems from the lack of a connection between vassalage (his loyalty and his lord's returning love) and fief-granting, a suggestion that seems to assume that there ought to be a connection. On the other hand, having a peasant tell a plowman that the love of a lord is not the same as having a fief suggests that fiefs, or the hope for them, were not confined to the aristocracy or warrior classes.

16. On the variety and complexity of the ways military service was performed and armies were raised and the relationship of these to the ideals of chivalry, see Tony Hunt, "The Emergence of the Knight in France and England 1000–1200," *Forum for Modern Language Studies* 17 (1981): esp. 100–104.

17. For the role of clerks in creating and spreading chivalric ideals, especially when writing genealogies of noble families, see Keen, 30–34. See also Duby, "Youth in aristocratic society"; and Flori, "Seigneurie" and "Aristocratie."

18. Perhaps this suggestion of something other than the job searching of a knight is a signal that Eliduc, for all his warrior vocation, is not a landless knight. As Flori points out, Eliduc has not only left a home in the care of his wife in Brittany, but he is able to bring along a troop of his own household knights ("Seigneurie," 203). Whether the peasant's implication that Eliduc is without a fief is then false or inconsistent with the facts is not clarified by Marie, and it is perhaps unfair to question too closely the details of a fictional story for socioeconomic consistency. Without being guilty of the "how-many-children-had-Lady-Macbeth" fallacy, I think we can assume that Eliduc's holdings are minimal (but probably his outright) and not sufficient to support him in the style to which he has been accustomed. On the other hand, we may simply have here, as I have suggested, a reminder that we are in the world of romance, which some scholars have stressed is a world "broadening on practically every front," a world opening up its imaginative, as well as its geographical, boundaries (Hanning, "Chivalric Epic and Romance," 97–99).

19. According to Flori, although precise terms vary from region to region, "obligations militaires féodales . . . n'excédaient pas 40 jours" [feudal military obligations . . . did not exceed 40 days] ("Seigneurie," 203; my translation). This kind of contractual arrangement was thus fairly common in Marie's world.

20. Hanning and Ferrante, 231.

21. On the dynastic wars in England in the mid-twelfth century, see Austin Lane Poole, *From Domesday Book to Magna Carta, 1087–1216* (Oxford: Clarendon Press, 1951), 131–66, 271–75, 291–94, and 303–12. In assessing the extent of "the anarchy" of 1135–54 (the period between Henry I's death and Henry II's coronation), Poole says that the situation was not all that disastrous but that the "English people had been 'spoilt,' as we

might say, by more than half a century of peace and strong rule, for a state of things which on the Continent was almost a commonplace" (150). On the actual place names of Exeter and Totnes and their appearance in another twelfth-century romance, Wace's *Brut*, see Rychner's editorial note to lines 88–91 (282).

22. *Deus Amanz* (252 lines), *Laüstic* (160 lines), *Chaitivel* (240 lines), and *Chievrefoil* (116 lines) are all shorter than the first part of *Eliduc*, while several other *lais* are not much longer.

23. On the desiring female, see Paxson, 13–14, in the introduction to this volume.

24. Eliduc's reference to his wife here perplexes editors and translators, who have difficulty punctuating and reading the lines. The text reads: "Mis sires m'ad par brief mandé / E par serement conjuré / E de ma femme d'autre part / Or me covient que jeo me gart" (595–98; Rychner ed., but with punctuation removed). The question is whether the line about "ma femme" goes with what precedes or what follows. Hanning and Ferrante translate as though "ma femme" goes with what precedes: "my lord has sent for me by letter / appealed to me by oath / and my wife, too, for her part" (595–97). Rychner, however, believing that the reference to his wife is an additional concern for Eliduc, puts a period after line 596, so that line 597 goes with line 598; the latter lines would therefore be translated: "and as, for my wife too, on her part, now I must take care that I be concerned for her" (my translation of Rychner's text, using his translation into modern French [285, note to 597]).

25. The Sign of Jonah owes its preeminence to two features: one the centrality of its significance—no less than the death and resurrection of Christ—and two, the source of its exegesis—Jesus himself in the Gospel of Matthew (12:39–40).

The Talking Wounded: Desire, Truth Telling, and Pain in the *Lais* of Marie de France

ROBERT W. HANNING

Early in Marie de France's *lai Guigemar*, there is a moment that obliquely and provocatively defines Marie's relationship as a love poet to Ovid, the *magister amoris* of ancient Rome and (from her perspective) modern France. How it does this also tells us much about Marie's sense of her status as woman and poet in her own court world. The moment involves the description of a *chaumbre*—"suz ciel n'en out plus bele," Marie's narratorial voice assures us[1]—in which the young wife of a jealous old *sire* is forced to spend her days, imprisoned there on account of her husband's fear of being cuckolded. The description of the chamber is well known but bears repeating:

> La chaumbre ert peinte tut entur:
> Venus, la deuesse d'amur,
> Fu tresbien [mise] en la peinture,
> Les traiz mustrez e la nature
> Cument hom deit amur tenir
> E lealment e bien servir;
> Le livre Ovide, ou il enseine
> Coment chascun s'amur estreine,
> En un fu ardant le gettout
> E tuz iceus escumengout
> Ki ja mais cel livre lirreient.
> Ne sun enseignement fereient.
> La fu la dame enclose e mise.
>
> (233–45)

[The room was painted with images all around; / Venus the goddess of love / was skillfully depicted in the painting, / her nature and her traits were illustrated, / whereby folk might learn how to behave in love, / and to serve love loyally. / Ovid's book, the one in which he instructs / lovers how to manage their love, / was being thrown by Venus into a fire, / and she was excommunicating all those / who ever perused this book / or followed its teachings. / That's where the wife was locked up.]

The room's decoration is dominated by the image—perhaps a series of images?—of Venus engaged in a variety of symbolic activities: she exemplifies or teaches (the text is teasingly ambiguous) love's nature and characteristics and the proper ways she/it should be served; she burns Ovid's book that instructs how love is to be managed (a key theme of the *Ars amatoria*), or perhaps suppressed (the stated lesson of the *Remedia amoris*); and she excommunicates those who would follow the Roman poet's teachings rather than her own.

Several aspects of this ekphrastic and emblematic moment demand attention. It would appear, first of all, that Marie—under the guise of Venus condemning Ovidian lore, destroying its authoritative textual matrix and punishing its adherents—here enacts her displacement of Ovid as *magistra amoris*. (In the "General Prologue" [GP] affixed to the collection of *Lais* in BL Ms Harley 978, she defines herself implicitly as a modern engaged in a rivalry of some sort with ancient writers, and explicitly as an adapter of [Breton] "lais" rather than Latin texts, among which Ovid's works were apparently the most imitated and translated in Marie's day; cf. GP 9–16, 28–42; cf. G 19–21).[2]

What makes Marie's claim all the more remarkable is that she not only assimilates herself, as love poet, to the goddess of love (thus by definition capable of excellence beyond any to which a mere mortal could aspire), but also shows Venus performing actions—teaching the truth about love, burning a heretic's books, excommunicating his followers—that any twelfth-century reader (or audience) would immediately recognize as appropriate to an ecclesiastical authority—a priest, even a bishop—and for that very reason, completely inappropriate to a woman.[3] (It is worth noting, by contrast, that when, at the end of Alan of Lille's *Plaint of Nature*—a work probably contemporaneous with, or known to, Marie—another goddess, Nature, decides to "burn with the brand of anathema men who are ensnared in the tangle of the vices" that threaten her rule of the world, she announces that "it is fitting . . . to consult Genius who serves me in a priestly office. . . . [L]et him, with the pastoral staff of excommunication, remove [the offenders] from the catalogue of the things of Nature." Genius, a grammatically male abstraction, dons "priestly dress with its distinguished ornaments" and pronounces "the prearranged formula of excommunication.")[4]

Hence, even as she claims authority for herself, through the *persona* of
Venus, as a poet of love, Marie suggests the transgressiveness of such a
claim. Nor does she refrain from representing the cultural obstacles it
faces, for the beautiful room over which Venus presides is also the young
wife's prison. It is placed in a *clos* next to her husband's castle and
surrounded by a high, impassable wall (which is, however, open on one
side to the sea). The only gate in the wall is kept locked, the key in the
possession of an old priest who is trusted as her guardian only because he
is sexually mutilated ("les plus bas membres out perduz: / autrement ne
fust pas crëuz" [G 257–58]). This collocation of details suggests that in
addition to offering an inscribed allegory of the powerful woman poet,
the painted chamber also functions as a rueful pun—a "chambre de
Vénus" with its dangerous "entrance" locked and guarded—indicative of
the fact that a woman, whatever her gifts and achievements, whatever her
ability to impart knowledge or wisdom, remains, for men, the
embodiment of a dangerous sexuality that they must perpetually control,
and perpetually distrust. (A propos the old, wounded priest, see further
below, note 18.)

Marie's representation of herself in this passage as a post-Ovidian
female court poet in whose sociopoetic situation (aptly figured as a
beautifully decorated prison) insight and victimization, willed authority
and unwelcome restriction, radically interact offers an important clue to a
major project of the *Lais*: the depiction of women for whom creative or
authoritative utterance is intimately connected with victimization, loss,
and even destruction. By exploring instances of this linkage between
voice and suffering in characters whom I shall collectively denominate
"the talking wounded," I undertake to argue for the presence in the *Lais*
of a distinctive voice, that of the "truthteller from the margin," whose
message, inseparable from the pain that attends it, gains in authority and
poignancy precisely because of its forced distance from loci of
institutionalized power. It is, I believe, in her capacity as marginalized
truthteller about the imperatives and frustrations of desire that Marie
makes one of her most significant contributions to twelfth-century
Europe's post-Ovidian, vernacular discourse of desire.

* * *

From the very beginning of *Guigemar*, Marie creates female
surrogates whose message is inseparable from the pain that attends it and
through whose experiences her sense of the complex relationship
between (female) speech and woundedness is vividly communicated.

The opening eighteen lines of *Guigemar*, constituting a kind of prologue to the *lai*, introduce a voice that can barely be called a surrogate for Marie's, since line 3, "Oëz, seignurs, ke dit Marie," appears to identify its origin as authorial. In fact, however, the passage, like analogous ones in many contemporaneous vernacular narratives, uses both first- and third-person verb forms, implying, at least at the grammatical level, a distinction between poetic authority (third-person) and narratorial "presence" (first-person). The first fourteen lines, presented as a series of enthymematic generalizations about "hummë u femme de grant pris" (G 8), specifically describe the difficult relations that often obtain (and thus, by inference, obtain in her case) between a poet of high competence and high standards—one who chooses good subject matter (G 1), worries about living up to its challenge (G 2), and does not shirk her responsibilities to it (G 4: "en sun tens pas ne s'oblie")—and her audience, which responds to her achievement and reputation (G 6), as envious people often do, with "vileinie" (G 10) and "traisun" (G 14) instead of the praise she deserves (G 5).[5]

The climax of these lines is Marie's (melo)dramatic comparison of her detractors to "malveis chien coart felun, / Ki mort la gent par traïsun" (G 13–14). But at this point the text moves from third- to first-person narration, in what can best be described as a declaration of defiant perseverance: "Nel voil mie pur ceo leissier, / Si gangleür u losengier / Le me volent a mal turner; / Ceo est lur dreit de mesparler" (G 15–18). If the first fourteen lines describe the (female) poet's situation as an *exemplum* of a general social dynamic, the next four communicate the impact of that dynamic on the emotions and the will of one who has become its particular target—but not, the first-person narrative voice insists, its helpless victim.

The effect of this juxtaposition of two perspectives, and two voices (one detached and sententious, the other subjective and resistant), at the beginning of *Guigemar* is to suggest vividly Marie's situation as one who has been "bitten" by cowardly, disloyal "dogs" for speaking well and conscientiously and who, fully understanding the larger context of such unjust behavior, chooses to speak again, wounded as she is, in order to relate "les contes . . . dunt li Bretun unt fait les lais" (G 19–20). If this prologial statement is thus to be understood as introducing not just one *lai* but the collection, then the *Lais* become part of a (potentially) ongoing process that not only defines Marie's activity as "talking wounded" but herself, in her poetic vocation, as (one of) *the* "talking wounded." That is, Marie's situation admits of no easy establishment of cause and effect: speaking, she is wounded; wounded, she not only continues but seems inspired (out of sheer determination) to speak.

The basic dynamic of Marie's poetic production revealed in the prologue to *Guigemar* can be further elucidated by referring to the "General Prologue," a statement of origin and intention that must have been written after some, if not all, of the *lais* that follow it.

Marie begins her introductory statement by announcing her felt imperative not to conceal or withhold her "escience / e de parler bone eloquence" (GP 2–3; obviously the bases of the "grant pris" she claims for herself at the beginning of *Guigemar*). She continues, "quant uns granz biens est mult oïz, / Dunc a primes est il fluriz; / E quant loëz est de plusurs, / Dunc ad espandues ses flurs" (GP 5–8). The point of these lines, as I understand them, is that a poet/performer at court needs the approbation of her audience to flourish and advance in her art (*espandre ses flurs*, with a likely play on the *flores rhetoricae*). Marie's reliance here on an organic metaphor to describe her ideal poetic trajectory suggests an understanding of poetry less as a process of topical invention than as a creative process of growth in which a reciprocal relationship with a sympathetic audience plays a major role.[6]

It is this need, or desire, for an audience that impels Marie to render herself vulnerable, to risk being wounded by envy as she pursues her goal of "bone matiere . . . bien faite" (G 1–2). It is not, I believe, fanciful to hear in the flower metaphor of the "General Prologue" an echo of the symbiotic relationship between the honeysuckle and the hazel that Tristram applies to his love for (and with) "la reine" Isolde at the affective center of the *lai* of *Chievrefoil* [C] (C 68–78). But such ideal mutuality stands in sharp contrast to the (back)biting Marie must endure from her "partner." Always already wounded, she will speak on.

In the final lines of the "General Prologue," Marie offers her *Lais* to a "noble reis [Henry II of England?] . . . / En ki quoer tuz biens racine" (GP 43–46); the image incorporates the monarch, as patronal "root," into her organic representation of the social system that nourishes, but also wounds, her. The king himself appears to partake, at least potentially, of this ambivalence as the intended recipient of the *Lais*: "Si vos les plaist a receveir," Marie declares, "Mult me ferez grant joie aveir"; but she adds, "Ne me tenez a surquidie / Si vos os faire icest present" (GP 51–52, 54–55). To speak—or, by extension, to offer one's writings—promises joy but risks wounding reproof.[7]

It can, of course, be argued that any court poet, male or female, must deal with the ambiguities of patronage, even as any "hummë u femme de grant pris" must, according to Marie, endure envy (rather than enjoying praise) for having achieved something noteworthy. But I am convinced that Marie's ingeniously displaced and emblematic self-representations throughout the *Lais* collectively emphasize the problematics of gender as a crucial component of her difficulties as a poet, even as they articulate a rare (for the twelfth century) female-centered (or -sensitive) perspective on the expression and pursuit of desire. Furthermore, in a few remarkable instances, Marie dramatizes how the burden of "talking wounded" paradoxically endows some women (including the poet herself?) with the power to tell, from a marginalized position, profound if troubling truths about the general "woundedness" of the human condition, and even to indicate difficult but salutary paths toward alleviation or cure.

The most spectacular such instance occurs once again in *Guigemar*, where the young male protagonist encounters, and wounds, a marvelous deer at (and as) the turning point of his life. While hunting a *grant cerf* (G 81) with his companions, Guigemar, only son of a vassal of the King of Brittany and a skilled warrior who shows no interest in love, encounters a white *bise* endowed with the antlers of a stag and accompanied by a fawn (G 90f.). Guigemar shoots an arrow that wounds the *bise* (G 95), but the arrow rebounds, striking him deeply in the thigh (G 99). As he lies on the ground next to the *bise*, she grieves for her wound (G 104), then speaks, announcing her own death and telling Guigemar his *destinee*: his wound can only be healed by a woman who will suffer unprecedented pain out of love for him, as he will for her; their situation will be a marvel to all past, present, and future lovers (G 106–21).

A hunter's encounter (intentional or unforeseen) with a marvelous beast figures in several twelfth-century vernacular narratives; the episode appears to have its roots in Celtic initiation legends, in which the hunt signifies the subduing of the "female" land by its aspiring male ruler.[8] However, several features of Marie's version—among them the deer's androgyny, the rebounding arrow that wounds its shooter, and the wounded animal's ability not only to talk but to announce to its assailant his future—distinguish it from such contemporaneous analogues.

Antecedents can, however, be suggested for some of these features as well. The androgyny of the *bise* possessing both a stag's antlers and a fawn's may have been inspired by the domesticated deer, pet of the Laurentian maiden Silvie, whom Ascanie, son of Enéas, kills while hunting in the *Roman d'Eneas* (3525 f.).[9] Silvie has trained the deer to sleep in her bedroom, eat and drink from her utensils, and act as a candelabrum for her and her father at dinner: "Mervoilles ert sa teste belle, / quant uns granz cierges li ardoit / sor chascun rain que il avoit" (E 3556–58). When Ascanie sees this creature in its usual daily haunt, among a "herde de bisches" (E 3585; cf. 3538–41), he wounds it mortally with an arrow, whereupon the dying animal seeks out its mistress: "devant sa dame vint a poine; / ja li aloit faillant l'aloine, / jus a ses piez chaï a terre / et fist samblant de merci querre" (E 3613–16).

Silvie's deer, while not biologically androgynous, focuses attention on issues of gender boundaries and interactions. In the shooting of the deer, "male" aggression and hegemony (epitomized in Ascanie, a hunter who, like Guigemar, is a noble son and heir) wounds, indeed destroys, the possessor of aestheticized, decorative (as well as useful) skills, "civilized" qualities instilled in him through a nexus of affection with a woman who possesses them. From one angle of vision, the deer, so domesticated by a woman that it prefers female to male company (its cohort of *bisches*), appears to be a baleful exemplum of the consequences of feminization on male warriors; from another, however, this image of peaceful intergender association suggests a countervailing, possibly resistant ideal of "cultural androgyny" that finds spectacular emblematic embodiment in the magnificent antlers of the *cerf* transformed into a source of illumination for the lord's table. In short, the tame *cerf* functions as a compelling image of the power and limits of a female-sponsored courtliness—a cultural force enlightening a feudal world but incompatible with (and wounded by) ideals of aristocratic masculine aggressiveness.[10]

Another type of contemporaneous narrative, hagiography, could have supplied Marie with models or suggestions for the rebounding arrow, the talking *bise*, her prophetic message, and the odd sense of intimacy her text implies between man and beast, after both have been wounded. For instance, in the widely diffused story of St. Eustace, a virtuous, pagan Roman soldier called Placidus (later baptized as Eustace) encounters, while hunting, a stag with a cross, bearing Christ, between its antlers. The image on the cross, speaking through the stag, urges Eustache to accept the true faith, promising that if he does he will have God's protection during hardships that will follow his conversion.[11] The legend of St. Giles tells how the saint, retiring to a cave in the wilderness of France, is "adopted" by a hind who lives there and who nourishes him with her milk. (He becomes her "fawn," in effect.) When one of the king's hunters shoots an arrow that, though intended for the beast, "grievously" wounds Giles instead, the holy man—who is found, the *Legenda aurea* says, with the hind's head in his lap—refuses the king's offer of medical treatment, preferring to remain wounded as a spur to holier living.[12]

Especially suggestive as a parallel to, or stimulus for, details of Marie's episode—an assaulted animal, an arrow rebounding on its shooter, and the unleashing of a numinous voice of power and warning—is a widespread account of the dedication of the Sanctuary of St. Michael the Archangel atop Mt. Gargano, in Apulia, an account she could easily have known because the dedication was celebrated each 8 May at Mont

Saint Michel in Normandy. According to the tale, a wealthy land- and cattle owner possesses "quidam taurus nimis superbus," which refuses to return home after grazing at the top of Mt. Gargano. Seeing the recalcitrant animal standing in the mouth of a cave, the *dives* orders a servant to kill it, but the arrow the servant shoots rebounds, striking and killing him. Shortly thereafter, St. Michael appears in a dream to the local bishop, identifies the cave where the bull was shot as his own dwelling place, and instructs that an altar in his honor be erected there.[13]

Against this varied background of possible antecedents and influences, the uniqueness (and, I would argue, the thematic importance) of Marie's *bise* episode stands out all the more sharply. Thus, if the "feminized" stag of *Eneas* inspired Marie, she, as it were, reverses the figure's androgyny, creating a true female (as the fawn testifies) who is "masculized" both biologically—"perches de cerf out en la teste"[14]—and culturally through the authoritative voice with which she announces to the fallen Guigemar his *destinee* (a voice, incidentally, quite free of any imputation of celestial origin). Similarly, the putative impact of Silvie's stag dying pitifully at the feet of its mistress (perhaps reinforced by the image of St. Giles's nurturing hind putting her head in the lap of her wounded "fawn") is transmuted, in *Guigemar*, into the simultaneous wounding of man and beast (suggested perhaps by the St. Michael story, in which, however, only the human who shoots the arrow is harmed by its rebound).

The effect of the *bise* episode in *Guigemar* depends on its elements of *reversal, specularity,* and *paradox,* the latter centered on the phenomena that I have named "talking wounded" and "truthtelling from the margin." At the beginning of the scene, Guigemar is the subject and the dominant force. Heir of a powerful lineage, already invested with social recognition (*pris*) because of his martial abilities, he is (with apologies to W. S. Gilbert) the very model of the warrior aristocrat, indulging his *talent* (desire) for hunting as a way of extending his lordship over nature as well.[15] Even his complete lack of interest in, and desire for, women— a flaw of, or offense against, "nature" (G 57) because of which "le tienent a peri / E li estrange e si ami" (G 67–68)—can be understood, from the perspective of the present discussion, as a sealing of emotional boundaries consistent with a life that revolves around mastery, and is therefore "naturally" indifferent, or hostile, to any relationship involving mutual dependence and need.[16]

Hence the arrow Guigemar shoots at the *bise,* wounding her, describes the trajectory of dominance that characterizes his life "en la flur de sun meillur pris" (G 69).[17] But at this moment the distribution, between them, of roles and power appears to reverse itself radically. The arrow

rebounds; Guigemar, the hunter, becomes the prey—his own prey, in
effect—while the *bise*, until now merely the unconsidered, momentary
object of his *talent* for mastery, becomes a speaking subject, addressing
to the young man, now her helpless audience, an authoritative account of
his *destinee*. And at the center of her discourse is the message of his
radical woundedness, neediness, and (if he is to be cured) dependence
upon a reciprocal (as opposed to dominant) relationship with a woman:

> "E tu, vassal, ki m'as nafree,
> Tel seit la tue destinee:
> Jamais n'aies tu med[e]cine!
> Ne par herbe ne par racine
> Ne par mire ne par pociun
> N'avras tu jamés garisun
> De la plaie ke as en la quisse,
> De s[i] ke cele te guarisse
> Ki suffera pur tue amur
> Issi grant peine e tel dolur
> Ke unkes femme taunt ne suffri;
> E tu ref[e]ras taunt pur li."

$$(G\ 107–18)^{18}$$

[And you, vassal, who have wounded me, / this be your destiny: / may you
never get medicine for your wound! / Neither herb nor root, / neither
physician nor potion, / will cure you / of that wound in your thigh, / until a
woman heals you, / one who will suffer, out of love for you, / pain and grief /
such as no woman ever suffered before. / and out of love for her, you'll suffer
as much.]

Her last words to him, couched like her entire utterance in the familiar
form, constitute an abrupt, almost contemptuous dismissal, such as a
weary mother might issue to a bothersome child (or *foün*): "Va t'en de ci!
Lais m'aver pes" (G 122).

The *bise*'s power, at this moment of reversal, is thus the power to
reveal a truth about a young, noble male's life that requires the upending
of his behavior, assumptions, and expectations until that moment. It
matches, and reverses, the authority over him demonstrated by the king
who had earlier fostered him and sent him off into the world a dubbed
knight, armed "a sun talent," ready to seek *pris* by the exercise of arms
all over northwestern Europe (G 41–56; quote at 48). Like its antlers, the
bise's authoritative voice is a *surplus* beyond our (and Guigemar's)
expectations; as it informs the young man of his (and his unknown
female "healer's") suffering in love, it establishes the plot of the first half

of Marie's *lai* and also defines her ideal audience: "tut cil s'esmerveillerunt / Ki aiment e amé avrunt / U ki poi amerunt aprés" (G 119–21).

That is, the voice of the *bise*—the first in the *lai*, besides that of the narrator, "Marie," to speak in direct address to an audience—stands in for, and transmits, the voice of the poet. And the antlered female deer embodies the "marvel" of this poet—a woman endowed with "male" attributes of *escience et eloquence*—who communicates to an audience of "lovers"—in other words, of those whose esteem she needs to flourish vocationally—the remarkable message that men and women suffer the same vulnerability, hence share a single destiny.[19]

But if the *bise* episode thus suggests the equation of speaking poet and speaking animal—of creator and creature—it also implies a complex, interconnected set of specular equivalences. The parallel between the self-absorbed, woman-scorning Guigemar, dealt a sexually suggestive wound "en la quisse" (G 99) by his own rebounding arrow, and an equally self-absorbed Narcisus, who falls in love with his reflection, has been noted by Stephen Nichols and Sarah Spence; but the precise nature of this parallel requires clarification. Guigemar and the *bise*, wounded by the same arrow, become mirror images of pain; but the nature of the wound and pain is implied by the disposition of their stricken bodies, next to each other on the grass (G 101–2) in a manner recalling postcoital lassitude. This union in pain is a proleptic emblem of the mutual love-wound suffered by Guigemar and his *amie* (cf. G 483: "Amur est plaie dedenz cors"). But it is also, as we have just seen, metaphoric, for Marie, of the ideal relationship between poet and audience. The members of these pairs, Marie appears to say, can and must find the reflection of their own pain in that of their opposite—an insight far removed from the impulse toward heedless domination that characterizes the pre-*bise* Guigemar, his *amie*'s jealous husband, and Meriaduc, the Breton castellan who would keep Guigemar's beloved for himself.[20]

But this insight forces us to confront the third major affective component of the *bise* episode: the paradox that the animal speaks, and speaks powerfully, to Guigemar only after he has wounded her, apparently to the death. It would seem that the *bise* embodies Marie's sense of herself (and other speaking women) as always already wounded—as speaking from a woman's permanent cultural situation of marginalization, which is only aggravated if she adopts an authoritative voice.

* * *

Marie's representation of herself, as woman and poet, through the figures of the wounded *bise* and the imprisoned Venus in *Guigemar* responds to several dominant tendencies and developments of her cultural milieu. The increasing institutionalization (and rivalry) of religious and secular power in western Europe throughout the twelfth century required both church and "state" to rely more and more on literate, trained clerical administrators to staff bureaucracies, keep records, and produce texts supporting their respective claims to dominion. This expanding administrative class, trained at cathedral and other urban schools, was exclusively male; its increasing importance to ecclesiastical and secular rulers resulted in a corresponding decrease in the authority and power of noble women, and its frequently misogynistic outlook permeates both learned, Latin texts and the vernacular literature of entertainment.[21] In an era when, as Beryl Smalley has indicated, the Pauline epistles were among the most widely studied and commented books of the Bible, the famous strictures against women teaching or preaching (1 Tim 2.11–12) were constantly read and reinforced in the classroom. Exegesis of the Genesis Creation stories frequently drew negative conclusions about the seductive power of the female voice, which therefore required careful regulation and restraint.[22]

This is not to say that there were no women who spoke with authority in the twelfth century—one need think only of Heloise, Hildegard of Bingen, or Christina of Markyate. Men, including men of high lay and clerical estate, constantly profited from their wisdom and insight.[23] Marie herself depicts, within the *lai* of *Guigemar,* occasions when the protagonist asks for female counsel. When Guigemar is discovered aboard the marvelous, crewless boat by his future *amie*, the distraught, wounded young man begs his "hostess" to advise him: "Cunseillez mei, vostre merci! / Kar jeo ne sai queil part aler" (G 334–35). And again, after Guigemar realizes he has fallen in love with the *dame* but cannot decide if he dare tell her his feelings, he implores her *pucele*, who has recognized the signs of love in him and in her mistress, "cunseillez me, ma duce amie! / Que ferai jeo de cest' amur?" (G 458–59).

Despite such real and fictive instances of women as astute and forthright imparters of wisdom and counsel, male clerics repeatedly composed, for women of Marie's generation and shortly after, instructional texts such as the *Ancrene Wisse*, which stress the danger of the unbridled female tongue.[24] No wonder the situation of Marie de France (whoever she was) as a learned, insightful, eloquent, and praise-seeking woman rendered her something of an anomaly and vulnerable to both general courtly envy and specifically male resentment, even at a court so involved in the patronage of writers as that of Henry II of England (which, until 1170, was also that of Eleanor of Aquitaine).[25] To borrow a phrase from Victor Turner's description of another woman writer, Lady Murasaki, who had to develop her gift in the face of misogynistic prejudice, "a truly learned woman in that court was indeed a liminal figure."[26]

Turner's notions of the liminal status of cultural performance, and of its function as bearer of "culture's 'subjunctive' mood, defined by Webster as 'that mood of a verb used to express supposition, desire, hypothesis, possibility, etc.,'" underlies my argument that through the androgynous *bise* of the *lai* of *Guigemar* Marie represents herself as a liminal figure, operating perilously along the gender boundaries, or fault lines, of her culture, and that the *bise*'s articulation of Guigemar's *destinee*, and of Marie's own ideal audience of (her) lovers, proposes to that culture, again in Turner's words (and Lady Murasaki's), "a reflexive, subjunctive world of characters who . . . 'lived at the Court of an Emperor (he lived it matters not when).'"[27]

What Marie adds to this awareness of the liminality of her status and subjunctivity of her poetic vision is the wrenching sense that the latter proceeds from, and is given depth by, her experience of woundedness and marginalization. "Nel voil mie pur ceo leissier," Marie says *in propria voce* at the beginning of *Guigemar* (G 15), and perhaps we should understand the locution, *pur ceo*, as giving the line two possible meanings: "*just because* detractors attack me like treacherous, biting dogs doesn't mean I'm going to stop speaking/writing," and "*for the very reason that* I have been wounded, I will not stop speaking,"—in other words, because of the power given her voice by her acquaintance with the pain of abjection.

To entertain the second reading is to place Marie with the tradition of marginalized truth-telling, which has in our own time and culture been so strikingly and salutarily instanced in so-called "minority" writers, and especially African-American women novelists and essayists. bell hooks has written movingly of her early life in an African-American community:

> As black Americans living in a small Kentucky town, the railroad tracks were a daily reminder of our marginality. . . . Living as we did—on the edge—we developed a particular way of seeing reality. We looked both from the outside in and the inside out. We focused our attention on the center as well as on the margin. We understood both. This sense of wholeness, impressed upon our consciousness by the structure of our daily lives, provided us an oppositional world view—a mode of seeing unknown to most of our oppressors that sustained us, aided us in our struggle to transcend poverty and despair, strengthened our sense of self and our solidarity.

hooks insists that marginality is "much more than a site of deprivation. . . . [I]t is also the site of radical possibility, a space of resistance. . . . [I]t offers the possibility of radical perspectives from which to see and create, to imagine alternatives, new worlds."[28] Her analysis complements Turner's as a guide to, and explication of, an aspect of Marie's *Lais*—its articulation of a woman's perspective; its inscription of what feminist criticism has named the "female signature"—that has only begun to be fully appreciated within the last fifteen years.[29]

* * *

The dying *bise* leaves her fawn behind as her legacy; similarly, Marie leaves us her *Lais* as a record of both her pain and her marginalized, culturally subjunctive vision. Throughout the *Lais*, various figures join the *bise* in the ranks of "the talking wounded," reenacting the meeting of power and pain in their lives and voices. In *Laustic*, a wife creates the fiction of staying up at night to hear the nightingale's song—even as Marie worked late to obey the call of her *escience* and *eloquence* (GP 42)—in order to disguise her exchange of words with her lover.[30] Her angry husband traps and kills the nightingale and throws its corpse at her, leaving a stain of its blood on her front of her gown. Thus washed (as it were) in the blood of the nightingale, the *dame* wraps the dead bird in "une piece de samit / A or brusdé e tut escrit," a striking emblem of the *Lais* as a body of writings created to enclose (and reveal) a mortally wounded singer but also to perpetuate the voice of a culturally subjunctive, reciprocal desire between men and women.[31]

In *Yonec* (Y), Marie audaciously appropriates and rewrites a canonical Christian story to craft a powerful, complex exemplum of "talking wounded." In a stunning reversal of the Annunciation, a young wife married to a jealous old husband asks God to do her will by sending her a secret lover of the type she has heard of in stories. It is done to her according to her desire: a bird (Marie's reimagined Holy Spirit, an eagle rather than a dove) flies in the window of her prison and becomes a handsome prince, who announces he could not come to her, despite his love for her, until she desired his presence.[32] He then assumes her shape to take communion—a daring reimagining of the Incarnation and Eucharist, two events increasingly linked in Marie's day in the scholastic evolution of the doctrine of transubstantiation[33]—and the two begin a love affair that ends with the mortal wounding of the bird-knight by the husband.

The temporary sharing of the wife's body by the bird-knight allows us to see his wounding (a reimagined Crucifixion) as a displaced version of her own painful entrapment in a loveless marriage, even as the fact that she willed him into her life in the first place allows us, as Freeman suggests, to read his communication to her, on his death bed, of the rest of the plot of the *lai* as a displacement of her own imagination at work.[34] At the climax of the *lai*, the *dame*, speaking like a prophet "a haute voiz" (Y 526), reveals to her now grown son (by her lover), Yonec, his true paternity, transforming him into the son and successor of lords (the people of his father's land "lur seignur firent de Yonec" [Y 549]); simultaneously, she gives him his real father's sword (the existence of which, incidentally, suggests that the love affair really happened), an act of both symbolic equivalence (word equals sword) and transgressive *surplus* (she appropriates the role of the older male dubbing the younger one knight). In the *lai*'s version of the Last Judgment, Yonec kills his supposed father (and his mother's oppressor), the old *jaloux*. But his mother, whose voice, focused and strengthened by the double pain of unhappy marriage and lost love, has brought about this (culturally subjunctive) conclusion, does not live to enjoy it. Having spoken the truth and empowered her son, she dies and is buried in her lover's tomb. "Talking wounded," this ending suggests, primarily benefits others' desires—nor does it earn one a tomb of one's own.

Perhaps Marie's most shocking version of herself (recently noticed, though very differently interpreted, by Michelle Freeman)[35] occurs in the *lai* of *Bisclavret*, when the werewolf's wife, like Marie herself, offers a gift to her king and is attacked and wounded by her enraged husband, who tears off her nose in revenge for her stealing his clothes (and thus condemning him to inhabit his bestial shape indefinitely)—a gesture uncannily duplicating, and recalling, the biting dog that attacks Marie out of envy in the opening lines of *Guigemar*. In my "resistant" reading of this *lai*, the woman is taught the terrible lesson that she has no right to make autonomous decisions such as abandoning her husband out of fear of his bestiality; her wound thus invites decoding as a displaced emblem of her lack of the phallus, i.e., of the status and authority that belongs in her world only to men.[36] Hence, when the wife in *Bisclavret* is tortured by the king to reveal what we might well call her "surquidie," she becomes a particularly grotesque embodiment of "the talking wounded."

* * *

In recent years, several readers of Marie's *Guigemar* have noted that the *lai* is in some sense organized around three homonymic, or quibbling words: *plaie* (wound), *plait* (plea or argument; by extension persuasive speech), and *plait* (knot).[37] The perspective from which this essay has been written clarifies the significance of this architectonic word play, providing a satisfactory ending point for my discussion. Each of the homonyms is associated with a different character and moment of the *lai*; taken as a sequence, they constitute an encrypted description of Marie's poetic trajectory.

First comes the wound, associated primarily with the *bise* that reveals to Guigemar his neediness, which is also his destiny. Next, counseled by women and inspired by love, Guigemar "descovre sun talent" (G 500) to the woman he desires via a persuasive *plait* that convinces her (in accord with her own desires) to go to bed with him and thus effect a satisfactory closure of the *lai*'s first "movement."[38] Finally, the *dame*, recognizing the lovers' vulnerability to discovery and, in that case, the danger to her happiness of her forced immobility as a woman vis-à-vis Guigemar's freedom of movement as a man, proposes the *plait* in his garment that, together with the belt he puts around her body, will serve as an implied "contract" of their mutual sexual fidelity. In thus resisting the buffetings of changeable fortune (G 538–40), the *dame* charts the second "movement" of the *lai*, even as the *bise* did the first; the climax will be reached when Guigemar's *amie* unties his knot, even though he must subsequently repossess her by force from the unaccommodating Meriaduc.

As for Marie, the sequence wound/speech/knot (-unknot) suggests that it is the pain of female marginalization that inspires her to adapt her gift for speech ("de parler bon' eloquence" [GP 2]) to the making of satisfactorily complex stories—a process conceived then, as now, in the imagery of knotting and unknotting, or denouement. The impressive results of Marie's "talking wounded" remain as a tribute to her skill and courage and as an object of wonder (and an interpretive challenge) to those comprising today's audience of (her) lovers.[39]

Notes

1. *Guigemar*, l. 231. All references to the *Lais* follow Marie de France, *Lais*, ed. Alfred Ewert (Oxford: Blackwell, 1952). Translations follow, with some modifications, *The Lais of Marie de France*, trans. Robert Hanning and Joan Ferrante (New York: Dutton, 1978, repr., Grand Rapids: Baker Book House, 1995). *Guigemar* is henceforth abbreviated as G.

2. For an elegant summary of Ovid's place in the clerically run schools of twelfth-century northern France, see John Baldwin, *The Language of Sex: Five Voices from Northern France around 1200* (Chicago and London: University of Chicago Press, 1994), 20–25.

3. See Elisabeth Vodola, *Excommunication in the Middle Ages* (Berkeley, Los Angeles, London: University of California Press, 1986), chap. 2, "Forms of Excommunication in the High Middle Ages," for information on developments in the theory and practice of excommunication under the "monarchical papacy" (28) of the twelfth century. Near the time Marie was composing the *Lais*, "the church was experiencing the first signs of a heresy crisis that would necessitate extraordinary legal measures. Excommunication *latae sententiae* ["a sentence that took effect immediately as the crime was committed" (28)] took its real impetus from the reaction of the church to the dangerously popular heretical movements of the second half of the twelfth century" (30). For an account (highly partisan, to be sure) of a celebrated book burning under the supervision of Archbishop Ralph of Rheims, see Peter Abelard's account of the burning, at the council of Soissons (1121), of his treatise on the theology of the Trinity, in *Historia calamitatum*, ed. J. Monfrin (Paris: Vrin, 1967), 82–89. For an analysis of the relationship between heresy and literacy in eleventh- and early-twelfth-century western Europe, see Brian Stock, *The Implications of Literacy* (Princeton, N.J.: Princeton University Press, 1983), chap. 2, "Textual Communities." Those who read Ovid's books are Marie's parody of an heretical community. Throughout the European Middle Ages, the presence of women preachers and/or priests within dissenting communities was regarded by the institutional church as particularly dangerous. See, e.g., Alcuin Blamires and C. W. Marx, "Woman Not to Preach: A Disputation in British Library MS Harley 31," *Journal of Medieval Latin* 3 (1993): 39–44, and Margaret Aston, "Lollard Women Priests?," *Journal of Ecclesiastical History* 31 (1980): 441–61. See further note 20, below.

4. See Alan of Lille, *The Plaint of Nature*, trans. James J. Sheridan (Toronto: Pontifical Institute of Mediaeval Studies, 1980), 206, 220. Sheridan (31–35) dates the work 1160–65.

5. On the enthymematic structure of medieval vernacular literary prologues, see the excellent introduction to SunHee Kim Gertz, *Poetic Prologues: Late Medieval Conversations with the Literary Past* (Frankfurt am Main: Klostermann, 1996). In the introduction to their translation of the *Lais* (Harmondsworth: Penguin, 1986), 10, Glyn S. Burgess and Keith Busby wonder whether any male author of Marie's era would have written "hummë *u femme*" in G 8. On Marie's understanding of, and response to, envy, see the important article by Sarah Spence, "Double Vision: Love and Envy in the *Lais*," in Chantal A. Maréchal, ed., *In Quest of Marie de France A Twelfth-Century Poet* (Lewiston, Queenstown, Lampeter: Edwin Mellen Press, 1992), 262–79.

6. On the role of topical invention in the narratives of the *lais*, see Douglas Kelly, "'Diversement comencier' in the *Lais* of Marie de France," in *In Quest of Marie de France*, 107–22.

7. Michelle A. Freeman speaks of Marie's "initiative," in offering her *lais* to the king, as "all the more arresting not only because it is a woman who dares address her male interlocutor first—an act often judged immodest, or uncourtly, in the twelfth-century romance tradition—but also because the person addressed is the King, namely, a dignitary to be spoken to only if he so requests." (See "Marie de France's Poetics of Silence: the Implications for a Feminine *Translatio*," *PMLA* 99 [1984]: 860.) Cf. Rupert A. Pickens's argument that "'[Marie's] fear does not lie in the presumption of bestowing largess on her king, but in the scandal of a woman who appropriates a male poetics and must take on a body of ambiguous sexuality in order to engage in fruitful public discourse" ("The Poetics of Androgyny in the *Lais* of Marie de France: *Yonec, Milun*, and the General *Prologue*," in Donald Maddox and Sara Sturm-Maddox, eds., *Literary Aspects of Courtly Culture: Selected Papers from the Seventh Triennial Congress of the International Courtly Literature Society* [Cambridge: D. S. Brewer, 1994], 219); cf. note 16, below.

8. See, for example, the anonymous *lais* of *Graelent* and *Guingamor*, ed. Prudence Mary O'Hara Tobin, *Les Lais anonymes des XIIème et XIIIème siècles* (Geneve: Droz, 1976), 83–125, 127–55; Chrétien de Troyes, *Erec et Enide*, ed. Mario Roques (Paris: Champion, 1963), ll. 27–76, 117–24, 277–84; *Partonopeu de Blois*, ed. Joseph Gildea, O.S.A. (Villanova, Pa.: Villanova University Press, 1967), ll. 584f. (In *Guingamor* and *Partonopeu*, the beast is a huge boar.) On the Celtic hunts, see Rachel Bromwich, "Celtic Dynastic Themes and the Breton Lays," *Etudes celtiques* 9 (1961): 439–74; cf. R. N. Illingworth, "Celtic Tradition and the Lai of Guigemar," *Medium Aevum* 31 (1962): 176–85. In *Partonopeu* and *Graelent*, the beast is associated with a beautiful woman whom the male protagonist rapes but who subsequently claims to have staged the rape in order to win his love. An analog to this plot, which constructs woman as the willing, highly sexualized object and inciter of masculine desire, constitutes the first part of "Pwyll, Prince of Dyfed," the first of "the four branches of the Mabinogi," tradition-based Welsh tales extant in two fourteenth-century manuscripts but much earlier in origin. See *The Mabinogion*, trans. Gwyn Jones and Thomas Jones (London: Dent; New York: Dutton, 1949), 3–5; in this version it is the dogs who hunt the stag, rather than the stag itself, which are marvelous in their coloration (white, with red ears). For a summary of some versions of the marvelous hunt analogous to Guigemar's, see Antoinette Knapton, *Mythe et psychologie chez Marie de France dans Guigemar* (Chapel Hill: University of North Carolina Press, 1975), 55–63. On rape as a frequent feature of twelfth- and thirteenth-century French narrative fictions, see Kathryn Gravdal, *Ravishing Maidens: Writing Rape in Medieval French Literature and Law* (Philadelphia: University of Pennsylvania Press, 1991); and on the deeply inscribed male fantasy that the land is a woman waiting to be forcefully taken by the man brave enough to possess her, see Annette Kolodny, *The Lay of the Land* (Chapel Hill: University of North Carolina Press, 1975).

9. All references to text of *Eneas* follow *Eneas: Roman du xiième siècle*, ed. J.-J. Salverda de Grave (Paris: Champion, 1929) and are henceforth abbreviated to E. For a recent consideration of Marie's response to the *Eneas*, which does not, however, allude to the passages under discussion here, see Earl Jeffrey Richards, "Les Rapports entre le *Lai de Guigemar* et le *Roman d'Eneas*: Considérations génériques," in Danielle Buschinger, ed., *Le Récit bref au moyen age* (Université de Picardie, centre d'études médiévales, 1979), 45–56. For the hypothesis that Marie's *lai* may have been influenced by the classical myth of Heracles and the horned hind of Artemis, see Knapton, 56–57, 71–73.

10. Eva Rosenn, "The Sexual and Textual Politics of Marie's Poetics," *In Quest of Marie de France*, 232, suggests that in the *Eneas* episode, "our sympathy is with the stag rather than the hunter." On women as patrons, see Jo Ann McNamara and Suzanne Wemple, "Sanctity and Power: The Dual Pursuit of Medieval Women," in Renate Bridenthal and Claudia Koonz, eds., *Becoming Visible: Women in European History* (Boston: Houghton Mifflin, 1977), 92–118, esp. 115–16; Diana B. Tyson, "Patronage of French Vernacular History Writers in the Twelfth and Thirteenth Centuries," *Romania* 100 (1975): esp. 185–86, 190–95, 219–20; and Joan M. Ferrante, "Whose Voice? The Influence of Women Patrons on Courtly Romances," in *Literary Aspects of Courtly Culture*, 3–18. For a reading of the *Eneas* outlining "the internal negotiations of the *Eneas*, between emerging claims of feminine power . . . and then ultimately dominant imperatives of male imperial conquest," see Christopher Baswell, "Eneas's Tent and the Fabric of Empire in the *Roman d'Eneas*," *Romance Languages Annual* (1990): 43–48 (quote from 43). My colleague, Prof. Sandra Pierson Prior, has pointed out to me that Silvie's name, recalling (or more properly anticipating) Silvius, Aneas's son by Lavinia, itself hints at an androgyny within Aeneas's lineage. Since the tame deer has assimilated to itself some of its mistress's virtues and skills, it is in a sense her surrogate, and

Ascanie's destruction of it can be read as a doubly displaced onslaught against the "feminized" part (or potential) of his lineage, once its role has evolved from fighting to ruling. (On the danger of warriors becoming feminized at court during intervals of peace, see the speech of Cador, Duke of Cornwall, to King Arthur, welcoming the challenge of the Roman Emperor, Lucius, as a call to arms, in Geoffrey of Monmouth, *Historia regum Britanniae* (the Bern MS), ed. Neil Wright [Cambridge: Brewer, 1985], 113.)

11. See, e.g., *La Vie de Saint Eustache*, ed. Holger Petersen (Paris: Champion, 1928): "Desus le cerf entre les cors, / Qui ierent gros et lons et fors, / Un signe li est apparu: / . . . une croiz resplendissant, / Plus clere que soleil luissant / . . . . L'ymage qui iert en la croiz / Au cerf donne raison et voiz, / A Placidum le fait parler" (301–13). At l. 321, the voice identifies itself as that of "li sauverez Jhesus." Cf. Knapton, 57–58, on the similar legend of St. Hubert, "patron des chasseurs. . . . Chassant un vendredi saint dans la foret des Ardennes, il vit un cerf blanc portant un crucifix entre les cornes" (57); the beast does not, however, address the startled hunter.

12. See, e.g., the account of St. Giles in Jacobus de Voragine, *The Golden Legend* (GL), trans. William Granger Ryan (Princeton: Princeton University Press, 1993), 2:147–49. GL was compiled ca. 1260, using earlier material.

13. Knapton, 76–77, notes the parallels between the wounding of the *bise* in *Guigemar* and aspects of "une légende mystique, celle de saint Michel du mont Galgano [sic], très célèbre au temps de Marie" (76), but give no documentation for her summary, which contains several errors. The Latin quotes in my text come from Bede, *Homiliae*, lib. 3, hom. CI, "In revelatione sancti michaelis" (PL v. 94, col. 502–3); the text in GL (2:201–2) is very similar to that transmitted by Bede but is part of a larger compendium (201–11) of apparitions of the archangel to which is appended an explanation of the angelic hierarchy. See further *Acta sanctorum* (PL v. 96, col. 1389–94) and, for other versions, see *Bibliotheca hagiographica latina antiquae et mediae aetatis,* Novum supplementum, ed. H. Fros (Brussels: 1986), 644. The "revelatio beati Michaelis in monte Gargano" is mentioned s.a. 506 in the twelfth-century *Annales du Mont-Saint-Michel*, ed. Léopold Delisle, in *Chronique de Robert de Torigni . . . suivie de divers opuscules historiques*, ed. Léopold Delisle (Rouen: Société de l'histoire de Normandie, 1873) 2:230, and is recounted in a narrative beginning, "De apparitione . . . sancti Michaelis in Monte Gargano," in Bibliothèque d'Avranches, ms. 211 [formerly ms. 204 in the library of Mont-Saint-Michel, where it was written], fol. 1; see Delisle, 2:209–10. For 8 May as the date on which the apparition at Gargano is celebrated, see GL 203, and for its celebration at Mont-Saint-Michel, see the "Calendrier du Mont-Saint-Michel entre le xie et le xve siècles," in *Millénaire monastique du Mont Saint-Michel*, vol. 1, *Histoire et vie monastiques*, ed. Dom J. Laporte (Paris: Lethielleux, 1966), 292–93. Marie places the tournament in *Milun* "al Munt Seint Michel" (387). The Abbot of the monastery, 1154–86, was Robert de Torigni, an intimate of King Henry II of England, putative dedicatee of the *Lais*; according to Robert's *Chronicle* (see reference earlier in this note), Henry came to Mont-Saint-Michel on the saint's major feast day (29 September) in 1158 to accept the surrender of Conan, Duke of Brittany.

14. Giraldus Cambrensis, in his *Itinerarium Kambriae*, recounts a story he heard in Wales concerning a hind with antlers, that had been hunted down, killed, and sent to the court of Henry II. See Urban T. Holmes, "A Welsh Motive in Marie's 'Guigemar,'" *SP* 39 (1942): 11–14; Knapton 69; and Leslie Brook, "Guigemar and the White Hind," *Medium Aevum* 56 (1987): 96.

15. On the expansion of the concept, and exercise, of lordship in northwest Europe during the twelfth century, see Thomas Bisson, "Medieval Lordship," *Speculum* 10 (1995): 743–59. Knapton, 55–56, discusses hunting as a quintessentially noble and mas-

culine activity. For a description of hunting practices and references to a variety of medieval treatises on hunting, see Marcel Thiébaux, *The Stag of Love: The Chase in Medieval Literature* (Ithaca and London: Cornell University Press, 1974), 21–40. As Marie
presents the hunt in *Guigemar*, what begins as a hunt of the stag *a force*, "by hunters
coursing with horses and hounds," turns into a "stalking" of the *bise* "with bow" (28).

16. For various theories about the nature and significance of Guigemar's lack of *talent*
for erotic relations with women, see Knapton, 40–48; Rupert T. Pickens, "Thematic
Structure in Marie de France's *Guigemar*," *Romania* 95 (1974): 328–35; Joan Brumlik,
"Thematic Irony in Marie de France's *Guigemar*," *French Forum* 13 (1988): 8–9;
Stephen G. Nichols, "Deflections of the Body in the Old French Lay," *Stanford French
Review* (spring-fall 1990): 31–32 (referring to Guigemar's "chivalric narcissism," on
which see further, below); Robert M. Stein, "Desire, Social Reproduction, and Marie's
Guigemar," in *In Quest of Marie de France*, 282–83; June Hall McCash, "The Curse of
the White Hind and the Cure of the Weasel: Animal Magic in the *Lais* of Marie de
France," in *Literary Aspects of Courtly Culture*, 199–204.

17. The contrast between the use of the botanical metaphor here and in GP 5–8
dramatizes the opposition between Guigemar's repute, in which love plays no part, and
Marie's, which derives from telling love stories. Pickens, "Poetics of Androgyny," 218–
19, notes the continuance of the metaphor in Marie's address to the "nobles reis" (GP 43).

18. Cf. the old priest guarding the *dame* (G 255–60, quoted above), whose analogous,
but more definitively unhealable "sexual wound" represents not a recognition of
neediness but the fact of being locked into institutionalized celibacy and thus, out of
frustration, into misogyny. On clerical celibacy as a major, and contested, initiative of the
institutional church beginning before, but integrated into, the "Gregorian reform" and
continuing into the twelfth century, see James A. Brundage, *Law, Sex, and Christian
Society in Medieval Europe* (Chicago and London: University of Chicago Press, 1987),
214–23, 226; 314–19 (for the thought and writings of the Decretists on clerical sexuality
during the period in which Marie was writing her *Lais*). Chaucer's Wife of Bath makes a
comment about the inevitable enmity between women and "clerkes" that may also be
relevant to this passage: "the clerk, whan he is oold, and may noght do / Of Venus werkes
worth his olde sho, / Thanne sit he doun, and writ in his dotage / That wommen kan nat
kepe hir mariage!" (*The Canterbury Tales*, 3:707–10, in Larry Benson, gen. ed., *The
Riverside Chaucer*, 3d. ed. [Boston: Houghton Mifflin, 1987], 114). Where the bise tells
Guigemar his *destinee*, the old priest reads the *dame* the divine service, with implications
of inculcating submission, even as the Venus pictures are supposed to inculcate her
submissive love for her *sire*.

19. Cf. GP, where Marie explains that the "anciens" wrote "oscurement," enabling
(challenging?) "ceus ki a venir esteient" to "gloser la lettre / E de lur sen le surplus
mettre" (9–16). The *bise*'s "curse"/prediction constitutes a *surplus* she adds to the life
Guigemar has led until now—a life exempt from sexual desire—and the antlers are, in
effect, an emblem of the authority her words will be shown to carry. (Cf. McCash, "Curse
of the White Hind," 202: "by providing the beast with antlers, [Marie] symbolically
attributes to the hind a special virtue and high moral stance, superior to that of
Guigemar.") Pickens, "Poetics of Androgyny," describes Marie's address to the "nobles
reis" (GP 43) as "androgynous," given her depiction of herself deriving "joie" (GP 52),
like a male suitor, from the "feminized" king's reception of her offered gift (219); Stein,
"Desire, Social Reproduction," argues that, in deciding to retell traditional Celtic tales
instead of translating Latin texts (GP 28–42), "Marie chooses oral (female) storytelling in
order to become a (male?) writer" (289).

20. See Spence, "Double Vision": "Much like the Narcissus story as told by Ovid, the deer clearly works as a reflection of Guigemar; the arrow returns to him as if reflected off the animal. . . . The deer is, indeed, Guigemar's double; his [sic] bisexuality is the perfect complement to Guigemar's asexuality" (266–67). Cf. Nichols, "Deflections of the Body": "Like Ovid's Narcissus, Guigemar has been too preoccupied with his literal identity as knight and hunter to contemplate more subtle conjugations of corporal signification. . . . In Marie's affective utopia, reciprocity of pain and pleasure plays a major role in defining male-female relations. . . . By connecting Guigemar's fate so fantastically to that of the white doe, Marie forcibly binds him to the blurring of gender alterity that the doe represents" (29–32). See also Stein, "Desire, Social Reproduction," 283: "The doe speaks in mirroring syntax, and its promise sets Guigemar henceforth in opposition to a figure (the doe, the lady, Meridauc) that will mirror him." Interestingly, the twenty-fourth of Marie's *Fables*, in a clear recollection of Narcissus, tells of a stag that admires his antlers in a reflecting pool and is then trapped by pursuing hunters when his antlers become caught in the branches of a tree.

21. See Jo Ann McNamara and Suzanne Wemple, "The Power of Women Through the Family in Medieval Europe, 500–1100," in Mary Erler and Maryanne Kowaleski, *Women and Power in the Middle Ages* (Athens and London: University of Georgia Press, 1988), 95–97; McNamara and Wemple, "Sanctity and Power," 110–14; Georges Duby, *The Knight, the Lady and the Priest: The Making of Modern Marriage in Medieval France*, trans. Barbara Bray (New York: Pantheon, 1983), 15–21, 211–26.

22. See Beryl Smalley, *The Study of the Bible in the Middle Ages*, 2d ed. (Oxford: Blackwell, 1952, repr. Notre Dame: University of Notre Dame Press, 1964), 77. On the seductive power of diabolically instructed female speech as a cause of humanity's fall and a constant concern of Christian moralists, see Eric Jager, *The Tempter's Voice* (Ithaca and London: Cornell University Press, 1993); cf. Lee Patterson, "'For the Wyves love of Bathe': Feminine Rhetoric and Poetic Resolution in the *Roman de la Rose* and the *Canterbury Tales*," *Speculum* 58 (1983): 660–64; and Blamires and Marx, "Women not to Preach."

23. See, for example, the description of the twelfth-century English recluse Christina of Markyate's role as unofficial but authoritative advisor to Geoffrey, abbot of the powerful monastery of St. Albans, ca. 1124–47, in *The Life of Christina of Markyate*, ed. and trans. C. H. Talbot (Oxford: Clarendon, 1959), 134–75, 192–93. (Like Marie, Christina was, according to her biographer, the object of a good deal of envy because of her saintliness and her influence on Abbot Geoffrey; see, e.g., 172–73. For a survey of medieval women who spoke authoritatively, see Danielle Régnier-Bohler, "Literary and Mystical Voices," ed. Christiane Klapisch-Zuber, in *Silences of the Middle Ages*, vol. 2 of *A History of Women in the West* (Cambridge, Mass., and London: Harvard University Press, 1992), 427–82.

24. See *Ancrene Wisse*, ed. J. R. R. Tolkien, Early English Text Society, vol. 249 (London, etc.: Oxford University Press, 1962), pt. 2, "Þe heorte warde Þurh Þe fif wittes," 35–43, on the perils of speech for an anchoress, who should follow the example of the Virgin Mary—she speaks only four times in the gospels (41)—rather than that of "te cakele eue" (cackling Eve [35]).

25. As it happens, there is extant a precious instance of Marie being "bitten" by a contemporary: in the prologue to his *Vie seint Edmund le Rei*, Denis Piramus, a self-described court poet turned hagiographer, comments negatively on the *matire* of some of his contemporaries, which, although in its fictionality it "resemble sounge" (30), is much praised "en ces riches curz" (34). He singles out "dame Marie . . . / Ki en rime fist e basti / E compassa les vers de lais, / Ki ne sunt pas del tut verais" (35–38); not only is her work

admired by "Cunte, barun e chivaler" (42), "Les lais solent as dames pleire, / De joie les oient e de gré, / Qu'il sunt sulum lur volenté" (46–48). See Ulrich Mölk, ed. *Französische Literarästhetik des 12. und 13. Jahrhunderts. Prologe-Exkurse-Epiloge* (Tübingen: Max Niemeyer, 1969), 92–93.

26. Victor Turner, "Liminality and the Performative Genres," in John J. MacAloon, ed., *Rite, Drama, Festival, Spectacle: Rehearsals towards a Theory of Cultural Performance* (Philadelphia: Institute for the Study of Human Issues, 1984), 29.

27. "Liminality," 29. The bise's "prophecy"/plot summary is in fact couched largely in the subjunctive, leading some readers (incorrectly, I believe) to describe it as her "curse." Cf. Michelle A. Freeman's comment (in "Dual Natures and Subverted Glosses: Marie de France's 'Bisclavret,'" *Romance Notes* 25 [1984/85]) on another binatured creature, the werewolf: "Like his, Marie's nature is at once dual and marginal, equally enigmatic and potentially repulsive to some, in that she is both female and court poet. . . . Marie's . . . behavior . . . exhibits a new, androgynous poetic vision—an appropriate maneuver that allows for authentic poetic expression within, and yet apart from, the stereotyped ideology of courtliness" (299–301).

28. The quotations come, respectively, from *Feminist Theory: From Margin to Center* (Boston: South End Press, 1984), ix, and "marginality as site of resistance," in *Talking Back: Thinking Feminist, Thinking Black* (Boston: South End Press, 1989), 341. Interestingly, the character Marie-Thérèse in Toni Morrison's 1981 novel, *Tar Baby*, has certain characteristics that recall Marie de France's oblique self-presentation in the *Lais*: Marie-Thérèse is "wounded" (in this case, nearly blind), and marginalized by those who control the power in the novel's world; but she is also a storyteller endowed with prescience who, by her words and vision, shapes the destiny of the novel's male African-American protagonist at a crucial moment. And she has about her an aura of androgyny (her name, blindness, and famous breasts—she is a noted wetnurse—recall the figure of Teiresias, the most famous androgyne of classical mythology).

29. On the female signature see, e.g., Nancy Miller, *Subject to Change: Reading Feminist Writing* (New York and London: Columbia University Press, 1988), 12–18.

30. See Freeman, "Poetics of Silence," 867; S. Nichols, "Working Late: Marie de France and the Value of Poetry," in Michel Guggenheim, ed. *Women in French Literature* (Stanford French and Italian Studies, Saratoga, Calif.: ANMA Libri, 1988), 58:7–16.

31. For a somewhat different reading of this image—from which, however, I have much profited—cf. Freeman, "Poetics of Silence," 869–70. As she says, "Naturally, we note the parallels between Marie and the Lady of the *lai*." (870).

32. The *dame* prays, "Si ceo peot estrë e ceo fu, / Si unc a nul est avenu, / Deu, ki de tut ad poësté, / Il en face ma volenté!" (Y 101–4). The disparity in age between Mary and Joseph was, of course, a commonplace of medieval retellings and depictions of the Nativity. Michelle Freeman interprets these events as "a secular, seemingly marvelous, courtly reenactment of the Annunciation," in "The Changing Figure of the Male: the Revenge of the Female Storyteller," in *In Quest of Marie de France*, 249–50; she does not, however, note the Mary-Joseph parallel or the *dame*'s reversal of Mary's acquiescence in the will of God.

33. See Miri Rubin, *Corpus Christi: The Eucharist in Late Medieval Culture* (Cambridge: Cambridge University Press, 1991), 142–47, "Mary of the Eucharist." Cf. Freeman, "Changing figure," 248–49, who notes the transubstantiation parallel but stresses instead Marie's use of it to refer to her own "transformation of the *malmariée* form, so that the Lady, and Marie as well in solidarity, *font semblant de vivre et d'écrire un lai ensemble*" (248–49; emphasis Freeman's).

34. Freeman, "Changing figure," 254, says of the dying lover's prophecy and instructions, "The motive for justice and revenge in this text becomes all the stronger as a result, which makes me even more willing to accept the premise that these events constitute episodes in an oppressed woman's fantasy."

35. "Dual Natures and Subverted Glosses: Marie de France's 'Bisclavret,'" *Romance Notes* 25 (1984–85): 296.

36. See M. Faure, "Le *Bisclavret* de Marie de France, une histoire suspecte de loup-garou," *Revue des langues romaines* 83 (1978): 345–56. Pickens, "Poetics of Androgyny," 219, refers to "*Bisclavret*, with the lady who loses her phallic nose."

37. See R. W. Hanning, "'I shal finde it in a maner glose': Versions of Textual Harassment in Medieval Literature," in Laurie A. Finke and Martin B. Shichtman, eds. *Medieval Texts and Contemporary Readers* (Ithaca and London: Cornell University Press, 1987), 35 n.15; R. Howard Bloch, "The Medieval Text—'Guigemar'—as a Provocation to the Discipline of Medieval Studies," *Romanic Review* 79 (1988): 72; Stein, "Desire, Social Reproduction," 283–86. I believe there is a parallel (and analogously important) instance in *Bisclavret*: a quibble on *curuz*, anger (35, 249) and *curut*, ran (146, 198, 233) linking the two parts of the man-beast's identity; the use of the verb form to describe the king's behavior (300) may suggest his reduction to a quasibestial level in his implicitly homoerotic embrace of the metamorphosed Bisclavret and exile of the latter's wife.

38. Guigemar reveals his love to the *dame* after being counseled by her *meschine*, "vus amez; / Gardez que trop ne vus celez" (GP 445–46). The parallel between this exhortation that Guigemar announce his passion and Marie's defense of her own poetic utterance— "Ki Deus ad duné escïence / E de parler bon' eloquence / Ne s'en deit taisir ne celer, / Ainz se deit volunters mustrer" (GP 1–4)—has often been noted.

39. I would like to thank Mary Agnes Edsall, Prof. Suzanne Conklin Akbari, Elizabeth Weinstock, and the members of the "group of New York medievalists" (especially Prof. Sandra Pierson Prior) for their invaluable assistance at various stages of this project. A very early version of this essay was presented at a meeting of the Columbia University Seminar in Medieval Studies, members of which, especially Prof. Elizabeth Brown, provided useful information and made helpful suggestions. Only after completing this essay did I read Nancy Vine Durling's excellent article, "The Knot, the Belt, and the Making of *Guigemar*," *Assays* 6 (1991): 29–53, which, although its focus is quite different, anticipates some of the interpretations offered here.

3

Chaucerian Discourses of Desire

Reading the Language of Love:
Boccaccio's *Filostrato*
as Intermediary between the *Commedia*
and Chaucer's *Troilus and Criseyde*

NANCY M. REALE

For the Christian poets who followed him, Dante's *Commedia* transformed the relationship between poetry, secular love, and divine truth—"l'amor che move il sole e l'altre stelle" [the love that moves the sun and the other stars].[1] Following the example of Petrarch and the *stil novisti* poets, he claimed for the transformative nature of romantic love an ability to awaken in the lover a desire to know divine truth and for (classical epic) poetry a visionary capacity that could lead the way to recognition of this truth. Dante the pilgrim needs the inspiration of and his deep love for both Beatrice and Virgil to undertake his journey; his two principal guides represent both his profound ties to the beauty and passion possible in the sublunary world and his impulse to transcend those pleasures for still greater rewards.

By electing to address directly in the *Commedia* the relationship between his experience of love, his poetic craft, and his Christian faith, Dante redefined medieval literary self-consciousness in ways that tremendously affected—and often apparently disturbed—the poets who followed him. Some, like Boccaccio, responded by asserting the realities of diurnal life through parodies of Dantean language and form (this in itself is testimony to the powerful effects of the *Commedia*), while others followed the Dantean example of trying to work out a theory of poetics that was consonant with their faith. In his *Troilus and Criseyde*, Chaucer wrestled with the relation of language to different kinds of love in the wake of Dante's accomplishment. I want to argue here that Chaucer used

Boccaccio's *Il Filostrato* as an intermediary between *Troilus and Criseyde* and the *Commedia*; through the filter of the Boccaccian poem, Chaucer found a form with which he could engage the claims Dante makes for love and poetry while recognizing the extent to which both are operative only in the sublunary world of mortal men. Chaucer's response to Dante was made possible by his reading of the *Filostrato* because he found in his Italian model not only his *matière* but also a way of thinking about love in a post-Dantean world.

Recent work by Karla Taylor, Nicholas Havely, and others calls attention to Chaucer's complex references and responses to the *Commedia* in the *Troilus*. Other scholarship on the latter poem emphasizes Chaucer's alterations and elaborations of and omissions from the *Filostrato*. To date, however, Chaucer criticism has not adequately addressed Chaucer's use of the Boccaccian poem as a mediating text through which Chaucer articulates his response to Dante and struggles with his own position regarding poetic practice and Christian doctrine.

Here I will address *one* of the connections Chaucer saw between himself and his Italian predecessors as he was at work on the *Troilus*. I will demonstrate that Chaucer's expansion of and insistence on Pandarus's role represents his affirmation of Boccaccio's faith in language as pure human artifact in the face of Dantean claims about proper uses for language. Chaucer celebrates linguistic artistry through Pandarus, yet his own ambivalence about the limits of language and its relation to faith pervade the *Troilus*. The central energies of the poem are profoundly conflictual as they simultaneously demonstrate the practical and aesthetic uses of language and call into question its efficacy in the face of Christian truth.

As Chaucer's narrator recounts the development of the love affair and its ultimate failure, he also repeatedly demonstrates Pandarus's indispensability as a skillful intermediary and wordsmith who is always eager to "newe his tong affile" (2.1681).[2] Pandarus propels the action of the plot by encouraging Troilus to confide in him, by creating fictions intended to persuade Criseyde to consider Troilus's suit, and by serving as literary consultant in the correspondence between the lovers. Indeed, it is largely the action of Pandarus that Chaucer's narrator describes (and admires) even as he proclaims his interest in the passions of the lovers.

After establishing the centrality of Pandarus's art, the poem undermines precisely what it so carefully asserts, first as it eliminates Pandarus in book 5, next as it demonstrates the failure of the love affair, and finally as it presents in the envoi a narrative voice that desperately seeks the assurances available only through faith in Christ and Mary as divine intermediaries. By looking briefly at book 3 and the envoi of the

Troilus, I shall show first how Chaucer responds to Dante and then how he finds in Boccaccio's *proemio* the direction for that response. Finally, I shall suggest that Chaucer locates the distance he sees between his own poetic practice and Christian faith in the discordant relations between Pandarus's role, the degree to which Troilus is measured against conventional standards of courtly love, and the envoi of the poem, in which the narrator reaches toward a view of love in the absence of Pandarus as poet-mediator.[3]

Windeatt, Fyler, and others have remarked on the unnerving presence of Pandarus in the consummation scene in book 3 of the *Troilus*, on the intervention of this intermediary in a tryst that "ought ben secree" (1.744). The fact that Pandarus, the creator and "narrator" of the love affair, never absents himself from the scene of "hevene blisse" (3.704) demonstrates the contingency of the meaning of the lovers' fulfillment on the craft of the artist. It is not enough that the lovers finally come together for their mutual pleasure; the intermediary must be present to bear witness to what transpires and to make the consummation real—by means of a report, presumably—to the public world beyond the room. As the maker of Troilus and Criseyde's romance, Pandarus must be present, even if sitting out of the way by the fire, for their love to exist at all (3.974–80). He is an author creating a scene and directing his characters to speak, and as he gives aural and physical form to the romance of his construction, he also serves as its primary audience.[4]

Pandarus's involvement in the lovers' interview is highlighted as he actively reintroduces himself to the scene in the face of their temporary loss of control. Troilus swoons, and Pandarus realizes that he must set things right:

> This was no litel sorwe for to se;
> But al was hust, and Pandare up as faste,—
> "O nece, pes, or we be lost!" quod he,
> "Beth naught agast!" but certeyn, at the laste,
> For this or that, he into bed hym caste,
> And seyde, "O thef, is this a mannes herte?"
> And of he rente al to his bare sherte;
>
> And seyde, "Nece, but ye helpe us now,
> Allas, youre owen Troilus is lorn!"
> "Iwis, so wolde I, and I wiste how,
> Ful fayn," quod she; "Allas, that I was born!"
> "Yee, nece, wol ye pullen out the thorn
> That stiketh in his herte, quod Pandare,
> "Sey 'al foryeve,' and stynt is al this fare!"

(3.1093–106)

Chaucer uses Pandarus's presence in this scene to call attention to his literary methods as if to answer Dante with the practical political possibilities for language offered by Boccaccio. The secular love we see consummated in this scene of "privitee" is a poet's making, and it is the same kind of love that Boccaccio's Pandaro creates in the *Filostrato*, which stands as a sublunary counterpoint to the divine love of the *Commedia*. This secular system of meaning asserted in the consummation scene is later contrasted with a divine system of meaning in the envoi as Chaucer explores where language stands in relation to each.

Once Chaucer establishes Pandarus's role as an indispensable wordsmith and intermediary, he fully intertwines making literature and making love by having Troilus himself describe his experience of Criseyde as a literary process. Just prior to the lovers' exchange of tokens, Troilus makes the following apostrophe to his beloved's eyes:

> . . . "O eyen clere,
> It weren ye that wroughte me swich wo,
> Ye humble nettes of my lady deere!
> Though ther be mercy writen in youre cheere
> God woot, the text ful hard is, soth, to fynde!
> How koude ye withouten bond me bynde?"
>
> (3.1353–58)

Troilus here has come up against a critical limitation in his relationship with Criseyde. He cannot fully see (and perhaps cannot fully know) what she feels or wants despite Pandarus's actions as go-between. In order to pursue the object of his desire, however, Troilus must give himself over to "blind passion," even as he marvels at his inability to fully know his beloved. This scene that conjoins love, privacy, and the transgression of privacy thus highlights the degree to which Pandarus's presence, Troilus's knowledge of his beloved, and the requirements of the love affair are in discord. Chaucer would have his audience see that not only is Troilus unable to read the text in his beloved's eyes in the most intimate of situations, but that the paradoxically necessary role of the pander need not work in conjunction with the lover's "good reading." Indeed, the lovers' knowledge of one another is shown to be irrelevant— and perhaps even counterproductive—to Pandarus's goal of bringing them together.

One way to understand Troilus's words at this point is to see that Chaucer contrasts Troilus's poor command of courtly love language with Pandarus's linguistic mastery. Perhaps more important, however, is the fact that Troilus's comment on Criseyde's eyes has behind it romance and *dolce stil nuovo* traditions about love entering through the eyes and the Dantean emphasis on vision that pervades the *Commedia*. Chaucer's Troilus cannot see in Criseyde's eyes what Dante's pilgrim learns to see through Beatrice's, so we see that from its inception the relationship is flawed, despite the great success that both Pandarus and Troilus claim. We will discover later in the poem that Criseyde lacks the knowledge and spiritual purity of Beatrice, but at this point it is crucial that we see the inability of the lover to comprehend the very beloved whom he seeks to know and with whom he seeks union.

For Dante, emphasis on vision demonstrates that the process of conversion experienced by the pilgrim is in fact a removal of the shadows of hell, which offer only images of reality, and a movement toward a paradisal clarity in which images refer perfectly, making mistaken, confused, or partial vision an impossibility.[5] In the *Commedia*, this process of clarification and movement toward God is intimately tied to the poet's writing project, the means by which he is able to communicate truth to his reader and thereby cause him to experience a conversion analogous to the pilgrim's. In the *Troilus*, on the other hand, Troilus's recognition that he cannot see the "soth" in Criseyde's eyes is counterproductive. In order for Pandarus's secular romantic program to be realized, Troilus must resign himself to not knowing his beloved. The closer Troilus comes to Criseyde, the deeper becomes his mystification, his inability to discern "soth" from "fals," and the more important becomes Pandarus's fiction. Pandarus must remain in the bedroom because he is the glue that holds the relationship together in the absence of transcendent knowledge. He is the Virgil, the Bernard, the Beatrice of the sublunary world who uses language to construct beguiling fabrications capable of uniting lovers.[6]

Troilus's experience in this crucial scene is diametrically opposed to the experience of Dante's pilgrim, whose movement toward Beatrice represents a *de*mystification, a removal of the veil of false appearance. Moreover, it is a fundamental promise of the *Commedia* that the reader moves with the pilgrim through his progression toward truth, while *Troilus and Criseyde* operates by means of an ever-widening gulf—which finds complete expression in the envoi—between the world Troilus sees and that seen by the reader, who is repeatedly reminded by narrative interjections not to become enthralled by Criseyde, Pandarus, or love itself.

To fully see how Chaucer's tragedy of disillusionment is a response to the "unillusionment" of the *Commedia*, we must see how the *Filostrato* is a response to Dante's use of the epic form for religious purposes. By drawing heavily on Dantean language and alloying it with popular traditions (for instance, the practices of the *canterini*), Boccaccio creates in his poem a text that explores for human love what Dante's explores for divine love.[7] Boccaccio answers Dante as he turns to the world of pagan romance for his material, and it is precisely this challenge to the poetic voice of Christian authority that attracts Chaucer.

When we turn to the *proemio* of the *Filostrato*, we meet a narrative voice (Filostrato) who addresses his lady with a controlled, even distant, account of a courtly world in which love is the subject for debate rather than a passion experienced directly:

> Molte fiate già, nobilissima donna, avvenne che io, il quale quasi dalla mia puerizia infino a questo tempo ne' servigi d'Amore sono stato, ritrovandomi nella sua corte intra i gentili uomini e le vaghe donne dimoranti in quella parimente con meco, udii muovere e disputare questa quistione, cioè: uno giovane ferventemente ama una donna, della quale niun'altra cosa gli è conceduta dalla fortuna se non ii poterla alcuna volta vedere, o talvolta di lei ragionare con alcuno, o seco stesso di lei dolcemente pensare. Quale gli è adunque di queste tre cose di più diletto?[8] (Proemio 1–3)

> [Many times, noblest lady, it happened that I, who almost from my youth to the present time have been in the service of love, finding myself in his court among gentlemen and lovely ladies there like myself, heard this question introduced and discussed: a young man fervently loves a lady, concerning whom no other thing is granted to him by fortune except that sometimes he may see her, or sometimes he may talk to others about her, or that he may think sweetly about her to himself. Which of these three things seems to him the most delightful?]

Filostrato indirectly refers here to the absence of his own lady, and we will soon discover that his tale of Troiolo's love for Criseida is both a reflection of his own love and a medium through which his desire for reunion is communicated and perhaps even effected.

Through his fictional Filostrato, Boccaccio presents the space between what a speaker says and what prompts him to speak. This distance is precisely the gap the poet Dante seeks to close in the *Commedia* as he attempts to lead his reader along the pilgrim's path of spiritual revelation. In the secular world of the *Filostrato*, however, literary wooing persuades for selfish purposes, and love of the other and truthfulness—or at least full disclosure—are not necessarily compatible. Filomena's absence and Filostrato's desire to recover her recall Dante's pilgrim's effort to reach Beatrice. Here, however, the emphasis is on sensual pleasure, and Filostrato elects to recount a fiction about Troiolo to communicate his longing for his lady.

By opening his poem with Filostrato's reference to the court of love, Boccaccio engages medieval courtly love tradition and the language used to express it. This is the very world Dante is at such pains to reject in the *Commedia* because it encourages infatuation with sensuality and the squandering of poetic resources on unworthy subjects.[9] For Boccaccio to reintroduce this world and use it as a frame for his pagan romance is for him to validate a kind of discourse that his predecessor sought to dismiss in his Christian epic.

Filostrato's language is a challenge to Dante in yet another way since the question being debated concerns the relative merits of vision, speech, and thought as avenues by which desire can be satisfied. This takes the reader beyond the limits of a *fin amour* love relationship and suggests larger philosophical questions about theology and poetics outlined in the *Commedia*. While in the sublunary world lovers and poets cannot help but live in reference to vision, speech, and thought, these are for Dante to be understood as means by which one can reach the transcendent world of the *Paradiso*. The claims of the *Commedia* notwithstanding, Boccaccio announces in the very first sentences of his text that his subject will be the way real men love real women.

The importance of vision is stressed throughout the rest of the *proemio* as Boccaccio continues to borrow from the language of the *stil novisti* and the medieval conceit that love enters through the eyes. Filostrato refers, for example, to his lady's "angelico viso" [angelic countenance] (8), to "la vostra sembianza" [her appearance] (12), and to the "occulta letizia procedente dal vostro sereno aspetto" [the hidden happiness emanating from her calm expression] (16). The emphasis on the appearance of the beloved highlights the importance of her current absence (and prefigures Criseida's absence from Troiolo), but it also refers to one of the three possibilities referred to in the opening disputation. Once the benefits of vision are removed, what other criteria does the sublunary lover—who is not graced by divine revelation—have for experiencing, interpreting, and participating in the world outside himself? This will become Troiolo's problem as he loves an absent beloved and constructs for himself the model of a perfect woman, only to be eventually disappointed by his own solipsistic "vision."

Boccaccio also uses the proem as a means to explore the impulse to write poetry. Filostrato says he wants to convert his personal experience to a form that is transferable to others:

Né prima tal pensiero nella mente mi venne, che il modo subitamente con esso m'occorse; del quale avvenimento, quasi da nascosa divinità spirato,

certissimo augurio presi di futura salute. E il modo fu questo: di dovere in
persona d'alcuno passionato sì come io era e sono, cantando narrare li miei
martiri. Meco adunque con sollicita cura cominciai a rivolgere l'antiche storie
per trovare cui io potessi fare scudo verisimilmente del mio segreto e
amoroso dolore. Né altro più atto nella mente mi venne a tale bisogno, che il
valoroso giovane Troiolo, . . . Per che della persona di lui e de' suoi accidenti
ottimamente presi forma alla mia intenzione, e susseguentemente in leggier
rima e nel mio fiorentino idioma, con stilo assai pietoso, li suoi e li miei
dolori parimente composui; . . . (Proemio 26–29)

[No sooner had such a thought come to my mind than suddenly occurred to
me the means, as if inspired by a hidden divinity, to secure the most certain
augury of future well-being. And the way was this: to be able, in the mask of
someone as impassioned as I was and am, to tell my sufferings by reciting
them. So, I began with great care to consider ancient stories to find one that I
would be able to make accurately into a shield for my secret and loving
sorrow. No other figure came into my mind as more appropriate for such a
purpose than the valorous youth Troiolo. . . . And so in the guise of him and
his experiences, I fortunately found a form for my intentions; thereafter, I
wrote his and my own sorrows alike in light rhyme and in my Florentine
dialect with a very heart-rending style; . . .]

Filostrato emphasizes his renovation of old material, so the very
authority of the inherited text is overwritten with the novelty of the
contemporary moment. Boccaccio wants us to recognize that the merging
of present actual experience and past fictional experience is the very
nature of the writing process: the poet is engaged in acting as an
intermediary, changing and coloring antecedent texts with his own, and
in seeing his own texts circumscribed by an inherited past.

Boccaccio also works against the Dantean model by using authorial
borrowing and revision characteristic of medieval practice. He avoids the
claims of innovation and importance implicit in Dante's conversion of
classical epic into an expression of Christian truth and assertion that there
is only one story worthy of narration. Instead of using pagan language to
speak about the divine, Boccaccio uses Dantean Christian language in a
classical context to reestablish a value for secular love. In so doing, he
validates the depths of desire and frustration experienced by the lover.[10]

In the *Filostrato*, the lover's presumed audience is private, and his
goal is to widen the distance between his own experience and that of his
protagonist. In the *Commedia*, on the other hand, the audience is public,
and the goal is to provide a fictional model that should be emulated. The
fiction of the *Commedia* presumes the increasing correspondence
between Dante the pilgrim and Dante the poet. Boccaccio's poem asserts

the alternative reality that such identification is impossible, that incompletion and distance are inevitable, and that it is precisely for this reason that storytelling and storytellers like Pandaro—and even the text itself—are necessary. In the world of the *Commedia*, full comprehension of the text (God) is the ultimate goal. In the worlds of Boccaccio's and Chaucer's Troilus characters, comprehension of the text (the beloved) is an impossibility, but a goal to be striven for nonetheless.

Boccaccio's Troiolo dies a sorrowful death, and his story ends with his disappearance from the pagan landscape of the poem. All that remains is for the narrator to warn his reader against following the example of Troiolo and selecting the wrong object of devotion. Chaucer's narrator, however, provides us with Troilus's translation to the eighth sphere (and an implicit invitation to see the preceding action in light of this moment), and he then uses his envoi to superimpose on the Boccaccian "pagan" response to Dante his own version of a Christian vision, based largely on the *Paradiso*.

Here, at the end of the poem, it is up to Chaucer's narrator to find the "text" that his hero was unable to find in the eyes of his beloved. Chaucer's discomfort with the claims of linguistic indispensability and relativity in his redaction of the Troilus story drives him toward a Christian resolution in the face of a "pagan" absence of faith. By electing to work from Boccaccio's poem, Chaucer confines his own narrative to the range of moral and theological possibilities available to (his version of) the classical world, yet it is critical to Chaucer's enterprise that he situate this poetic choice in the context of Christian views of meaning and truth (represented most emphatically by the *Commedia*). It is nonetheless true that the poem celebrates the instrumentality of language, the fluidity and complexity of human relationships, and the realities— sometimes comforting and sometimes not—of the powers of romantic love and desire.

Troilus and Criseyde is thus a poem that appears to speak against itself. It pushes the reader toward uncertainty and despair, yet it seeks to provide the comfort of a Christian revelation. It stresses the polyvalence of language and the limits of knowledge and posits divine truth in the face of these. This could not have been possible for Chaucer without Boccaccio's treatment of the Troilus story. Chaucer combines Boccaccio's interest in the persuasive powers of linguistic skills to create private realities with Dantean notions about the nature and purpose of language. The result is a text fraught with internal tensions, as narrator, characters, inherited plot, and authorial strategy strive uncomfortably with one another.

Chaucer uses *Troilus and Criseyde* to explore the possibilities of linguistic agency, but the poem stops short of asserting ultimate claims for language. The implied conclusion, however uncomfortable for a poet, is that faith in language leads ultimately to despair. Chaucer's narrator finds himself faced with his own reliance on language, and he produces an envoi in which Mary and Christ assume the quality of literary tropes in a gesture toward an assurance of salvation that is not fully convincing:

> And to that sothefast Crist, that starf on rode,
> With al myn herte of mercy evere I preye,
> And to the Lord right thus I speke and seye:
>
> Thow oon, and two, and thre, eterne on lyve,
> That regnest ay in thre, and two, and oon,
> Uncircumscript, and al maist circumscrive,
> Us from visible and invisible foon
> Defende, and to thy mercy, everichon,
> So make us, Jesus, for thi mercy digne,
> For love of mayde and moder thyn benigne.
>   Amen.

(5.1860–70)

As the poem closes, we feel the force of the divergence of perspectives that pervades it since the strident assertions of Christian truth in the envoi are so uncharacteristic of the narrator whose subtlety we have come to admire. In the indeterminate distance between the narrator's language and his faith in what he says in these final stanzas rests the uneasy coexistence of Chaucer's yearning for a Dantean assurance of salvation and his insistence on the validity of his own poetic project.

Notes

1. Dante Alighieri, *Paradiso* 33.145, *La Divina Commedia*, ed. Natalino Sapegno, 3 vols. (Florence: La nuova Italia, 1983), 3:425. The English translation is from Mark Musa's translation, *The Divine Comedy*, 3 vols. (Harmondsworth: Penguin, 1984), 3:394.

2. *The Works of Geoffrey Chaucer*, ed. F. N. Robinson, 2nd ed. *Troilus and Criseyde*. (Boston: Houghton Mifflin, 1957), 397. All further references appear in the text.

3. As many readers of the *Troilus* have noted, the narrator often seems to be profoundly influenced by both the plot and the characters in his narrative. Pandarus is perhaps an obstacle for the narrator's development of a transcendent vision of love in that his machinations on behalf of Troilus firmly ground the lover, and by extension the audience watching the evolution of the love affair, in the material world of romantic love. In effect, the narrator removes Pandarus from the poem in order to clear the way for his own view of love, which stands in sharp contradiction to the one Pandarus has assumed

and has engaged both lovers in pursuing. On the subject of Boccaccio's and Chaucer's narrators in *Il Filostrato* and the *Troilus*, see chapters 2 and 3 of Laura Kellogg's *Boccaccio's and Chaucer's Cressida* (New York: Peter Lang, 1995). See also the articles by Carolyn Dinshaw and John Fyler in R. A. Shoaf, ed., with the assistance of Catherine S. Cox, *Chaucer's "Troilus and Criseyde": 'Subgit to alle Poesye'* (Binghamton, N.Y.: Medieval and Renaissance Texts and Studies, 1992).

4. Working from the romance of Pandarus's creation, the narrator in turn creates his own version, for which we are the primary audience. The two acts of creation are in some sense parallel, but it behooves us to remember that Pandarus's romance, though it does indeed bring two lovers together, is solipsistic in that its "author" becomes the voyeuristic audience of his own creative enterprise. This is not true of the work of Chaucer's narrator, which is clearly intended for a public audience and which advertises that fact in various places, including the address to the audience in the envoi. Perhaps Chaucer deliberately contrasts the authorial self-reflexiveness of Pandarus against the audience awareness of his primary narrator to demonstrate the narcissism of sublunary love and the (outwardly directed) selflessness of love directed toward God. For further discussion of the narrator's role, see Martin Stevens, "The Winds of Fortune in the *Troilus*" (*Chaucer Review* 13 [1979]: 285–307), in which Stevens contrasts Pandarus as poet, and therefore the voice of free human will, with the narrator as the spokesperson of historical necessity. See also Evan Carton, "Complicity and Responsibility in Pandarus' Bed and Chaucer's Art," *PMLA* 94 (1979): 47–61. Sherron E. Knopp, "The Narrator and his Audience in Chaucer's *Troilus and Criseyde*" (*Studies in Philology* 78 [1981]: 323–40) is also useful regarding the narrator's mediation of the poem's tensions and his competency. In her essay, "Paradis stood formed in hire yen: Courtly Love and Chaucer's Re-vision of Dante" (*Acts of Interpretation: The Text in Its Contexts 700–1600*, Mary J. Carruthers and Elizabeth D. Kirk, eds. [Norman, Okla.: Pilgrim, 1982], 257–77), Elizabeth D. Kirk sees Chaucer's technique as "that of juxtaposing multiple versions of the same event" in various voices in an effort to get to the "truth" of that event (276). Kirk believes that the *Commedia* and *Troilus and Criseyde* are the "two great retrospective analyses of 'courtly love' and its meaning in the larger universe of Christian revelation" (264–65). See Edvige Giunta, "Pandarus: Process and Pleasure in Artistic Creativity," *Medieval Perspectives* 6 (1991): 171–77 for a recent discussion of Pandarus as creative agent.

5. See R. A. Shoaf, *Chaucer, Dante, and the Currency of the Word* (Norman, Okla.: Pilgrim Books, 1983). Shoaf's argument that the reality of imagery means something different in hell, purgatory, and heaven is offered in succinct form on pages 22 ff., and it is an argument that informs his entire reading of the *Commedia*. Shoaf also discusses at some length the relationship between *speculatio*, or "the ascent to mystic vision of God" (21) and narcissism, a perversion of contemplative vision; in a consideration of the *Troilus*, this should invite us to recall the influence of the *Roman de la rose* on Chaucer. Here the two crystals in Narcissus's fountain (20439 ff.) are particularly relevant to Troilus's gaze into Criseyde's eyes.

6. There are suggestions throughout the *Troilus*, not the least of which is the implied sexual involvement with his niece, that Pandarus acts as a kind of diabolical go-between or guide for lovers, perhaps reminiscent of the serpent in the garden. Nonetheless, we do not perceive him as a fully evil figure, in part because he does indeed seem to be loyal (in his way) to Troilus and to help him win Criseyde, in part because he is liked and appreciated by the other characters, and in part—and perhaps most important—because of his humor and his extraordinary capacity for practical negotiations.

7. For a good, brief summary of Boccaccio's indebtedness to the lyric tradition for his composition of the *Filostrato*, see David Wallace, "Chaucer and Boccaccio's Early

Writings," in *Chaucer and the Italian Trecento*, ed. Piero Boitani (Cambridge: Cambridge University Press, 1983), 141—62. Another essay by Wallace, "*Troilus* and the *Filostrato*" in Shoaf and Cox's collection, is a useful piece on the uses Chaucer makes of Boccaccio.

8. Giovanni Boccaccio, *Il Filostrato*, Proemio 1–3, *I Classici Mondadori: Boccaccio II*, ed. Vittore Branca (Milan: Mondadori, 1964). All further references appear in the text, and all translations of the work are my own.

On the Chaucerian treatment of the material of the *proemio* of the *Filostrato*, see Robert W. Hanning's "Come in Out of the Code: Interpreting the Discourse of Desire in Boccaccio's *Filostrato* and Chaucer's *Troilus and Criseyde*," in Shoaf and Cox.

9. See Karla Taylor, *Chaucer Reads the "Divine Comedy"* (Stanford: Stanford University Press, 1989). Also note the essays by Richard Neuse and Karla Taylor in Shoaf and Cox.

10. Boccaccio's intimate knowledge of the *Commedia* can be seen throughout the *Filostrato* in various kinds of allusions (especially important are references to light and vision), but Boccaccio also takes the much more direct step of establishing in the "*Prima Parte*" that his poetic voice is moved by love of a lady and not divine love: "ma Amore / novellamente m'ha fatto mutare / il mio costume antico e usitato, / po' fui di te, madonna, innamorato" [but recently Love has made me change my custom since I fell in love with you, my lady] (1.1). This kind of renewal and inspiration for the renovation of inherited poetic material is simultaneously an imitation of and a challenge to Dante's use of Beatrice and Virgil.

Presence, Absence, and Difference: Reception and Deception in *The Franklin's Tale*

CYNTHIA A. GRAVLEE

For many years, readers of Geoffrey Chaucer's *The Canterbury Tales* accepted the bland assumption of the Franklin that his tale illustrated an ideal marriage distinguished by mutual understanding and appreciation.[1] To many contemporary scholars, however, the tale seems problematic as a manifesto on marriage. This change in perception can perhaps be accounted for by applying Hans Jauss's theory of aesthetic reception, which posits that both author and audience have a "horizon of expectations" that is shaped by history and culture; moreover, each generation of audiences has a wider horizon because of the accumulation of diachronic responses to the work. Authorial anticipation of an audience's response can be derived from the following presupposed factors:

> First, through familiar norms or the immanent poetics of the genre; second, through the implicit relationships to familiar works of the literary-historical surroundings; and third, through the opposition between fiction and reality, between the poetic and the practical function of language, which is always available to the reflective reader during the reading as a possibility of comparison.[2]

Although neither Chaucer nor the Franklin were students of literary theory or historiography, the text shows that they are both aware of an audience's generic expectations, engendered by literature and experience, and are both alert to the power of poetic language not only to reflect but to create reality. The modern reader, receiving and benefiting from centuries of Chaucer scholarship, can discern that Chaucer's broad horizon of expectations encompasses the Franklin's limited horizon, which is influenced by his fellow pilgrims and their tales, the courtly and mythic traditions, and the social conditioning of his era.

Having received these influences, the Franklin is attempting to establish a discourse with his contemporaries on courtship, love, marriage, and gender roles. However, the tale outwits the teller by thwarting the Franklin's efforts to validate his notions of appropriate behavior. The ostensible theme on the nature of marriage is subverted by the rhetorical interplay of differences. Such courtly concepts as truth, honor, freedom, and courtesy, which are present in the surface text and privileged as determinate, are displaced by their absent opposites from the subtext. These are displaced in turn, resulting in a dispersal of potential meaning and a deferral of textual closure. The continual subversions and displacements demonstrate the limitations and subjectivity of human perceptions as well as the deceptiveness of discourse and the concepts derived from it.

The Franklin, who claims to be a simple man unskilled in the "colours" of rhetoric (726),[3] tells a rhetorically complex tale characterized by struggles for dominance between such opposites as freedom/confinement, generosity/selfishness, patience/restiveness, and illusion/reality. The reversals of these concepts are compounded by the characters' discourses, which reveal misapprehensions about themselves and one another. Because of its state of flux, the tale resists closure. The Franklin's final question, "Which was the mooste fre?" (1622), shows that the issues raised by the tale have not been resolved. The Franklin, who seemed confident of his aims at the start, cannot answer his own question and is reduced to admitting, "I kan namoore; my tale is at an ende" (1624). Truth remains elusive as the Franklin relinquishes his authority.

In fact, the Franklin's credibility has been suspect all along, since the values he admires and attributes to the characters are absent, just as the mutuality he alleges is present in the marriage of Dorigen and Arveragus is subverted by Arveragus's assertion of authority. Whether we interpret "fre" as "generous" or "at liberty," it is clear that none of the characters qualify as "fre." They are motivated by self-interest and only give away what they cannot possess anyway or do not value highly.[4] Moreover, they are captives of their illusions, as well as society's mores. Qualities associated with Chaucer's redoubtable knight—truth, honor, freedom, courtesy, worthiness, and *gentilesse*—are declared to be present in the characters but are actually absent, along with the quality of patience, which is a virtue that none of them possess. The characters' actions consistently contradict their self-images as well as the Franklin's judgments of them.

Dorigen, during courtship, offers her "trouthe" to Arveragus to be his "humble trewe wyf" (758–59), yet she is inclined to defer truth and is dominated by illusion. Although she accedes to Arveragus's public mastery, she is uncomfortable with his decisions, brooding over his absences and desiring his presence. She frets about present reality, indulges in "derke fantasye" (844), and wishes the black rocks would miraculously disappear to insure her husband's return and her own happiness. The sea of troubles that Dorigen observes from the cliffs of Brittainy could be a metaphor for her marriage, which is rockier than she admits. She swears that she is a true and loyal wife, but she plays a game with Aurelius, promising to be his mistress if he will remove the rocks. Dorigen professes to believe that this miracle is impossible, yet she has already importuned God to bring it about. Aurelius's suffering is evident, and Dorigen—like a capricious courtly mistress—is willing to prolong it with a promise she thinks she will not keep.[5]

Although she persuades herself that it cannot happen, Dorigen too readily accepts the illusion of the disappearing rocks when it occurs, not even considering that time and tide could be responsible. Moreover, she ignores the reality that her own rash promise has caused her plight. Instead, she blames Fortune: "On thee Fortune, I pleyne / That unwar wrapped hast me in thy cheyne" (1355–56). Faced with the daunting prospect of yielding to Aurelius or the dishonorable alternative of breaking her promise, she contemplates suicide. Yet her lengthy catalogue of desperate women from the classical tradition seems to be an expedient for postponing death. Regardless of her invocation of suicidal role models, Dorigen clearly does not want to die or she would act instead of temporizing. She prefers games with no penalties for the losers, so she defers death, just as she has delayed consummation of Aurelius's desire.

Dorigen's voluntary confession to Arveragus indicates that she does not expect vengeance from him. She probably has the illusion that her lord will handle the situation by protecting her and confronting Aurelius, as would be natural and customary for any husband dealing with the attempted seduction of his wife. However, this "worthy" man, who has forsworn dominance, orders her to "trouthe holden" (1474) and to satisfy Aurelius as long as nobody knows the truth but the three of them. When Dorigen tells Aurelius that she is going "unto the gardyn, as my housband bad, / My trouthe for to holde—allas, allas!" (1512–13), she seems to lament not only the fulfillment of her promise but her husband's command that she do so.

Absolved of honoring her rash promise by Aurelius, Dorigen is supposedly "trewe" to Arveragus "for everemoore" (1555), yet the Franklin's contention seems unlikely. Neither Dorigen nor Arveragus have met one another's expectations in this situation, so recriminations seem inevitable. Moreover, the illusion of mutuality would be difficult to retain after Arveragus's assertion of mastery when he had once vowed to "take no maistrie / Agayn hir wyl, ne kithe hire jalousie, / But hire obeye, and folwe hir wyl in al" (747–49). The Franklin, who attests to a happy ending, seems to contradict his earlier warning that "Love wol nat been constreyned by maistrye. / Whan maistrie comth, the God of Love anon / Beteth his wynges, and farewell he is gon!" (764–66).

Dorigen's "honor" is allegedly saved, but she was not honorable or honest in gaming with Aurelius and arousing expectations that she did not intend to satisfy. She is hardly generous, since she never planned to give herself to Aurelius and dreads doing so at Arveragus's orders. She is not free of illusion and is a prisoner of convention throughout. Dorigen perhaps exhibits courtesy—or courtly behavior—by playing the decorous lady, first with Arveragus, then with Aurelius, yet the nobility of character inherent in *gentilesse* is not present. The patience in love extolled as "an heigh vertu" (773) by the Franklin is not practiced by Dorigen. She is impatient for Arveragus to return, she is impatient for the rocks to be covered and then uncovered, and she is eager to blame her problem on Fortune and then let Arveragus handle it.[6] Dorigen is obsessed with her own needs and avoids the truth she swears by.[7]

Her husband, Arveragus, is often cited for his "worthynesse" (735), but he does not seem to merit the accolade. At the start of their relationship, he is not only a long-suffering lover but also an opportunist pursuing a lady of high estate. With the movement from courtship to marriage, he will go from the subservient position of a suppliant lover to the superior rank of Dorigen's "lord" (742). Although he forsakes private mastery, he wants his "soveraynetee" (751) publicly acknowledged in order to preserve his manly image. Still, he exerts mastery over Dorigen when he leaves for England "To seke in armes worshipe and honour" (811) and remains for two years while she mopes at home. Once returned, he is impatient to be gone, for he is out of town when the rocks are covered. Indeed, he tends to be absent at key moments when his presence could be vital. It seems that he cherishes authority but shuns responsibility.

When the forlorn Dorigen confesses to him, Arveragus fails to challenge Aurelius for the sexual harassment of his wife. Instead, "with glad chiere in freendly wyse" (1467), he tells Dorigen to keep her promise. This is *noblesse oblige* carried to the extreme! A man who truly loved and respected his wife would not dismiss potential adultery so amiably.[8] It seems that Arveragus's real concern is neither Dorigen's honor nor her feelings but his public image. When he realizes that could be besmirched, he begins to weep and tells Dorigen not to *tell* the truth about what happens while she is *being* true to her vow.

Arveragus disregards Dorigen's suffering in his fidelity to a misconception of honor. Moreover, he does not trust the wife he supposedly loves, for he threatens her with death if she ever reveals the truth, and he sends servants to escort her to the garden where she will meet Aurelius. In spite of his promises, Arveragus is not free of his need for mastery, and he is more generous to his wife's aspiring seducer than to her. His plans seem directed toward humiliating Dorigen while he feigns generosity. He also subtly punishes Aurelius by lending Dorigen, then taking her away. A prisoner of his insecurities, Arveragus plays the role of worthy knight to meet public expectations and claims to honor the truth while suppressing it.

Arveragus's rival, Aurelius, could be his ironic doppelgänger. Both men are aspirants for the favors of a lady of higher estate, Dorigen, whom they eventually seek to dominate. Strangely, Arveragus and Aurelius never meet, for Arveragus is absent when Aurelius is present and vice versa. Aurelius's pursuit of Dorigen seems a reprise of her earlier courtship by Arveragus, but with sinister overtones that discredit his courtly facade.[9]

Although Aurelius thinks of himself as exhibiting *gentilesse* worthy of a knight, his motives are selfish throughout. In addition, he ignores truth, honor, freedom, courtesy, and patience. He meets the image of the stereotypical courtly lover in his years of nursing his hopeless passion for Dorigen, but he does not evince true chivalric behavior in trying to seduce a married woman who does not want him. When his pleas fail, he willingly resorts to black magic to attain his goals. He appears as the proverbial "snake in the grass" from the start, when he accosts Dorigen in the garden, trying to corrupt her as Satan did to Eve. And the magician, releasing Aurelius from his debt, seems to view him as an underworld denizen when he says, "I releesse thee thy thousand pound, / As thou right now were cropen out of the ground" (1613–14). And when Aurelius lusts for Dorigen, he "langwissheth as a furye dooth in helle" (950).

Aurelius, like Arveragus, has cultivated a respectable public image. Dorigen has known him as a "man of worshipe and honor" (962); hence, she is not on guard against him. In their first garden encounter, Aurelius seems carefree and debonair. The Franklin describes him much like the Knight's son, also a squire: "Daunced a squier biforn Dorigen / That fresher was and jolyer of array, / As to my doom, than is the month of May" (926–28). Moreover, he is "yong, strong, right vertuous, and riche and wys, / And wel biloved, and holden in greet prys" (933–34). But this "lusty squier, servant to Venus" (937) has a dark inner nature that does not match his pleasant exterior.

With Dorigen's stipulation about the rocks, the text moves from the garden world of warmth, light, tranquillity, and life to a psychological nether world of cold, darkness, madness, and death. Aurelius turns to pagan gods to help in his despair, approaching the sun god, Apollo, to intercede with his sister, Lucina, goddess of the moon, to send high tides and sink the black rocks into darkest Hell. The fire and brimstone of that domain are reminiscent of the elements used by alchemists and practitioners of the occult arts, such as the magician he eventually consults at Orleans, the known enclave of astrologers and necromancers. Aside from his brother, Aurelius confides in no one but keeps his guilty love more secret "than evere dide Pamphilus for Galathee" (1110). Just as Pamphilus secured a go-between to arrange an occasion for the rape of Galatea, Aurelius hatches his own plans to consummate his passion by using his brother and the magician to help him dupe Dorigen.

While his brother, who has once studied the occult, guides Aurelius to Orleans, they encounter a clerk who mysteriously knows their "entente" (1178). After leading them to his home, the clerk produces marvelous illusions to entertain his guests.[10] A hint of doom is introduced when this magician reveals that the brother's former comrades are all dead, but Aurelius is undeterred. Posing as a man of honor, Aurelius swears, "Ye shal be payed trewely, by my trouthe" (1231), to the magician. This rash promise is made when Aurelius is surely aware that he cannot comply with it. Later, he will reluctantly offer only half of the promised sum.

Aurelius has exacted Dorigen's promise in the bright romantic month of May; he now conspires with the powers of darkness in cold and bleak December. Storm and darkness accompany the magician's calculations on the high tides that enable him to cover the rocks temporarily, so Aurelius can urge Dorigen to honor her rash promise, although he is unable to honor his. Moreover, he willingly purveys illusion while demanding truth from Dorigen.

When Aurelius finally releases Dorigen from her promise after all of his machinations, it is surely not generosity on his part but the realization that his love will be forever unrequited and that her body is merely a loan, not a possession. He can, however, demonstrate his power over Dorigen by releasing her. She is at his mercy until he says, "I yow releasse Madame, into your hond" (1533). In addition, he can improve his image by manifesting the *gentilesse* expected of a knight, although he is only a squire. He asserts, "Thus kan a squier doon a gentil dede / As wil as kan a knyght, withouten drede" (1543–44). This apparently generous deed is actually a way of competing with Arveragus, who may surpass Aurelius in love but not in courtesy.[11]

Aurelius also knows that he does not have the thousand-pound fee for the magician, and he may hope that relinquishing Dorigen can clear his debt, as indeed it does. Aurelius has been impatient, untruthful, dishonorable, selfish, and uncourtly in attempting to fulfill his needs. He only gives up Dorigen when he realizes she has come because of the grace of Arveragus, to whom she will return. Like Arveragus, he has never sought mutuality in his relationship with Dorigen but has used servility to inspire pity initially and "generosity" to attain psychological mastery ultimately.

Aurelius's handy brother does not deserve a commendation for generosity either. Watching Aurelius languish in misery, the brother becomes impatient for his recovery, but he does not seek a constructive cure for the lovesickness. Instead, he begins to weep and wail himself, but "pryvely" (1116). Like Aurelius and Arveragus, he hides weakness. When he remembers that the black arts he once studied could remove the black rocks, the brother seems just as interested in punishing Dorigen as in helping Aurelius. He decides that Aurelius can be "warisshed of his wo," but also that Dorigen "nedes holden hire biheste / or elles he shal shame hire atte leeste" (1162–64). The brother then conspires to damage a marriage; he educates Aurelius in the black arts; and he encourages uncourtly, ungenerous, and unmanly behavior.

The accommodating magician is hardly generous for waiving his fee, since he knows that Aurelius is unable to pay it. Also, it could be convenient to have Aurelius forever grateful and forever obligated. The magician's statement, "Thou hast ypayed wel for my vitaille" (1618), could imply that in nourishing and endorsing a practitioner of the diabolic arts, Aurelius has unwittingly sustained a spiritual loss. The magician's earlier ambiguous question, "Have I nat holden covenant unto thee?" (1585), could hint at a more sinister agreement than Aurelius supposes, for once bound to the devil or his disciples, one is never "fre." And the magician's release of Aurelius can be seen as a form of control. Just as Aurelius has sought to rival Arveragus in generosity and to establish power over Dorigen by releasing her from her vow, the magician plays the role of benefactor. Echoing Aurelius's words to Dorigen, he swears: "But if a Clerk koude doon a gentil dede / As wel as any of yow, it is no drede! / Sire, I releesse thee thy thousand pound" (1610–13). This seems yet another power play masquerading as generosity.

Although the Franklin has purported to speak of mutuality in relationships, each character seeks sovereignty: Dorigen over Aurelius; Arveragus over Dorigen; Aurelius over Dorigen; the magician over Aurelius; and the brother as a controlling mentor to Aurelius. Each has a different notion of truth: it is always what serves him or her best. Dorigen, in believing she is true to Arveragus, compromises truth with her game-playing; Arveragus and Aurelius hold Dorigen to "truth" that can only hurt her and them while evading truth themselves; the brother and the magician are eager to portray illusion as truth. Honor, in each case, is concerned with image and reputation and not with ethics. Although superficial courtliness is depicted through role-playing, true *gentilesse* is not shown.

Patience is absent from everyone's agenda. Arveragus is impatient to pursue his career while love can wait; Dorigen is impatient for his presence and for her satisfaction; Aurelius is impatient to sate his lust; the brother is impatient to please Aurelius and to relieve himself of being a caretaker; and the magician is impatient to prove his skill and to claim his reward. All are guilty of appropriating tradition and manipulating others to suit their own devices. All of the qualities stated as present are actually absent, displaced by their opposites, regardless of the Franklin's plan or the perceptions of the characters. All of the characters are illusionists who create and believe in their fantasies.

Even the Franklin seems to suffer from illusion. Despite his pretensions to sophistication, he exhibits naiveté through his notions that the tale portrays mutuality in marriage and that his characters are exemplars of courtliness. The Franklin possibly believes that his tale and his support of courtly principles can enhance his image with his peers and his superiors. His flattery of the Squire for telling an inchoate tale and for being a role model for his own flawed son shows that the Franklin has some social insecurity that prompts him to curry favor with those of higher rank. He is easily coerced by the Host into telling a tale that he hopes "may plesen" (707).[12]

The Franklin has tried to meet generic expectations and to observe social conventions with his tale, but he may have misconceived his mission and misjudged his audience. Although the Franklin's question, "Which was the mooste fre, as thynketh yow?" (1622), is in the tradition of the *demande* that sometimes is used at the end of folktales or romances to generate discussion, none ensues. Despite the debates on marriage that have already taken place, the pilgrims seem at a loss to sort out "truth" from the ambiguous tale and provocative question.[13] In fact, the Franklin does not wait for an answer. He may think that all of the characters are so "fre" that it is difficult to choose the most exemplary, or he may suddenly perceive that he has subverted his own assertions throughout. He quickly adds, "I kan namoore; my tale is at an ende" (1624).

While the pilgrims may be pondering the nature of an effective marriage, the modern reader, who has received almost six centuries of responses, can perceive that marriage is not the central issue in the tale. It may be the Franklin's ostensible subject; however, it is a subject fraught with more complexities than he has anticipated. The subject of marriage actually serves as a vehicle for Chaucer's ultimate object: to illustrate the illusory nature of rhetoric and the difficulty of establishing univocal truth or of bringing any issue to complete closure.

The open ending of this tale that is allegedly about "open marriage" is in accord with the modus operandi of *The Canterbury Tales* as a whole.[14] The structure of the text as a frame story indicates that closure is intended. Yet, the tales within the frame never reach the boundaries set up at the start. Moreover, "The Franklin's Tale" does not follow the linear direction that the Franklin intends. Instead, it constantly surprises, overturning and re-turning itself in cycles of displacement and replacement. However, nonclosure does not mean stasis. In "The Franklin's Tale," as in the entire work, the "horizon of expectations" is always expanding, so the possibilities for an aesthetic of reception are boundless.

Notes

1. See George Lyman Kittredge, "Chaucer's Discussion of Marriage," *Modern Philology* 9 (1911–12): 435–67, who argues that the tale is a culmination of the marriage discussion and that the Franklin expresses Chaucer's view of an ideal marriage; see also Kathryn Jacobs, "The Marriage Contract of the *Franklin's Tale*: The Remaking of Society," *Chaucer Review* 20 (1985): 132–43, who thinks the marriage is a microcosm of an ideal society; and see Anne Scott, "'Considerynge the Beste on Every Syde': Ethics, Empathy, and Epistemology in the *Franklin's Tale*," *Chaucer Review* 29 (1995): 390–411, who claims that the tale "asserts and reasserts the stabilizing influence of the spoken word, of promises made and fulfilled, and of faithful love" (390).

2. Hans Robert Jauss, *Toward an Aesthetic of Reception*, trans. Timothy Bahti, intro. Paul de Man, vol. 2 of Theory and History of Literature (Minneapolis: University of Minnesota Press, 1982), 24.

3. Geoffrey Chaucer, *The Riverside Chaucer*, gen. ed. Larry D. Benson, 3d ed. (Boston: Houghton Mifflin, 1987), based on *The Works of Geoffrey Chaucer*, ed. F. N. Robinson, 2d ed. (1957) . All quotations will be from "The Franklin's Tale," Fragment V (Group F), and will be listed by line number in my text.

4. See D. W. Robertson Jr., "Chaucer's Franklin and His Tale," *Essays in Medieval Culture* (Princeton: Princeton University Press, 1980), 273–90, who thinks that no one is

generous, because it is "impossible to be generous with something to which one has no right" (290).

5. See Robert B. Burlin, *Chaucerian Fiction* (Princeton: Princeton University Press, 1977), who is unsympathetic to Dorigen, seeing her treatment of Aurelius as "maliciously parodic of the 'daungerous' courtly mistress—professing to be motivated by pity . . . but pitiless in its seeming impossibility" (200–201). Also see Susan Crane, *Gender and Romance in Chaucer's Canterbury Tales* (Princeton: Princeton University Press, 1994), who believes that Dorigen's behavior is shaped by the romance genre and that her "desire to refuse is at odds with courtly discourses that do not admit a language of refusal" (65); see also Angela Jane Weisl, *Conquering the Reign of Femeny: Gender and Genre in Chaucer's Romances*, Chaucer Studies 22 (Cambridge, England: D. S. Brewer, 1995), who agrees that Dorigen is constrained by gender and genre, trapped "between the conventions of romance and the reality of the outside . . . in which she is forced to function" (114).

6. See A. M. Kearney, "Truth and Illusion in *The Franklin's Tale*," *Essays in Criticism* 19 (1969): 245–53, who believes Dorigen and Aurelius are similar: "querulous and impatient" (248).

7. See Effie Jean Mathewson, "The Illusion of Morality in *The Franklin's Tale*," *Medium Aevum* 52 (1983): 27–37, who defends Dorigen and explains, "For Dorigen, to be *trewe* is to be faithful to Arveragus" (28). See also Ann Thompson Lee, "'A Woman True and Fair': Chaucer's Portrayal of Dorigen in the *Franklin's Tale*," *Chaucer Review* 19 (1984–85): 177, who believes that Dorigen is a lovable person, central to the tale, and that the Franklin sympathizes with her because "his deepest allegiance is to the truth of the human heart, not the truth of abstract moral values." Mary R. Bowman, "'Half As She Were Mad': Dorigen in the Male World of *The Franklin's Tale*," *Chaucer Review* 27 (1993): 239–51, thinks that Dorigen is undervalued and that "both the narrator and his male characters show frequent disregard for Dorigen as a person" (241); moreover, they see her as a commodity—"property that men exchange among themselves to demonstrate their moral worth" (242). Carolynn Van Dyke, "The Clerk's and Franklin's Subjected Subjects," *Studies in the Age of Chaucer* 17 (1995): 45–68, believes that "Chaucer makes Dorigen comparable to the male characters in moral agency" (52–53); she is more fully developed than her prototype in Chaucer's source: "not simply more sympathetic but also more reflective, serious, and deliberate—in short, a more fully human subject" (53).

8. See Derek Pearsall, "*The Franklin's Tale*, Line 1469: Forms of Address in Chaucer," *Studies in the Age of Chaucer* 17 (1995): 69–78, who argues that Arveragus is not kindly attempting to comfort Dorigen; instead, the use of the vocative can be seen as a condescending attempt to assert power.

9. See Lee, who thinks Aurelius's portrait is "distressingly similar to that of Arveragus" (172); see also Crane, who agrees that "Aurelius tries to double the absent Arveragus in the *Franklin's Tale*" (29).

10. See Mary Flowers Braswell, "The Magic of Machinery: A Context for Chaucer's *Franklin's Tale*," *Mosaic* 18 (1985): 101–10, who shows that the technology for such special effects was known and available and that illusion was used for entertainment. See also Joyce Tally Lionarons, "Magic, Machines, and Deception: Technology in *The Canterbury Tales*," *Chaucer Review* 27 (1993): 377–86, who sees both the usefulness and the danger in such technology. "It . . . can be used to deceive; . . . it can sometimes deceive the technician" into believing he has God-like powers (385).

11. See Alan T. Gaylord, "From Dorigen to the Vavasour: Reading Backwards," in *The Olde Daunce: Love, Friendship, Sex, and Marriage in the Medieval World*, ed. Robert R. Edwards and Stephen Spector (Albany: SUNY, 1991), 177–200 and 284–87,

who thinks that there is some ambiguity over who is speaking in lines 1541–49. The Franklin could be taking over from Aurelius in 1541–44, and perhaps Chaucer himself enters the text, since line 1549, "it were impossible me to wryte," seems to preclude the Franklin, who doesn't have writing materials at hand (179–82). In any case, the speaker seems to cite Aurelius's generosity, which I contest.

12. See Robertson, 273–90, who says that the Franklin's "gentilesse" is in accord with his "concern for externals" (290). Mary J. Carruthers, "The Gentilesse of Chaucer's Franklin," *Criticism* 23 (1981): 283–300, takes a more tolerant view of the Franklin as a gentleman with sound principles.

13. See Janemarie Luecke, "Dorigen: Marriage Model or Male Fantasy," *Journal of Women's Studies in Literature* 1 (1979):107–21, who argues that the Franklin "cannot include Dorigen in the closing *demande d'amour* . . . since she is not an active agent" (118). On the other hand, David Raybin, "'Wommen, of Kynde, Desiren Libertee': Rereading Dorigen, Rereading Marriage," *Chaucer Review* 27 (1992): 65–86, considers Dorigen "the most fre" because of her independent and noble spirit that inspires the men.

14. See Michaela Paasche Grudin, "Discourse and the Problem of Closure in the *Canterbury Tales*," *PMLA* 107 (1992): 1157–67, who notes that Chaucer avoids a "conventional closure" and instead "focuses our interest on the processes of communication, on the dynamics of discourse as social interaction itself" (1157). The "oral quality" of the *Canterbury Tales* "shows Chaucer's pronounced interest in the social interactions of discourse" (1163).

The Conquest of Femenye:
Desire, Power, and Narrative
in Chaucer's *Knight's Tale*

ROBERT M. STEIN

It is a commonplace of criticism that Chaucer's *Knight's Tale* is concerned with the problems of two kinds of order: on the one hand, there is the problem of artistic control that appears throughout the tale in various registers—the Knight-narrator's performance with intractable materials, for example, or Chaucer's elaborate cutting of the *Teseida* and his return to Statius's *Thebaid* for elements of both matter and style; on the other hand, there is the problem of political control that forms the *content* of the tale and indeed the content of the tale's sources, the question, as Muscatine and then Hanning put it, of the struggle between a "noble design and chaos."[1] Let us remind ourselves, to begin with, that both matters appear in the text from the side of the negative. Artistic control is visible primarily as a set of doubts and questions about how to order the material. It is especially visible in the employment of the narrative device of *occupatio*, the refusal (in many cases to be sure an ironic refusal) to narrate. But that is not all. The Knight-narrator is present throughout the tale, shifting perspective, dropping one thread to pick up another, telling the audience how much more there is to say, and at one moment even saying that if his listeners want more information than he has time for, they can find it in Statius.[2] Similarly, Theseus's activities as a warrior and as a prince, which are in the realm of politics what the narrator's are in the realm of aesthetics, are throughout the narrative reactive: his favorite word is "'amendment'" (which appears in a rhyming position both at the beginning of the tale and at the end, in its verbal form, in each case rhyming with "offend") (909–10, 3065–66). There is always a preexisting situation to fix or change, and Theseus as a prince unleashes violence in the name of *pax et iustitia* to subdue outbreaks of private or political violence, defiance of law, or violations of right.[3] In both cases then, the assertion of control appears to be a negation of a previous state, an imposition of order on something by its nature disorderly, chaotic, and needing control. Part of my purpose in this essay is to investigate the structure of this appearance. Is chaos, as our conventional reading of the *Knight's Tale* suggests, the true beginning?

Where does the *Knight's Tale* begin? We may answer this question in several ways. Narratively, the tale begins most obviously with the voice of the Knight: "Whilom as olde stories tellen us." Yet, in referring to "olde stories," these words make an immediate acknowledgment that the tale in fact does not begin with the Knight's narration but preexists this telling. This most marked beginning is not a beginning at all. Rather, the first narrative act is a citation, the appropriation and transformation of a tale that once belonged to someone else. Perhaps, then, the tale begins with the actual citation, "Iamque domos patrias, Scithice post aspera gentis / Prelia, laurigero subeuntem Thesea curru." That is to say, it begins not with the Knight-narrator at all but with a piece of text, the manuscript inscription lifted from Statius's narrative of the destruction of Thebes.[4] Considered this way, the *Knight's Tale* begins by marking a position for itself in an intertextual array, an array with a preexistent set of political and aesthetic meanings, for in the epic, as the genre was understood in Chaucer's time, the political and aesthetic are inseparable. The generic marks of epic—language, meter, elevated style—also signify the presence of a political, indeed world-historical content. Moreover, those generic marks are also inseparable from the epic's claim to practical seriousness: the epic, whose content is political action on the grandest scale, was most often read as a book of advice for princes.[5]

Or perhaps the *Knight's Tale* has begun already in the *General Prologue* with the choice of the first teller in Harry Bailey's game:

> Were it by aventure or sort or cas
> The sothe is this: the cut fil to the Knyght,
> Of which ful blithe and glad was every wyght.
>
> (844–46)

The Knight goes first in the game, as the Knight's profile comes first "accordant to resoun" in the *General Prologue*, and as most readers agree, this coincidence of reason and chance is too good to be true. Donaldson surely is not the first to have had the suspicion: the draw must have been fixed.[6] But then the game itself may well be fixed: the Knight goes first, the Knight finishes first, and "ful blithe and glad was every wyght." Or at least they should be, as the coincidence strongly implies. If the draw can be fixed, the storytelling contest threatens to become merely a pretense with nothing at stake, not even a supper at Harry's bar. Perhaps the Knight's constant anxiety about the success of his performance is actually an ironic indication of his superior gamesmanship in the quintessentially chivalric game of the renaissance courtier *avant la lettre*, the predetermined winner playing as if there were a real game:

> I wol nat letten eek noon of this route;
> Lat every felawe telle his tale aboute,
> And lat se now who shal the soper wynne?

> (889–91)

And the close? The closure of the *Knight's Tale* is a problem of form that looks like a problem of content.[7] Because the peace of the state is not the elimination of violence but rather its monopolization, the very possibility of aesthetic closure in a story of princely success is the sign of the control of violence purely by princely means, namely political stability, dynastic continuity, and the permanence of the state. The *Knight's Tale* thus closes with the dynastic wedding of Emily and Palamon, a wedding that solves two related political problems. On the one hand, it makes possible the continuation of the Theban blood line and therefore of Thebes itself; on the other hand, the wedding is also the sign and instrument of the alliance between Athens and Thebes. The alliance is made on Athenian terms and it serves to neutralize Thebes as a political threat to Athenian hegemony: the wedding implements an Athenian parliamentary decision

> To have with certein contrees alliaunce,
> And have fully of Thebans obeisaunce

> (2973–74)

This desirable alliance has been made possible by the prior conquest of the *regne* of Femenye, Emily in the process becoming Theseus's sister so that he has gained, in his power as *paterfamilias*, the legal disposition of her life. Aesthetic closure in the *Knight's Tale* thus rests on the political figure of Theseus in his three different and theoretically quite separable abilities to wield power—as prince of Athens, as the warrior who conquered the reign of Femenye, and as a great lord who has in his proprietary power the disposition of lives and property.[8] Or else dramatically considered, narrative closure allows others to compete for the prize supper. The sign of the continuity of the state in the political sphere, closure is in the social sphere the sign of the continuation of the game of storytelling. The story thus closes with blessings on "al this faire compaignye" (3108). Or else the story closes in a response from the company itself, where it immediately reveals in the fellowship of sundry folk what has always been denied in their characterization by the Chaucerian narrator, the fact of class division:

> In al the route nas ther yong ne oold
> That he ne seyde it was a noble storie
> And worthy for to drawen to memorie,
> And namely the gentils everichon
>
> (3110–13)

And thus it instigates what looks like political violence, an expropriation of the game by a new teller of a new tale performed under new rules. But this tale, too, has also already begun. For, as we all know, the Miller rewrites what the Knight has already spoken by taking the words out of his mouth.

What I have been suggesting, then, is that at the edges of the story we may find the same contradictions that motivate the telling of the story and that are inscribed within it as its content and its aesthetic mode. They are already in play before the story has properly begun, and they are still in play after narrative closure has properly been reached. And at the edges of the story these same contradictions are alternately visible in the sphere of politics and in the sphere of art.

With what then does the *Knight's Tale* properly open? With an act of state violence and with the refusal to narrate. Theseus is a warrior, prince, and feudal *dominus*, a multiple status insisted upon immediately by the rhyming combinations of his introduction at the very beginning of the tale:

> Whilom as olde stories tellen us,
> Ther was a duc that highte Theseus;
> Of Atthenes he was lord and governour,
> And in his tyme swich a conquerour
>
> (859–62)

This lord, governor, and conqueror has conquered the "regne of Femenye" and is bringing back Hippolyta, now his wife, and Emily, now his sister, in triumph to Athens. The opening scene of the story, a glorious homecoming, is immediately interrupted twice: the first time by the narrator, who deflects the narrative from the direct presentation of the scene to the problem of what to tell; the second time by the "compaignye of ladyes," who petition the state for redress of grievance. Lamenting their unburied husbands at Thebes, an atrocity of state violence, they instigate a new act of state violence as Theseus leaves his triumphal return home for a military raid to avenge them. No sooner, then, does the tale open than it is opened by its own mechanisms. In the sphere of narrative and in the sphere of content, the story is interrupted and deflected. These interruptions have many functions. Among them, they establish a narrative principle of deflection and discontinuity that structures the tale as a whole.

I want to isolate and look briefly now at five structural entities, each of which comes into being in this interruption. Any more than a brief look would involve untying the complex knot of the text, a procedure that can only be done slowly and in detail. Here I will isolate only the five entities as a preliminary indication of what needs to be done. The five structural entities that I want to discuss can each be understood as a rhetorical/imagistic/narrative series: what I call the series of political action, the series of desire, the series of storytelling, the series of explanation, and the series of suffering flesh.[9] I will briefly present each series and then return to this moment of textual opening to draw some conclusions about the political and aesthetic textualization of the *Knight's Tale*.

The Series of Political Action

The series of political action can look like the content of the *Knight's Tale*. It serves to install Theseus as a narrative center and to articulate the genre of the tale as epic. In brief, Theseus conquers Femenye, intervenes in Thebes to avenge and correct the atrocity of the unburied dead, arrests Palamon and Arcite, releases and banishes Arcite, intervenes in their private battle, and enforces the peace of the state by arranging the tournament. He builds the theater, hosts the knights, rewards them and escorts them out of town, buries Arcite, and arranges the marriage of Palamon and Emily at the end. It is no accident that this series is in the first instance organized as a plot, which we may justly call the Theseus plot since, as my summary intends to make clear, Theseus is the busy agent of all the action. But the Theseus plot is not the only action in this series although there is a strong desire within the tale to assert his sole agency. There is also the constant threat, imagined variously and at various times by Palamon and Arcite, of public or private war and of armed uprising against Athens by Thebes. There is moreover the private battle between Palamon and Arcite, the unforgettable Homeric simile of the hunter standing at the gap in the "regne of Trace," hearing the lion or bear charging through the bushes and becoming in the simile the hunted rather than the hunter (1638–46), and the many notations throughout the tale of the existence of political violence, "the murmure and the cherles rebellyng" (2459). Essentially, this series is structured by a simple binary opposition between activity and passivity, or to put it more accurately, the series structures the tale into a logic based on active/passive oppositions, a structure of force. As such, the whole series of political action becomes in the text itself a sign of the logic of force and declares that force is the underlying reality of all action even as it wants to legitimize the action of Theseus alone.

The Series of Desire

The series of desire looks like the other content of the *Knight's Tale*. Within this series the *Knight's Tale* is no longer the story of Theseus but of Palamon and Arcite. Not Theseus but Emily, the object of the cousin's desire, is the narrative center, and by means of such centering the genre is marked as romance rather than epic.[10] The relationship of Theseus to Hippolyta, their imminent wedding and the celebrations attending it, all transform a scene of military conquest into the setting for enamorment, both their own and especially the enamorment of Palamon and Arcite, whose story the *Knight's Tale* principally becomes. Just as we find it in Ovid's love poems, the world of epic action loses its political focus and forms merely a background to a story of private experience, the story of Palamon, Arcite, and Emily, the vicissitudes of their love longing and its resolution. Violence becomes romance performance, an occasion for chivalric display, as the narrator underscores in his reflections on the desire of all the knights in the land to be invited to participate in the tournament:

> To fighte for a lady, benedicitee!
> It were a lusty sighte for to see
>
> (2115–16)

In the series of desire, the fact of gender and gender difference is crucial in its relation both to the generic possibilities of romance and to the continual creation of the positions of subject and object in the text.

Although the love plot converges on Emily, she is little more than a device of narrative centering, subject to the necessities of romance resolution. The two cousins fall in love with what the narrative presents as a view of her from behind, a long golden braid hanging down her back (1049–51). And Theseus, finding the two men fighting for love of her, is amused by how removed she is from any agency in the plot:

> But this is yet the beste game of alle,
> That she for whom they han this jolitee
> Kan hem therfore as muche thank as me.
> She woot namoore of al this hoote fare,
> By God, than woot a cokkow or an hare!

(1806–10)

Just as the political resolution rests on the multiple positions of power occupied by Theseus, the resolutions of desire rest on Emily's double subjection both to Theseus, who will arrange her marriage ultimately to Palamon, and to the imaginative necessities of the romance genre—to what Adrienne Rich has memorably termed "compulsory heterosexuality."[11] Although Emily prays to Diana that she be allowed to remain her devotee, a virgin huntress, and thus to have a place, as it were, out of the story, her prayer is the one prayer in the poem that will not be granted in any way; in a tale filled with alternative possibilities, there is no alternative to the constraints of the genre that requires Emily thus to love and marry.[12] The series of desire gives rise to the structured opposition of subject/object and to the gendering of that opposition. The language of subjectivity in the poem emerges from it primarily as masculine love longing in the lyric mode but also in many other reflective modes, always a property in the poem of a male character.[13] The poem's first part, for example, ends with the narrator addressing the audience as "yow loveres" and inviting them to judge and debate which of the two men is in the worst situation (1346–54). Similarly, the poem is filled with other male self-reflective moments such as Theseus's revisions of earlier decisions rashly made, and his nostalgic recollections of his feelings as a young man. In all such moments, the masculine subject comes into being as such by taking his own past actions and feelings as the object of his attention, an attention that is always accompanied by a degree of erotic investment.

The Series of Storytelling

The series of storytelling comprises the whole mechanism by which the text overtly acknowledges artistry. We have in this series not only the activity of the narrator, who at times refuses to narrate, narrates at other times in detail, and moves around in the story from one character or incident to another. We have also the building of the tournament theater, the descriptions of the temples, the notations about Theseus's hiring artists, how "lifly" they painted, and how much the materials cost—the acknowledgment in both the narrative performance and in the narrative content that art comes into being by human work. The series makes for an independent layer of content in the tale, a reflection on human work, but the independent content nevertheless continually brings the first two series into play: the discourse of art and artistry is either in the language of force—as for example, when the narrator refuses to narrate, as he says, in order not to hinder others from telling (or from the passive side, "But al that thyng I mot as now forbere" [885])—or in the language of desire—the desire for the story and the simultaneous desire for the end of the story. What enters the text in the series of storytelling is always a metonymy because, by acknowledging that it is the outcome of a series of deliberations, it always presents itself as only one part of a larger supply of material that could have entered the text at that moment but did not. Narrative practice such as this, which overtly acknowledges the continual decisions that result in the story we happen to be reading at the moment, is a very particular form of narrative self-consciousness. It stands in the sharpest contrast, for example, to an equally self-conscious practice that results in the effacement of the role of the narrator and the concomitant denial of choice within the story world. In the Old French *La Mort le Roi Artu*, for example, the continual narrative linking by means of such expressions as "Mes atant lesse ore li contes a parler de lui" [But now the story stops speaking about him] or "En ceste partie dit li contes que " [In this part, the story says that] serves to create a sense of tremendous inevitability to the action and of finality to the tale.[14] The tale asserts itself over and over again as a body of information existing independent of any particular telling of it. And the tale as it has been told before stands behind the particular instance of discourse as its guarantee of truth. In fact, we should not speak here of tale-telling at all but rather of recording or of writing in the sense of writing down or documenting. Within the framework of *La Mort Artu*, there is no possible imaginative alternative to what happens to the characters or to what the tale tells, and the text confronts its reader as an unalterable document. In the *Knight's*

Tale, on the other hand, we are always confronted with the fact that the tale, in the process of its unfolding, could be otherwise, that in order to do one thing, something else equally plausible to entertain will not be done, and in order to narrate one thing, something else equally likely to have been narrated at that moment will not be told. The whole tale thus becomes an instance of something that could well have gone otherwise, just as what enters the text inevitably needs to be read against what did not enter the text but could have. In this way the possibilities for both political and artistic agency become in the *Knight's Tale* analogous centers of attention in their own right.

The Series of Explanation

Sooner or later in the poem, every character—with the singular exception of Hippolyta, who uniquely remains totally silent throughout—attempts to give an account of what has been going on in the poem, to make sense of the situations they find themselves in. What is most important about this series is that all the characters assert a passive position with respect to events, or, again more accurately, they all see themselves as passive constructions of the rest of the text. This applies as well to the Knight-narrator's language as to the characters' language regarding themselves and their actions. The structure of this series is the logic of the allegorical sign: event, situation, the material—this is the signifier; intention is the signified. The signifier appears as the outside or visible manifestation of an intention that lies either deep within or far beyond. Whatever can be seen must be endlessly scrutinized to discover what it can reveal about the will of the gods, or fate, or chance.

The Series of Suffering Flesh

What I call the series of suffering flesh is most important. As content, it appears independent and independently organized, but it is neither. This series emerges from all the others and appears as their exterior. It appears, that is to say, as what needs to be controlled, what needs to be explained, what forms all demand. Passivity, objectivity, and the signifier all coalesce as dead matter and imprisonment; activity, subjectivity, and signification as desired and impossible release. In this series are all the calamities of desire depicted in the temple of Venus, all the uncontrolled and pathetic violence of Mars, all the identity changes and personal transformations of Diana. The text of the *Knight's Tale* is littered with corpses—the unburied bodies being eaten by dogs outside of Thebes or the pile of bodies after Theseus's raid, where the pillagers do their business; "the careyne in the busk with his throte ycorve" (2013) in the temple of Mars, or Palamon, who starts up "out of the buskes thikke" "with face deed and pale" (1578–79). Arcite is imprisoned in that pile of corpses and then imprisoned in a tower, imprisoned in love sickness, imprisoned in his armor, imprisoned in his rotting body, imprisoned in the "foul prison of this life," imprisoned in his grave, "alone withouten any compaignye." Theseus's great Boethian speech on the perfection of a creation knit together by "the faire cheyne of love" (2988) is a precise demonstration of this exteriority: creation, life, and universal power, all objects of desire, manifest themselves in experience solely as death and destruction.

All but the last of these series is an independent body of content structured on its own principles. Each series is itself a metonymic chain that nevertheless functions as a metaphoric equivalent of all the others; each may at any time substitute for another or refer to another by a kind of analogy. Without ever "standing for" a preexistent reality, these first four series form a surface of representation that gives rise, by what is necessarily jettisoned from them, to the effect of a preexistent, natural, unstructured reality—the fifth series: the inevitability of death, the missing object of an overwhelming desire, or of chaos waiting for a noble design. And this reference always makes for a sense of activity as controlling something by its nature out of control, as attaining something by its nature beyond reach, or especially of amendment, as stabilizing something corrupted. Thus the imagined end of action—unity, harmony, private fulfillment—is always asserted to be its true beginning, and the end is conceived to be the recovery of a lost origin and lost happiness:

> For nature has not taken his bigynnyng
> Of no partie or cantel of a thyng,
> But of a thyng that parfit is and stable,
> Descendynge so til it be corrumpable
>
> (3007–10)

Let us return now to the opening of the text. The opening scene of the story, I have said, is interrupted twice. From the standpoint of the romance that the first interruption inaugurates, the conquest of Femenye need not be narrated because it is mere background, a device to get Emily into the garden in Athens. And the second interruption is similarly merely a device to get Theseus to Thebes so that he can bring back

Palamon and Arcite to begin the love plot, the real story. Boccaccio, in fact, suggests this very reading in one of his glosses to the *Teseida* while nevertheless devoting the whole first book of the poem to Theseus's campaign against the Amazons and another elaborately narrated section to the war against Thebes:

> Con cìo sia cosa che la principale intenzione dell'autore di questo libretto sia di trattare dell'amore e delle cose avvenute per quello, da due giovani tebani, cioé Arcita e Palemone, ad Emilia amazona, sì come nel suo proemio appare, potrebbe alcuno, e giustamente, adimandare che avesse qui a fare la guerra di Teseo con le donne amazone, della quale solamente parla il primo libro di questa opera. Dico, e brievamente, che l'autore a niuno altro fine queste cose scrisse, se non per mostrare onde Emilia fosse venuta ad Attene, e perciò che la materia, cioè li costumi della predette donne amazone, è alquanto pellegrina alle più genti, e perciò più piacevole, la volle alquanto più distesamente porre che per avventura non bisognava; e il simigliante fa della sconfitta data da Teseo a Creonte, re di Tebe, per dichiarare donde e come alle mani di Teseo pervenissero Arcita e Palemone.

> [Because the principal intention of the author of this little book is to treat of the love of the two Thebans Arcita and Palemone for Emilia the Amazon, and to narrate the events that happened because of it, just as appears in the prologue, perhaps someone could justly ask what Theseus's war against the Amazon women, of which the whole first book of this work speaks, is doing here. I say, briefly, that the author wrote these things with no other purpose than to show how Emilia was led to Athens; and since the material—that is to say, the customs of the aforementioned amazon women—is somewhat strange to many people and therefore rather pleasant, he wanted to set it down somewhat more at length than perhaps was necessary. And he does this similarly with the defeat given by Theseus to Creon, king of Thebes, to explain how and why Arcita and Palemone fell into the hands of Theseus.][15]

Chaucer eliminates the first book of the *Teseida* and replaces it with the narrator's refusal to narrate. The main narrative line is thus broken open shortly after it has begun in the *Knight's Tale* and resumed with Theseus's successful return home from Thebes "with laurer crowned as a conquerour" (1027), Chaucer's rendering of the lines from Statius that form the epigraph. While making a show of getting the story underway and eliminating material deemed unnecessary even by the author of his source, nothing of what is left out is mere background and none of the narrative maneuvering is merely play; it is all essential. Chaucer in effect ironically refuses the Ovidian choice of making epic action into the scene for romance, a story of the private play of desire, as Boccaccio's rendering suggests. Rather, in the narrative opening of the *Knight's Tale*, epic and romance confront each other continually as all the series are put into play from both the active and passive sides—Power, in the conquest of Femenye and in the lament of the Theban ladies, Storytelling in the narrator's interruption and in Theseus's demand for the story of the ladies, Desire in the wedding of Hippolyta and in the bereaved ladies' grief, Explanation in Theseus's own interestingly mistaken interpretation of the ladies' lament and in their self-presentation as signs. The revelation of a heap of dead bodies becomes the occasion for all the action, and the result of this revelation is the creation of a second heap of dead bodies out of which Palamon and Arcite will be torn to dwell in prison perpetually. The logic of force, all subject-object relations, all demands for action, and the accumulation of death and suffering are all constituted here and constituted in the particular relations to one another that create the texture of the *Knight's Tale*.

In this opening, the mechanisms for closure are also fully put in play. The crisis in the Theban royal bloodline is resolved in a political alliance between Athens and Thebes that contains the threat to the state represented by Palamon and Arcite's very existence and the threat to the patriarchy represented by the existence of a realm of Amazon women. As I noted before, the political resolution is made possible only by the prior subjection of Femenye that puts Emily into Theseus's *familia*. This closure is the third return in *patrias domos*, and by doubling the wedding of Theseus and Hippolyta with the wedding of Palamon and Emily, it intends to be its final celebration, the triumph of succession, of the patriarchal state, indeed of patriarchy itself in the guise of the victory of joy over sorrow, of the political and aesthetic will over death:

> And er that we departen from this place
> I rede that we make of sorwes two
> O parfit joye, lastynge everemo
>
> (3070–72)

In the light of this desire for a final celebration, we may notice the play of meanings in the double rhyming of "chivalrie" and "Femenye" with which the poem opens. The first time it appears, chivalry carries the strong suggestion of Ovidian love-conquest, Theseus's wooing Hippolyta and winning her love by his worthiness:

> What with his wysdom and his chivalrie,
> He conquered al the regne of Femenye
> That whilom was ycleped Scithia,
> And weddede the queene Ypolita
> And broghte hire hoom
>
> (865–69)

In these lines, chivalry is coupled first of all with wisdom, a Chaucerian rendering of the value-saturated ethical ideal of *clergie et chevalerie* that runs through the romance tradition from at least as early as Benoît's *Roman de Troie*. Similarly, the narrative moves directly to the wedding of the victorious conqueror with a lady of the highest status and their voyage home, "with muchel glorie and greet solempnytee" (870), with no hint of intervening action. "Chivalry" thus seems here to indicate an ethical ideal, the character of nobility. The second time "chivalry" appears, it loses these overtones entirely and unequivocally denotes simply a cavalry raid, a means to effect the conquest of the warrior women by force:

> And certes, if it nere to long to heere,
> I wolde have toold youw fully the manere
> How wonnen was the regne of Femenye
> By Theseus and by his chivalrye;
> And of the grete bataille for the nones
> Bitwixen Atthenes and Amazones;
> And how asseged was Ypolita,
> The faire, hardy queene of Scithia

(875–82)

Hippolyta, "the wedded queen" of the first lines, is here the "faire, hardy queene," a collocation of adjectives that unsettles the gender-exclusive language of romance ("faire" is of course the principal romance attribute of ladies; "hardy" is the standard epithet for a warrior)[16] to foreground her as a warrior-prince and thus a direct counterpart of Theseus, governor and conqueror. She is "beseiged" not metaphorically by wooing but literally by the invading military force of another prince, "[b]y Theseus and by his chivalrye." The romance meaning of "chivalry" is (mis)presented *in* the narrative line; the second meaning is ironically given directly only within what is excluded, inside the *occupatio*, where the narrator tells us what a story he could tell if only he wanted to tell it. This play on "chivalry" is of course the meeting place of violence and eroticism, the place where the series of power and the series of desire cross, and it enacts the same contradiction between public action and private fulfillment that destabilizes the self-identity of the warrior-prince himself. On the one hand, as Lee Patterson explains,

[b]y defining its values almost entirely in terms of personal worth, chivalry tended to privatize all historical action. ... [I]ts deepest ambition was to produce not a better world but a perfect knight. It was committed to codes of behavior not as programs of action but techniques of self-fashioning: the

chivalric life was its own goal. Becoming ever more elaborate in its self-articulation, chivalry sought to create a form of life that was autonomous and self-sustaining, complete in itself and requiring no authentication from outside.[17]

This is indeed one side of Theseus. The other is precisely his identity as prince, which enacts not "its own self-articulation" but uses that enactment to undertake programs of action justified from outside by the political and dynastic ends of statemaking. Such action is always violence, either as threat or as deed, performed in the name of *pax et iustitia* and in no other name, neither ethical nor aesthetic. This is the primary contradiction at the core of the *Knight's Tale*, the unresolvable contradiction between political action and ethical being according to the norms of *any* code.

Let us note here, too, what happens in the tale's "laying bare of its device" toward the conclusion. The funeral of Arcite is fully narrated in a refusal to narrate elaborated to the point of self-parody (2919–66). The narrative of Arcite's funeral, however, is a doubling of the final scene of the *Thebaid*, the longed-for funeral rites and burning of the dead bodies that Theseus had successfully avenged in his victory over Creon at Thebes.[18] The military victory and its celebration, coupled with the funeral rites for the dead soldiers and the mourning of their wives, all of which form the closure of the *Thebaid*, form in the *Knight's Tale* not a closure but an opening for violence that finds its real resolution in yet another funeral and a dynastic marriage and complex set of alliances that both neutralize a potential enemy after military devastation and rearticulate the power of the prince at home and abroad. The *Knight's Tale* never calls into question the success of the warrior-prince, but it is uncompromising in notating the state of continuous conflict that makes it possible and the tremendous cost in lives and suffering that is its result. The tale presents the victory celebration of the conquerors without ever quite wholeheartedly joining in.

And the tale can never quite close, much as it wants to. What it intends to be the final celebration is not final at all. Out of the undercurrent of political violence, the Miller restructures each of the series I have been writing about to reinscribe the *Knight's Tale* with words stolen from the Knight's own mouth. Readers have often been struck by the "homely simile" with which the Knight first excuses his narrative performance:

> I have, God woot, a large feeld to ere,
> And wayke been the oxen in my plough.

> The remenant of the tale is long ynough.
> I wol nat letten eek noon of this route,
> And lat se now who shal the soper wynne.

(886–91)

But listen to the Miller speak a version of power, storytelling, desire, and explanation that simultaneously is and is not entirely his own:

> Why artow angry with my tale now?
> I have a wyf, pardee, as wel as thow;
> Yet nolde I, for the oxen in my plough,
> Take upon me moore than ynogh,
> As demen of myself that I were oon;
> I wol bileve wel that I am noon.
> A housbonde shal nat been inquisityf
> Of Goddes pryvetee nor of his wyf.

(3157–64)

Clearly, more here is at stake in this reinscription than a supper. And as such reinscriptions show, much more was always at stake, even from the very beginning and certainly at the end.

Notes

Earlier versions of this essay were presented at the conference, *Europe in the Age of the Hundred Years' War*, Fordham University, New York, 1989, and at the Medieval Association of the Pacific annual meeting, Seattle Wash., 1993. I want to thank the participants for their comments and questions.

1. Charles Muscatine, "Form, Texture, and Meaning in Chaucer's *Knight's Tale*," *PMLA* 65 (1950): 911–29; Robert W. Hanning, "The Struggle between a Noble Design and Chaos: The Literary Tradition of Chaucer's *Knight's Tale*," *Literary Review* 23 (1980): 519–41. This reading has since Hanning become central to criticism of the *Knight's Tale*. Even if, as John Ganim notes, Muscatine overestimated the efficacy of the forces of order, and now the "consensus position . . . is that the elements of chaos in the poem are not sufficiently ordered or explained by its structure or plot," the binary opposition of order and chaos and the analogy between artistic and political control are still central to virtually all readings of the *Knight's Tale*. See John Ganim, "Chaucerian Ritual and Patriarchal Romance," *Chaucer Yearbook* 1 (1992): 65–86. For the persistence of the "consensus position," see works as diverse in critical interest and theoretical approach as Donald Howard, *The Idea of the Canterbury Tales* (Berkeley and Los Angeles: University of California Press, 1976); H. Marshall Leicester, *The Disenchanted Self* (Berkeley and Los Angeles: University of California Press, 1990); Lee Patterson, *Chaucer and the Subject of History* (Madison: University of Wisconsin Press, 1991).

2. In his careful analysis of the narrative syntax of the tale, Jerold Frakes notes the appearance in the text of the deliberation of the narrator at the seams joining one episode to another. See Jerold C. Frakes, "'Ther nis namoore to seye': Closure in the *Knight's Tale*," *Chaucer Review* 22 (1987): 3. For the reference to Statius, see line 2294. All citations of Chaucer are from *The Riverside Chaucer*, 3d ed., ed. Larry D. Benson (Boston: Houghton Mifflin Company, 1987).

3. R. H. Nicholson, "Theseus's 'Ordinaunce': Justice and Ceremony in the *Knight's Tale*," *Chaucer Review* 22 (1988): 194, points out that while in the *Teseida* the Theban ladies appeal to Teseo as "a famous avenger of any wrong in behalf of anyone who appealed to him" (citing Boccaccio's gloss to 2.10), in the *Knight's Tale* the ladies appeal to Theseus, as prince of Athens, for an act of justice and princely favor. This shift of emphasis from lord to prince is a point that cannot be overstressed and to which I will return later.

4. In his explanatory note in the *Riverside Chaucer* to the epigraph, Vincent di Marco writes that the motto (from the *Thebaid* 12.519–20) found in many manuscripts of all groups is "perhaps by Chaucer himself" (828). In *Anelida and Arcite*, Chaucer begins the story proper by translating these same lines immediately after the invocation (*Anel.* 22–28). Several manuscripts of *Anelida and Arcite* in fact insert the Latin lines before line 22.

5. See David Anderson, *Before the Knight's Tale: Imitation of Classical Epic in Boccaccio's* "*Teseida*" (Philadelphia: University of Pennsylvania Press, 1988). For an excellent discussion of the epic received as a manual for princes, see Paul A. Olson, "Chaucer's Epic Statement and the Political Milieu of the Late Fourteenth Century," *Mediaevalia* 5 (1979): 61–87. See also Robert S. Haller, "The *Knight's Tale* and the Epic Tradition," *Chaucer Review* 1 (1966): 67–84. In all classical discussion of genre, aesthetic characteristics such as metrical practice are strictly speaking the only generic indicators, and particular subject matters are seen as specifically appropriate to particular genres. For an especially clear indication of this relationship, see Ovid, *Amores* 1, where the transformation of the dactylic hexameter line into elegiac couplets (because Cupid snatched a foot) necessitates the change in subject matter from history to love, that is, from the public to the private realm. It is Ovid's poetic brilliance to bring about this change by audibly introducing the pentameter, in the line "edere materia conveniente modis," precisely on the word "conveniente," the decorous linking of subject matter with style, which the line simultaneously enacts and destroys, being the principal aesthetic concept of antique rhetoric.

6. Donaldson was fond of this observation and expressed it in a variety of places. For one convenient example, see the note on Harry Bailey in *Chaucer's Poetry: An Anthology for the Modern Reader*, ed. E. Talbot Donaldson (New York: Ronald Press, 1958), 800: "Initially we are told only of his [Harry's] competence as a social manager and of his great virility. We see the former in operation at once when—by what the narrator considers the most extraordinary bit of luck—the Knight somehow draws the straw that makes him the first storyteller."

7. See Frakes, 1: "Closure is more than merely the resolution of conflict in events of the narrative; it is also the resolution and logical end point of the *structure* [his emphasis] of the narrative." On content as formal in the way I discuss it here, see Georg Lukács, *Theory of the Novel: A Historico-Philosophic Essay on the Forms of Great Epic Literature*, ed. and trans. Anna Bostock (Boston: MIT Press, 1971).

8. The social history of these relationships has recently become an object of careful inquiry. For the crucial distinction between public and private power, see Georges Duby, "Private Power, Public Power," in *A History of Private Life* (Cambridge, Mass.: Harvard

University Press, 1988), 2:3–31. In his magisterial 1995 presidential address to the Medieval Academy of America, Thomas Bisson discussed the extreme overestimation of medieval governmental and institutional regularity in classic American medieval historiography. He draws attention rather to lordship, the personal exercise of proprietary power, as the form of power characteristic of medieval experience. While Bisson focuses his discussion primarily on evidence drawn from the twelfth century, his shift of emphasis from structure to practice and his questioning of the adequacy of such concepts as government and office to describe the reality of political life have very important applications to the later middle ages. See Thomas N. Bisson, "Medieval Lordship," *Speculum* 70 (1995): 743–59; see also the essays collected in *Cultures of Power: Lordship, Status, and Process in Twelfth-Century Europe*, ed. Thomas N. Bisson (Philadelphia: University of Pennsylvania Press, 1995). In *Chaucer and the Subject of History* (Madison: University of Wisconsin Press, 1991), Lee Patterson draws attention precisely to the same combination of seigneurial lord, warrior, and prince in the use of the Scottish campaigns of 1385 "to provide the eighteen-year-old king [Richard II] with an opportunity to come into his own not only as monarch but as the leader of the chivalry of England, a warrior king worthy of his glorious father and grandfather. Parliament granted money for the campaign only on condition that the king lead the army himself, and it noted that this was 'le primier Viage nostre dit Seigneur le Roy'" [quoting *Rot. Parl., 3:185*] (186–87). For this campaign, Richard invoked, "for the first time in almost a century and for the last time in English history, the ancient feudal levy" (187), an action whose ideological significance Patterson underlines: "By invoking the levy, Richard at least asserted, even if he could not in the event enforce, his role as the feudal overlord of England, the personal seigneur of all those who followed him to war" (188).

9. My terminology and critical practice here is drawn from M. M. Bakhtin, "Forms of Time and of the Chronotope in the Novel," in *The Dialogic Imagination*, ed. and trans. Michael Holquist and Caryl Emerson (Austin: University of Texas Press, 1981), esp. 167–206, who uses the term "series" to collocate a variety of similar entities in Rabelais; and from Jacques Derrida, *Of Grammatology*, trans. Gayatri Chakravorty Spivak (Baltimore and London: Johns Hopkins University Press, 1974), 152–64, who uses the term similarly in his discussion of "the chain of supplements" in Rousseau's *Confessions*. Both Bakhtin's and Derrida's discussions have as their common *point d'appui* a fundamental critical tool of Russian formalist criticism, the assertion that since a device is a function and not an essence, it therefore can appear in various modalities within a text. Structural entities such as "theme" or "plot" are too restrictive to identify what I want to attend to here because their identities are based rather on their mode than on their function. That is, as I will show, the series of political action, for example, or of desire, is sometimes created in narrative—we are given a story of conquest or of enamorment— while at other times it is created by a rhyme or by an image cluster while the narrative is occupied with other matters. That is, sometimes the same device is a theme while sometimes it is a plot, or even a rhetorical figure. Chaucer, I am suggesting, uses thematic, poetic, or narrative procedures to organize what is otherwise disparate material into a single entity. This entity I call a series because I am interested in this essay only in the fact that its elements are forced together and am indifferent at the moment as to how its elements are forced together.

10. See Susan Crane, "Medieval Romance and Feminine Difference in the *Knight's Tale*," *Studies in the Age of Chaucer* 12 (1990), and her *Gender and Romance in Chaucer's* "Canterbury Tales" (Princeton: Princeton University Press, 1994).

11. Adrienne Rich, "Compulsory Heterosexuality and Lesbian Existence," in *Selected Prose, 1979–85* (New York and London: Norton, 1986), 23–75.

12. The relations between the establishment of the genre of the *Knight's Tale* as romance and the specific performance of gender that is entailed by this establishment have been well studied by Angela Jane Weisl, *Conquering the Reign of Femeny, Gender and Genre in Chaucer's Romance*, Chaucer Studies vol. 22 (Cambridge: D. S. Brewer, 1995).

13. John Ganim, 70, notes a double suppression in the *Knight's Tale* that underlies Chaucer's transformation of the material into romance: the suppression of Emily's literary past as an Amazon and the transferring of the articulation of some of the most important philosophical issues of the poem, which had been given voice in the *Teseida* by Emilia, to the male characters Arcite, Theseus, and Egeus. As Ganim sees it, this amounts to a wholesale repression in the *Knight's Tale* of female agency.

14. *La Mort le Roi Artu*, ed. Jean Frappier, 3d ed. (Geneva: Droz, 1964). The quotations come from p. 19, but identical or similar expressions are the most usual way of linking one large scene to another in the tale and can therefore be found throughout the text. For a powerful analysis of the effects of such impersonal narrative linking in *La Mort le Roi Artu*, see Jean Rychner, *Formes et structures de la prose française médiévale: L'articulation des phrases narratives dans la Mort Artu* (Geneva: Droz, 1970). For similar observations regarding the narrative syntax of the Old French *Oueste*, See Tzvetan Todorov, "The Quest of Narrative," in *The Poetics of Prose*, trans. Richard Howard (Ithaca: Cornell University Press, 1977), 120–42.

15. Giovanni Boccaccio, *Teseida*, ed. Alberto Limentari, in *Tutte le Ocere di Giovanni Boccaccio*, ed. Vittore Branca (Milan: Mondadori, 1964), vol. 2. The translation is my own. See also Weisl, 52–53.

16. For a convenient example of the force of this discourse, one can do no better than what may well be the very first chivalric romance, Chrétien de Troyes, *Erec et Enide*. Arthur's court consists of "boens chevaliers, / Hardiz et conbatanz et fiers, / Et riches dames et puceles, / Filles de rois, gentes et beles" (31–34). In arguing against undertaking the hunt for the white stag, Gawain declares that each woman at court has for a lover a "Chevalier vaillant et hard" (54) who would maintain that his beloved "est la plus bele et la plus gente" (58). I cite the edition of Mario Roques (Paris: Champion, 1973).

17. Patterson, 175. See also Maurice Keen, *Chivalry* (New Haven and London: Yale University Press, 1984), esp. 143–61, which draws the important contrast between chivalry as a "self-authenticating" ethical imperative and the political creation for reasons of state of the nobility as a class.

18. *Thebaid*, 12.778–809.

The Semiotics of Character, Trope, and Troilus: The Figural Construction of the Self and the Discourse of Desire in Chaucer's *Troilus and Criseyde*

JAMES J. PAXSON

Recent Chaucer criticism proffers a surplus of theory-driven projects devoted to issues of gender, sexuality, and history—a success story that reaffirms poststructuralism's final entrenchment in the field of Chaucer studies.[1] In particular, *Troilus and Criseyde* continues to enjoy interpretations treating exchange, patriarchy, rape, incest, queerness, and the occulted residues of domestic or governmental practices in Ricardian England; few studies, for instance, have done more to advance our understanding of gender and social or hermeneutical patriarchy in the poem than Carolyn Dinshaw's discussion, entitled "Reading Like a Man," in *Chaucer's Sexual Poetics*.[2] Yet the rhetorical or structural dynamics of literary character have often been left behind in such poststructural (or indeed post-poststructural) interventions; perhaps the momentum of identity studies, a central component of 1990s theory, has dislodged or dislocated the rhetorical study of character from the agendas of medievalists and early modern scholars. But one might assert that this dislocation has been premature: even before the structural and rhetorical poetics of Chaucerian characterization have had a chance to redress the sense felt by Robert M. Jordan and many others that Chaucer studies seemed "to be reaching the point of exhaustion" under the older regime of New Criticism,[3] critical deconstruction itself garnered the reputation of an exhausted approach.

I therefore continue to press for the rhetorical study of literary character in the *Troilus*. I do not advocate a "new formalism" of character and poetic language in Chaucer studies (verily, "characterization studies" had already been prompted by the waning of New Criticism in the face of the language- or discourse-centered conceptual schemes inherent to poststructuralism). Rather, I emphasize that the formal dimensions of postmodern rhetorical criticism, semiotics, narratology, and critical deconstruction still offer tools useful to our understanding of how the discourse of desire sometimes works in Chaucer's texts. And although these tools involve the articulation of any number of semiotic constants employed by the gendering discourse of patriarchy in *Troilus and Criseyde* (insides or outsides, penetrations or eruptions, dispersals or encasements, blazons or defacements), I hope that the drift of my analysis deflects the charge that my project joins the paradigm of "reading like a man" identified by Dinshaw. I in fact proceed forward from Dinshaw's conclusions, wishing only to place in relief the rhetorical or tropological minutiae of signal moments in the *Troilus* that crystalize Chaucer's poetics of desire, personality, and gender.

The heyday of semiotic and rhetorical character study in *Troilus* criticism came at the end of a trajectory that had gotten underway, more than eighty years ago, with the critical "novelization" of Chaucer's great romance. By the 1970s, many critics had parted from the view, first articulated by George Lyman Kittredge, that Chaucer's characters exhibited authentic personality and that this personality found literary expression through a kind of novelistic, psychological realism.[4] The anti-Kittredgian trend accorded with current histories of the premodern philosophy of mind,[5] as well as with established models of fictional character in ancient, medieval, or early modern drama and literature.[6] Such models have employed a now familiar battery of adjectives for premodern conceptions of character or personality: "emblematic," "iconic," "anti-realistic," "anti-psychological," "non-mimetic," "allegorical," "figural," "tropological," and so forth. The rhetorical basis for Chaucerian characterization, narrative generation, and lyrical posturing had of course been canonized in Robert O. Payne's *The Key of Remembrance*, one of the twentieth century's most important books on Chaucerian poetics that, although not a poststructural study itself, paved the way for tropological models of character that would come to reflect the tactics and sentiments of deconstructive criticism.[7]

In the essay that follows I will continue on this route—a route that, as I've already implied, has suffered some neglect in the face of enthusiasms felt for cultural or sexual poetics in the field of Chaucer studies. I will provide an ostensible semiological model for just *how* figural character gets invented or constructed and indeed thematized, particularly in terms of the suffering Troilus. The minutiae I addressed a moment ago will proceed from examination of how Chaucer conjoins crucial poetic tropes, in the field of the Narrator's discourse, during key moments of Troilus's characterization. Chief among these tropes are prosopopoeia, apostrophe or ecphonesis, pragmapoeia (reification), ethopoeia, and sermocinatio or dialogism. (Allow me to refresh: prosopopoeia or personification occurs when a nonhuman thing or concept is given human form and speech; apostrophe is the direct, verbal address of a nonhuman thing or an absent person; pragmapoeia occurs when a human character is treated as or converted into a speechless thing; ethopoeia involves the poetic creation of a programmatic, set speech or sententia; sermocinatio is the corresponding creation of bicharacter dialogue.)[8] Moreover, I hope to show that the poem stages a narrative experiment in the liminality or marginality of human language—an experiment that considers human language and speech in relation to noise, exclamation, and the emotive force of apostrophic utterance. The poem tests and compares the linguistic and poetic values of crying and laughter, silence and dialogue, thereby creating what Slavoj Žižek calls the "sublime body" or object of desire's discourse. In coveting his irrecoverable object of desire—Criseyde—the suffering Troilus himself metamorphoses into an object of the sublime. Via this methodological route I will convey a sexual poetics or "bodytheory," so to speak, of the phenomenology of gender and the psychodynamics of desire that inform poetic discourse in the *Troilus*.

* * *

Let me start by reviewing just a small sample of the iconic, rhetorical, or figural models of character in *Troilus* that comes out of recent criticism. Through a reader-response program reminiscent of the theoretical strategies of Wolfgang Iser, John Ganim argues that character early on in the poem is "pictorial" and emblematic.[9] Working towards similar hermeneutic ends, Robert W. Hanning has called for the allegorization of Criseyde's character as a text itself—one that must be penetrated as it is decoded by the suasive (as well as exegetical) male figures Pandarus and Troilus.[10] Henrik Specht reads the characters of *Troilus* as registers or nodes of rhetorical exercise: the characters exemplify ethopoeia or adlocutio (once again, the figure whereby set speeches, soliloquies, monologues, or *sentientiae* are attached to characters), but also prosopopoeia and sermocinatio in action.[11] And Eugene Vance has moved that character in *Troilus* functions as the exemplary and commodified essence of narrative speech-acts.[12] Two central matters from Specht and Vance— that prosopopoeia actually anchors characterization in the *Troilus* and that programmatic speech-acts frame out key "lyrical cores"—provide useful guidance through some of the problematic and peculiar moments of Troilus's characterization in the poem.

One such lyrical core and characterizational node involves book 4's memorable scene of the frenzy suffered by Troilus after he has learned that Criseyde must be handed over to the Greeks. The scene, which will serve as the focus of most of my remaining discussion, builds upon a complex interaction of tropological fields while it contains one of the poem's best-known metaphorical cruxes. It begins with a peculiar and striking phenomenological diagram of Troilus's "diminishment," a diminishment that gains realization not just on the level of actual story but on the level of the Narrator's discourse:[13]

> And as in wynter leves ben biraft,
> Ech after other, til the tree be bare,
> So that ther nys but bark and braunche ilaft,
> Lith Troilus, byraft of ech welfare,
> Ibounden in the blake bark of care,
> Disposed wood out of his wit to breyde,
> So sore hym sat the chaungynge of Criseyde.
>
> He rist hym up, and every dore he shette
> And wyndow ek, and tho this sorwful man
> Upon his beddes syde adown hym sette,
> Ful lik a ded ymage, pale and wan;
> And in his brest the heped wo bygan
> Out breste, and he to werken in this wise
> In his woodnesse, as I shal yow devise.
>
> (4.225–38)[14]

Winthrop Wetherbee has provided a thorough unpacking of this scene along with its source in *Inferno* 3, where Dante first sees the souls of the damned fluttering, like dead leaves, down to the river Acheron:

> Come d'autunno si levan le foglie
> l'una appresso de l'altra, fin che 'l ramo
> vede a la terra tutte le sue spoglie,
> similemente il mal seme d'Adamo
> gittansi di quel lito ad una ad una
> (As, in the autumn, leaves detach themselves,
> first one and then the other, till the bough
> sees all its fallen garments on the ground,
> similarly, the evil seed of Adam
> descended from the shoreline one by one)
>
> (3.112–16)[15]

Chaucer's borrowed image of a tree "bereft" of leafy cover initiates a sequence marked by the kinds of puns that pick up from the arboreal or botanical simile found in the Dantean source.[16] Subsequently, the characteristic withdrawal from the social setting, the silence, and the narratorial simile of the lover appearing as a "ded ymage" (a point straight out of Boccaccio's *Filostrato*) indicate a phenomenological and psychic diminishment characteristic of the medieval courtly allegory and the troubadour lyric. Such a condition of diminishment was called *dorveille*,[17] and in rhetorical terms it equates to the implementation of the trope reification or pragmapoeia—the figural conversion of a human character into an object. As a "ded ymage," Troilus has been reified or "thingified" into an aphasic, nonsentient, nonhuman thing; he becomes a nonliving simulacrum of a human form. This conversion, of course, occurs on the level of narratorial discourse, though on the level of narrated story he suffers from periodic catatonia. The figurative reification has a structural counterpart in the common local rhetorical personification or, as Morton Bloomfield often called it, the simple "animate metaphor."[18] The silence and pragmapoeia signal a chain of figural maneuvers that begin to constitute Troilus's characterization at this point in the poem.

In addition to Dante's figurative description of the scene at Acheron, Chaucer's simile of defoliation recalls Boccaccio's similar image that characterizes Troiolo the moment he hears of the decision to trade Criseida: "Even as the lily in the fields that has been injured by the plough droops and fades in the too hot sun . . . so . . . did Troilus . . . fall in a faint."[19] But whereas Boccaccio presented the simple image of a flower drooping, Chaucer's botanical simile gathers greater charge by developing a semiotic component latent even in the Dantean simile. The first figure in the book 4 scene conveys a sense of denudation or uncovering. The tree (or Troilus) was concealed by an outer sheath of leaves (comprised of "ech welfare") and is now left naked or exposed. Dante's text implies this sense too, with its reference to the tree's "garment" that gets stripped away. And whereas the Dantean simile employs a brief local personification (the bough "*sees* all its fallen garments"—*vede . . . le sue spoglie*) regarding the trunk and limbs of the tree, Chaucer's simile configures the leaves through a more tacit kind of (pseudo)personification. That is, each "welfare" (an abstract concept) lost by Troilus gets substantialized or objectified as a leaf that departs from a tree, leaving only bare bark and branches. And yet each welfare functions like an individual personage abandoning a community—a faintly implicit sense to the simile that prefigures the social isolation and abandonment felt by Criseyde or Troilus through books 4 and 5.

Chaucer's passage furthermore develops semiotic potential lacking in

Dante's simile by emphasizing the word *bark* through a pair of puns. Mad, or "disposed wood out of his wit," Troilus is "Ibounden in the blake bark of care"—bound or fettered in the black bark of care. The tree now serves as an objectification or hypostasis of the abstract concept *care* (sorrow or worry). Botanical allegory cascades along by drawing on the word "wood," which has a sylleptical (or pun-actuating) quality: *wood* = "mad" as well as the dense and pulpy matter of a tree. The vegetative or dendritic signification reinstalls the passage's inner/outer semiotic by next playing on the semantic value of the word "bark" as a casing or integument on a tree; Troilus, now made (of) wood, finds himself bound inside this black integument. The passage therefore provides, through simultaneous similaic operation, the conflicting figural images of botanical uncovering and botanical encasement: Troilus's social, psychic, and somatic status converts him, in the Narrator's discourse, to *both* a dendritic skeleton stripped of its folial skin or flesh, and a ligneous tree imprisoned in its exoskeletal sheath. Such figural aporia joins a chain of similar aporetical moments in the Narrator's discourse, a state of affairs that finds general underpinning elsewhere in the semiology of medieval romance: as Evelyn Birge Vitz has demonstrated in regards to *The Romance of the Rose*, the aporetical deployment of inside/outside auto-figures serves as one of the most prominent structures in the allegory of desire.[20]

Overall, the discursive or figurative equation between a person and a tree evokes the classical topos of dendrification, really a magical conversion or metamorphosis proper.[21] The tree topos can be traced back through Dante (*Inferno* 13.28–51) and Ovid (*Metamorphoses* 10.489–98) to the *Aeneid*, when Aeneas breaks off a branch of the tree that had once been the Trojan youth Polydoros (3.32–63). Important here is the idea that magical or supernatural dendrification can be taken as a literalization of pragmapoeia. It is the story-level actuation of a human's figurative, discourse-level translation into a nonhuman entity. This dramatized pragmapoeia or reification has its parallel in the narratorial depiction of the catatonic Troilus behaving or appearing as a "ded ymage," a lifeless, carved statue.

The text thus presents an oscillation between dendrification in the sense of a discourse-level metaphor and the sense of a story-level magical transformation that has classical reference. This oscillation also exists for the brief and almost latent personifications lurking in the book 4 frenzy sequence. That is, the objectified or pseudopersonified welfares, which are only discourse-level entities, call up the ontic domain of a more substantial allegorical person who likewise possesses classical reference or warrant. The Narrator's term "bark" also signifies, via syllepsis, a boat[22]—a secondary meaning supported by the text's recurring and programmatic metaphor of Troilus in Fortune's boat (1.416–17; 2.1–6) and by the allusion to the frenzy-passage's Dantean subtext. The "bark of care" can be taken as a *boat* of care, an echo of the very boat that traverses the river Acheron, loaded with the souls of the damned, piloted by the "demon Charon" in *Inferno* 3.109 (*Caron dimonio*). This allusion in turn might suggest an extended phonetic echo with the personification Care, the anthropomorphic embodiment of misery or anxiety or sorrow: Troilus now finds himself bound (as a maritime traveler) in the infernal boat of Care/*Caron*. Line 229 therefore marks the putative generation, in very tacit terms, of an allegorical "character"—or barely the ghost or effigy of one—as a corollary of Troilus's cognitive *dorveille*.[23]

The figural imagery of encasement continues in lines 232–38, where it finally gets literalized or narrativized on the story-level of the text through Troilus's own actions. Here, Troilus shuts the windows and doors in the room so that he may shut out the world. The Narrator then refocuses or readjusts this symbolic spatial arrangement as a feature of metaphorical discourse. He describes how the "heped wo bygan / Out breste" (4.236–37). The architectural dimension of the scene recalls a similar enclosing of Troilus in a confined space: prior to his emergence with the goal of seducing Criseyde, Troilus glimpsed her "Thoroughout a litel wyndow in a stewe, / Ther he bishet syn mydnyght was in mewe" (3.601–2; the word "mewe" itself connotes a locale for animals or livestock—a subtle dehumanization).[24]

But the book 4 reference to a frenzied "out-bursting" works in far greater contrast to Troilus's eventual emergence from mew, his active plans for seduction in hand. Contrary to the figural imagery of encasement and containment at the center of the frenzy scene are figurative images of explosion, eruption, outrage, madness, and, as in the defoliation simile, revelation and uncovering. The coeval operation of contradictory figural images ironizes and calls into question the function and value of the Narrator's figurative language itself. Another aporia opens wherein mutually canceling semes collide.

In elementary aesthetic terms, these contradictions constitute no threat to any thematic unities in the text. After all, the images could be a way of establishing the melodramatic sense of love-induced self-contradiction. Inexplicable contrariness or self-contradictory conceptualization features the thinking and behavior of romance characters locked in problematic amatory situations. For instance, in the *Metamorphoses* Ovid provides the classical commonplace for such contrariness in the guise of Myrrah, who, in the throes of love longing (but prior to her actual conversion into a tree), behaves at once explosive and petrified (10.380–420).[25] Here is a moment of mixed body language that, as my discussion of dendrification has already indicated, enjoys still greater resonance with the figural transformations of *Troilus and Criseyde*. The basis of Chaucerian aporia does have classical thematic warrant.

Yet, the array of figural oppositions evident in each of the lines I have anatomized carries a consequent semiotic charge that foregrounds or advertises the structural logic of the medieval paradigm of tropes and figures in ways that are far more than incidental or aesthetically convenient. Presaging the tropological common denominators utilized by current schools of rhetorical and poetic theory, the passage thematizes the conceptual, structural properties of figures like prosopopoeia and pragmapoeia.[26] In conventional poetics, such structural properties are to remain hidden. "Figure" seeks to establish itself—in other words, seeks to define itself in relation to nonfigure by concealing a secret manipulation or subversion of grammatical, semantic, or ontological codes. Yet in the book 4 frenzy passage, the Narrator of the *Troilus* stages the structural motor of characterizational tropes, engaging a chain of figural images built upon the structural oppositions living/nonliving, motion/stasis, eruption/contraction, revelation/concealment, covered/uncovered, external/internal, and so forth. Current semiotic descriptions of prosopopoeia and pragmapoeia—tropes that stand as binary oppositions of each other—reveal that of all tropes, these two are the dialectical expressions par excellence of the foundational sets of oppositions tallied here.[27] Prosopopeia entails the making of life and motion, while pragmapoeia entails transmutation of those alive and human into that which is static or inanimate. Furthermore, as Jon Whitman has demonstrated, the lexical status of "prosopopoeia" (along with the Hellenic concept *hyponoia* or "undermeaning"—the conceptual precursor of *allegoria*), involves the imaging of a mask or facade that covers an interior.[28] *Prosopon poein* means "to make a face or mask." The figure already serves as the (meta)figure of the container/content dichotomy upon which figuration itself depends for viability, for its lexical constitution conveys the image of a surface contour that conceals and yet lures toward a substrate. Pragmapoeia or reification, prosopopoeia's binary opposite, enjoys this metafigural property too. Traditionally, the trope has often been conceived in terms of its Thomistic or Aristotelian synonyms: hypostasis and holomorphism or hylozoism (the taking on of *morphe*, "form," by primal *hyle*, "matter"); indeed it is this more common and familiar usage of the neo-Latin term *reification* that denotes the distillation of a rarefied idea or abstraction down to a palpable substance or thing (*res*).[29] But as the characteristic imagery of the frenzy scene reveals, Troilus's

ontological reduction or reification is concomitant upon figurative strip-
ping away, unmasking, de-facement; it provides an occulted micronarrative of the negation of *facement* or prosopopoeia while it also narrates
the building up of containers and their secret contents.

The frenzy passage therefore stages the self-reflexive status of
"Troilus," a fictionally invented character. To repeat: on discourse-level,
Troilus suffers figural depiction as a reified entity, a human being translated into a wooden thing that's been robbed of motion, sentience,
speech. Yet the figural images of encasement depict Troilus *as the trope
prosopopoeia itself*, as an anthropomorphism of prosopopoeia, a personification of personification, if you will. One might conclude further that
the passage is an allegory of the invention of a prosopopoeia. More
precisely, it is the *mimesis* of prosopopoeia's semiotic structure—a move
achieved, paradoxically, through the metaphorical reduction of Troilus
via pragmapoeia or reification. The conjunction or compaction of two
mutually canceling tropes that are the very engines of characterization at
this site in *Troilus and Criseyde* (or in all allegorical narrative) marks an
unresolvable structural tension, a crucial aporia. Put another way, the
effective pragmapoeia is undermined or undone because the text narrates
the secret armature of *all* figures; the ludic disposition of insides/outsides
signifies both prosopopoeia and the semiology of *sign* itself. The combination of these aporias marks the dismantling or deconstruction of the
Narrator's (or the text's) rhetorical and formal enterprise—a state of
affairs that reflects, in the very least, the Narrator's well-known narratorial attachment to the trope *occupatio* as well as his well-known
diffidence.[30]

* * *

Although there are no actual, physical personification characters
walking about in *Troilus and Criseyde*—a matter that should not, like the
poem's absence of gods, go unquestioned[31]—Chaucer experiments with
conceptions or latent images of the trope in the tacit way I've charted
schematically here. Further implicit reference to the conceptual latency
of "dispersonation" or defacement in the frenzy scene comes at the close
of book 4, during Criseyde and Troilus's parting embraces and final
conversation. Just before Criseyde makes her ten-night pledge, she tries
to persuade Troilus of the heroic longevity of her devotion to him:

> This made, aboven every creature,
> That I was youre, and shal while I may dure.

> And this may lengthe of yeres naught fordo,
> Ne remuable Fortune deface.

                                        (1679–82)

The first "this" cited here refers to Troilus's nobility and self-control and its effect of securing Criseyde as his loving and loyal companion forever. In straightforward terms, Criseyde seems then to conclude that "many long years will not destroy such love or loyalty, nor will fickle Fortune deface it." But the periodic syntax engages a pun: the clause "ne remuable Fortune deface" contains grammatical ambiguity because the pronoun "this" of line 1681 can be, as typical construal reveals, the antecedent of the verb "deface," making Fortune the subject of the compound sentence; but at the same time, "lengthe of yeres" also could be the subject of the syntactical compound, making "Fortune" the direct object acted upon by the verb "deface." Thus a heroic claim about the durability of love gets haunted by a pessimistic afterthought representative of the kind of syntactical or assertional (hap)hazards we have seen before in the *Troilus*:[32] not even durable love can destroy the power of changeable Fortune, that personified agent of time's vagaries. The two clauses that yield, according to the second construal, a kind of anacoluthon[33] stand in mutual contradiction. This ironic result foreshadows the catastrophic failure of Criseyde's constancy as it relates to the forces of destiny and chance so central to the Boethian subtext of the poem.

Irony and foreshadowing aside, the foregoing grammatical calisthenics underline the semiotic import of a nearly incidental discursive micronarrative: *the defacement of Fortune*. The semiotic charge of "defacement" in relation to a personification character (indeed to the *only* personification, besides Love, who finds regular representation in the narrative discourse of *Troilus and Criseyde*) enjoys centrality in recent theoretical formulations about prosopopoeia. For Paul de Man, the poetic evocation of face, voice, mouth, or eyes had provided Romantic or modern poets with the opportunity to treat an important trope like prosopopoeia as a lyrical theme.[34] Chaucer's brief presentation of Fortune engages a similar mimesis of the structural properties constitutive of the trope prosopopoeia, properties visible in the strange frenzy scene of book 4. "Defacement" is the literal inversion of the trope that enables the invention of a *prosopon* or "face" for an intangible, alien, or ineffable essence, concept, faculty of mind, natural force, or absence. Tropological defacement can be thought of as a variant of pragmapoeia or reification, a point that makes Criseyde's latent assertion about "remuable Fortune" recall the conjunction of mutually canceling, oppositional tropes: as the Narrator conjures up one of the few discourse-level personifications in the text, the configuration is negated by a single verb ("deface") that connotes the structural apparatus needed for undoing personification or prosopopoeia. Since these tropes can also be shown to constitute a semiotic grid of structural relations (prosopopoeia vs. pragmapoeia vs. apostrophe vs. dialogism), Chaucer's semantics, syntax, and the latent tropes reflected therein allegorize their self-reflexive, structural turnings.[35]

The two stanzas of book 4 containing Troilus's strange figural transformation prefigure an eventual sequence powered by the semiotic grid of trope relations, allegorized or invoked by the defacement micronarrative, that I have suggested. But the figure *apostrophe* also takes on an its own important metafigural role. At the point in this sequence just following the initial moments of diminishment and encasement, Troilus rises up in a wild rage, hurling himself about the room like a raging beast. Indeed, on the level of narrative action, Troilus can produce nothing but "heighe sobbes" (248). As the narrator tells us, his crying and sorrow of "His speche hym refte" (249). That is to say, Troilus has been reduced to uttering no more than the cry of sorrow, the wordless, nonlinguistic vocalization of absolute emotional agitation or rational collapse. As we'd expect, Troilus's first but "unnethes" verbal utterance once this eruption has subsided is an apostrophe to Death personified: "O deth, allas! why nyltow do me deye" (250). This site in the *Troilus* marks the protagonist's ontological nadir: after configuring Troilus as a reified object *and* as the mimesis of the trope prosopopoeia, the text proceeds to characterize (or ontologize) him as (1) an entity poised on the boundary between human speech and nonspeech (or noise), as well as (2) one on the border of animation and inanimation. This second liminal status is reinforced by the fact that Troilus's first, difficult apostrophe (for apostrophe is the only verbal move the distraught Troilus can produce at this point) is to the personification character Death. Moreover, the cry or "sike"—an utterance at once human and nonhuman—finds synecdochic representation by the graphic inscription of apostrophe or ecphonesis: the ubiquitous and telltale "O."[36]

Following the initial apostrophe to Death, the Narrator cites a chain of apostrophes that occupy the next eighty-six lines of book 4. In this chain of apostrophes, Troilus addresses personified abstractions, parts of his body, and other characters in the poem. (The addressees of the apostrophes follow, for the most part, those of the apostrophe sequence composed by Boccaccio in the *Filostrato*: Death, Fortune, Love, Troilus's spirit, Troilus's soul, his two eyes, Criseyde, lovers in general, and finally Calkas, the proairetic motor or first cause of the poem's narrative action.)[37] Yet, even the lengthy and excessive chain of apostrophes supplied in the text, the Narrator tells us, serves as a small sample of

Troilus's complaint. The narrator is no doubt hyperbolic when he claims that "A thousand sikes . . . / Out of his brest ech after other wente" (337–38). Nonetheless, one trope (hyperbole) cannot assert itself over another (apostrophe) in the rhetorical scheme so far deployed in my discussion. The passage reveals an obsession with, or rather an abuse or excessive use of, the figure apostrophe. Allen Koretsky has argued that apostrophe serves as a central device in the *Troilus* and that the protagonist suffers from an excessive use of it.[38] If, as Eugene Vance claims, Pandarus represents an abuse of sermocinatio, Troilus represents the abuse of that figure's semiotic subcontrary in a hypothetical Greimas Square of sentience-tropes: apostrophe.[39] More an underling of Apostrophe than of Fortune, Troilus is the text's "linguistic innocent" who "seems woefully ignorant of the medium which all other characters seem so adept at manipulating to their own advantages," as Julian Wasserman has put it.[40] Troilus's excessive attachment to apostrophe enables his manipulation *by* language and rhetoric; it assures his characterization as the "function" or exemplum of a powerful trope, a *remuable* (if I may) trope that seeks to master one, like a narcotic, but that inscribes the *marginality* of linguistic systems through its homograph, the "O."

It is curious that Chaucer defines these apostrophes as *sikes*, or "sighs." Indeed, they are "fiery," emotionally charged exhalations that signal a consciousness so tormented and torn that it has reached the brink of ontological and epistemological vacuity or entropy. Like the cry, the sigh is no more than an exhalation, a (partial) feature of voice or pulmonary motility that is devoid of semantic content and significant of the boundary between human language and nonhuman noise. The cry, the moan, the painful "O" that signals and initiates apostrophe, is, as a vocal gesture, the last "speech act" of the dying consciousness, the para-speech-act that delimits all speech acts. The *sike*, so understood, serves not just as the vocal signal of boredom, distraction, pain, or even orgasm,[41] but as the final thoracic or pectoral motion in a man who has arrived at his mortal end.

Even the entropic ontology represented in this chain of apostrophes, however, reveals an opportunity for Troilus's escape and redemption. That is, Troilus's apostrophe to his own mind and spirit suggests a figural "standing outside" of himself.[42] On the face of things, the apostrophic address to a component of the physiological self implies a kind of auto-blazon and therefore a self-directed, figural dismemberment—a figural maneuver that results in yet another pragmapoeia or reification.[43]

However, the site provides a curious and confusing figural separation of "voice" from "self." The apostrophized "goost" and "soule" suggest the Aristotelian *pneuma*, while the ever-embodied *psyche* (signified by voice—or better yet, by what Aristotle in *The Poetics* calls *lexis* or "speech") must be making the apostrophic addresses that, in this case, posit their figurative address from a semiotic "outside" beyond Troilus's suffering body.

But this striking tropological turn might also be said to represent an uncanny *doubling* of body, as psychoanalytical theory would admit (in adjunct support to the rhetorical and philosophical registers so far delineated). It represents what Slavoj Žižek has described as the projection of a sublimely suffering "body within the body" characteristic of discourses concerning both common commodity exchange (in the desire-armature of late capitalism) and intense desire.[44] Žižek's sublime body coextends as a fictional materialization of the Lacanian Real—the extralinguistic or parasomatic Thing fantasized by psychoanalysis to stand behind language and consciousness, or inside will/desire and cognition. Projection or adoption of this body, particularly under the aegis of intense suffering or deprivation, marks an important juncture in the poetic discourse of desire.

This psychotropic escape or release, allegorically fantasized as the byproduct of desire's prominent tropes (apostrophe, ecphonesis, or prosopopoeia) in book 4, ultimately enjoys literal representation at the end of book 5 in the famous apotheosis scene presenting the image of Troilus's disembodied soul. Here, though, the distinctions between *psyche* and *pneuma*, between *lexis* and *ego*, are confounded. In quite literal terms, Troilus rises after death through the *primum mobile*; like Dante's elect, he undergoes the divine effect of "transhumanization." Troilus's transformation, however, takes a curious form. He dies at the hands of Achilles (1806), leaves earth and its temporal miseries, and, standing outside the concentric and encapsulated structures of the created world, looks back in. His response at this point, however, is not verbal. The Narrator points out how "in hymself he lough" (1821).

Conventional exposition of Troilus's laughter has pursued theological or ethical themes: it has been taken as a divine response to the human and finite;[45] or it captures Chaucer's satirical deference to comedy as the aesthetic mode of ultimate efficacy in such a poem.[46] But the human laugh, like the exclamatory *sike*—that is, the "O" of apostrophe—is an utterance without semantic content. It is a semiotic variant of the cry or the sigh, a vocal exhalation that indicates emotion but does not encode information, save that derivable from a circumscribing social or linguistic context. Troilus's final, disembodied laughter concludes a protracted but tacit textual critique of the structural roles occupied by soul, mind, and voice, or by society, language, and tropes. The acoustic and thoracic sign that is the most liminal of all signs marks the margin of final action in the poem. This final action, in Žižek's terms, reveals the purest of psycho-sexual sublimities.

But let me further clarify the semiotic link between crying and laughter. The laugh could be said to enjoy phenomenological identity with the cry, the apostrophic "O," which signals the shutting down of human cognition in the *Troilus*. This identity, however, has one physical (or material) difference despite the identity: while both the cry and the laugh are pure vocalizations, the cry comprises a stream of undifferentiated sound, like the unbroken playing of a musical note. It is a steady, unpunctuated exhalation of thoracic or pulmonary wind. The laugh, conversely, is broken, punctuated, or articulated by *silences*, by stops in the steady stream of wind. The cry or *sike*, represented by the graphic sign "O," conveys no information and is the phenomenal but latent image of voice, whereas the laugh incorporates in its phenomenal structure the regular, syntagmatic sequence of vocal sound-and-silence. (In English, laughter finds graphic representation in the inscription "ha-ha-ha," the mere inscription of phonological difference between phoneme and silence—a graphological move that Chaucer was first among English writers to employ.)[47] If the cry or "O" is the sign of pure voice, the laugh (although *not yet* linguistic itself) is the *differential* sign of language, the figure of linear, syntagmatically organized, sonorous or acoustic production. And voice is the precursor and phenomenal core of language.

The semiotic cooperation of precursory voice figured as "O," and language figured as the laugh, has further theoretical underpinnings. Through an inventive psychoanalytical and semiotic program that underwrites a psychogenic narrative of human infancy, Julia Kristeva has shown how the cry, which is the chronologically inaugural human utterance, by necessity evolves or mutates into its expressive consequent, the laugh, which is the second kind of human utterance.[48] For Kristeva, the transition of *anaclisis* from cry to laugh marks the developmental inception of human language, the preliminary step towards the opening of the cognitive Symbolic as opposed to the neonatal Semiotic.

The stakes of this semiotic explication are rich for the *Troilus*. Troilus's death signals a "rebirth" or spiritual mutation (a matter supported by traditional medieval theories of the spiritual apotheosis following death) that is figured, in the semiotic terms of Kristeva's system, as the acquisition of human language, the passage from nonspeech to speech, the step from cry to laugh. The text thus lifts Troilus from the characterological and ontological paradox presented in the figurally confounded frenzy scene of book 4—a scene that depicted him as a reified person, a personification of prosopopoeia, an embodiment of apostrophe, or as a Lacanian sublime body. Let me further specify that the frenzy scene is one self-contained parable, allegory, or, to use a term suggested by J. Hillis Miller, "emblem scene"[49] that expresses the temporary arrest of language and cognition in apostrophe and figural diminishment; the apotheosis scene serves as a corollary emblem scene that allegorizes the (re)discovery or (re)birth of language. The former scene figures the loss or end of voice and the loss of human substance; the latter figures the birth of voice and the winning of posthuman or transhuman substance.

Apart from Troilus's allegorical deliverance from what we may think of as a "tropological purgatory" in the frenzy scene, the poem's narrative concludes by continuing its play with images of encasement, encapsulation, and directed vocal address. The apocalyptic laugh is still a fragmentary version of *exclamatio* or *ecphonesis*—one directed downward or inward through a great core of material concentricity (the earth and its surrounding, sublunar sphere) toward unhearing and now phenomenologically incommensurate mortal ears. The effect can be thought of as analogous to the earlier, inward-directed apostrophes made by Troilus's ecstatic "voice" to his soul, spirit, and body parts. But it also underscores the phenomenology of containment that turns out to inscribe not only the semiotics of prosopopoeia and its related tropes but also the gendered phenomenology of the contained and penetrated female body. The sartorial, cosmetic, and somatic semiotics of allegory and personification resonate with the hermeneutical quandary that rests in the poem's "reading" of Criseyde, as Dinshaw's work has so decisively shown.[50] Troilus's figural characterization throughout the poem has been a specular version of his lady's de facto characterization.

So, despite its metaphysical uplift and Christian moralization, the end of *Troilus and Criseyde* does not find Troilus's characterization at all apart from figural quandaries. The patriarchal semiotics of embodiment, containment, penetration, and apotheosis (vertical release, or antipenetration) inform every turn of the narrative, and in concluding I reassert that my intention in the foregoing discussion has been to highlight a representative sampling of those turns.[51] Even the poem's most localized and incidental-looking liminal vocalizations or occulted patriarchal figurations get problematized accordingly: the final fact, conveyed in idiomatic Middle English, that Troilus "laughs *in* himself" subverts the phenomenology of pectoral exhalation (the "O" is supposed to dynamize the difference between the *inside* of a hypothetical body and its *outside*), for the apotheotic context of the action annuls the semiotic of insides/outsides, a semiotic pertinent, according to medieval pneumatology, only in the context of *living* humans possessed of embodied spirits.[52] Troilus's somatic "voice" is gone; his laugh is virtually one of silence, a phenomenologically unrealizable "exhalation," as Derrida would have put it—the prefixal or morphemic *ex* requiring palmipsizing by a graphemic "x" which thereby undoes the whole semio-spatial metaphorology underwriting discourses about "bodies" and "spirits." And has not this poetics of silence, bound up with the problematization of bodily interiors and exteriors, fully characterized Chaucerian women—Griselda and Criseyde preeminent among them?

Troilus and Criseyde, then, can be read in part as an allegorical narrative of the powers latent in poetic figuration, in the mimesis and deployment of human language, and in characterization. In the poem, Chaucer "is miming a certain sort of discourse in such a way as to bring out the assumptions that make it possible and to question them."[53] Above all, the text's metafictional handling of characterization and human ontology demonstrates that these elements can be seen as tropological domains accessible through the tactics of poststructural rhetorical criticism, a practice still effective in tracing the minutiae in desire's discourse. The fascinating thing about *Troilus and Criseyde* is that it examines these self-reflexive fictional concerns without the kind of overt allegorical machinery that we find in *Piers Plowman*, the *Psychomachia*, *The Romance of the Rose*, or *The House of Fame*.[54] *Troilus and Criseyde* can be read as a compelling narrative romance, as an apologue of Ricardian royal activity, or as a parable of patriarchy. But as a parable of patriarchy, it *must* be read as an autocritique of the sophisticated rhetorical devices used by medieval poets to create the literature of desire.

Notes

1. See Faye Walker, "Making Trouble: Postmodern Theory With/In Chaucer Studies," *Style* 26 (1994): 577–91.

2. Carolyn Dinshaw, *Chaucer's Sexual Poetics* (Madison: University of Wisconsin Press, 1989), 28–64.

3. Robert M. Jordan, *Chaucer's Poetics and the Modern Reader* (Berkeley and Los Angeles: University of California Press, 1987), 5.

4. See George Lyman Kittredge, *Chaucer and His Poetry* (Cambridge, Mass.: Harvard University Press, 1946)—the critical monument that came out of Kittredge's seminal lectures of 1914. I use the adjective "novelistic" to describe Kittredge's view of character primarily in *The Canterbury Tales*, although the more customary use of the designation "dramatic" that has been applied to Kittredge's well-subscribed theory incurs an explanation for the terms' identity. Although Kittredge read the individual tales of *The Canterbury Tales* as long, dramatic "speeches" provided by a string of performers, his understanding of such soliloquy-like speeches differed from the conventional understanding of the medieval soliloquy or sententia: the former involved the authentic crystallizations of speakers' realistic personalities; the latter involved the mouthed and nonpersonal

expression of preexisting discourses or areas of reference. The designations "dramatic" and "novelistic" thus express Kittredge's *expressive* rather than *formalist* poetics, to use M. H. Abrams's concepts.

5. See especially Richard Rorty, *Philosophy and the Mirror of Nature* (Princeton: Princeton University Press, 1979), for a still-vital discussion of how modern conceptions of human personality and textually represented character originated, in the seventeenth century, as nodes of "psychological interiority." According to Rorty, Descartes, Hobbes, and Locke were the chief proponents of these modern concepts. Rorty's assertions, along with those of the literary theorists of character cited below, conform to an insistent historicism. Note that a current exception to this historicism—one insisting on the *continuity* between medieval textual models of characterological generation or authorial self-presence and modern characterological models—can be found in Burt J. Kimmelman, *The Poetics of Authorship in the Later Middle Ages: The Emergence of the Modern Literary Persona* (New York: Peter Lang Publishing, Inc., 1996).

6. Valuable studies of premodern literary character include Robert C. Elliott, *The Literary Persona* (Chicago and London: University of Chicago Press, 1982); Warren Ginsberg, *The Cast of Character: The Representation of Personality in Ancient and Medieval Literature* (Toronto: University of Toronto Press, 1983); Rose A. Zimbardo, *A Mirror to Nature: Transformations in Drama and Aesthetics, 1660–1732* (Lexington: University of Kentucky Press, 1986); and Jonathan Goldberg, *Endlesse Worke: Spenser and the Structures of Discourse* (Baltimore and London: Johns Hopkins University Press, 1981). See also Goldberg's *Voice Terminal Echo: Postmodernism and English Renaissance Texts* (New York and London: Methuen, 1986), 68–100, for a strong discussion of constructed character ("Shakespearian Characters: the Generation of Silvia"). Zimbardo's analysis of emblematic, figural, and "iconic" character in Shakespeare finds more recent and succinct representation in her essays, "The King and the Fool: *King Lear* as Self-Deconstructing Text," *Criticism* 33 (1990): 1–29; and "One and Zero: The King-Fool Emblem in Medieval/Renaissance Dramatic Figuration," *Mediaevalia: A Journal of Medieval Studies* 18 (1995): 367–86. For an impressive analysis of iconic and "desire-structured" character used exclusively in medieval narrative, see Evelyn Birge Vitz, *Medieval Narrative and Modern Narratology* (New York and London: New York University Press, 1989), especially 176–212. I single out the projects of Zimbardo, Goldberg, and Vitz to promote the efficacy of structural and poststructural strategy in the study of literary character, consciousness, and desire.

7. Robert O. Payne, *The Key of Remembrance: A Study of Chaucer's Poetics* (New Haven: Yale University Press, 1963). H. Marshall Leicester Jr. would qualify as the most effectual poststructuralist Chaucerian who has benefited from the trajectory of rhetorical character study devoted to *Troilus and Criseyde* or *The Canterbury Tales*. His magnum opus, entitled *The Disenchanted Self: Representing the Subject in the "Canterbury Tales"* (Berkeley and Los Angeles: University of California Press, 1990), synthesizes with virtuosity the strands of rhetorical analysis, deconstructive characterology, psychoanalysis, and the legacy of humanist criticism in modern Chaucer studies.

8. The ultimate taxonomic source for thinking on these five tropes is the same for all tropes and figures inventoried in fourteenth-century rhetorical theory: Quintilian. See the *Institutio oratoria*, ed. and trans. H. E. Butler, Loeb Classical Library (Cambridge, Mass.: Harvard University Press, 1920), 1.7.3; 3.8.49 and 52; 4.1.63; 6.1.25; 9.2.29, 37 and 38; 9.3.24 and 26; and 11.1.41.

9. John Ganim, *Style and Consciousness in Middle English Narrative* (Princeton: Princeton University Press, 1983), 83.

10. Robert W. Hanning, "Come in Out of the Code: Interpreting the Discourse of

Desire in Boccaccio's *Filostrato* and Chaucer's *Troilus and Criseyde*," in *Chaucer's "Troilus and Criseyde" 'Subgit to alle Poesye': Essays in Criticism*, ed. R. A. Shoaf with the assistance of Catherine S. Cox (Binghamton, N.Y.: Medieval and Renaissance Texts and Studies, 1992): 120–37. Here in fact is a version of Chaucer's gender poetics that finds more intensive formulation in Dinshaw's pronouncements.

11. Henrik Specht, "Ethopoeia, or Impersonation: A Neglected Species of Medieval Characterization," *The Chaucer Review* 21 (1986): 1–15. In H. Marshall Leicester Jr., "The Art of Impersonation: A General Prologue to the *Canterbury Tales*," *PMLA* 95 (1980): 220–28, one finds the argument for a similar kind of rhetorical self-referentiality centered on the use of ethopoeia or impersonation in *The Canterbury Tales*.

12. See Eugene Vance, *Mervelous Signals: Poetics and Sign Theory in the Middle Ages* (Lincoln and London: University of Nebraska Press, 1986), 256–310. Vance applies the theoretical framework of Austin and Searle in his analysis of the *Troilus*, declaring that event and character involve "a complex texture of different kinds of utterances that tend to distribute themselves between the constative as narrative, the illocutionary, the perlocutionary, and the exclamatory" (272).

13. The ontological conversions that constitute Troilus's figural characterization function exclusively in the domain of narrative *discourse* as opposed to narrated *story*. The former is the complete verbal field in which all actions are embedded; the latter comprises all phenomenal events that actually take place in the poem's setting. For an elaboration of this basic division, common among most modern narratologists, see Seymour Chatman, *Story and Discourse: Narrative Structure in Fiction and Film* (Ithaca and London: Cornell University Press, 1978), 15–42; Gérard Genette, *Narrative Discourse: An Essay in Method*, trans. Jane E. Lewin (Ithaca and London: Cornell University Press, 1980), 25–32; and Mieke Bal, *Narratology: Introduction to the Theory of Narrative*, trans. Christine van Boheemen (Toronto: University of Toronto Press, 1985), 3–10.

14. Citations to *Troilus and Criseyde* are taken from *The Riverside Chaucer*, 3d. ed., ed. Larry D. Benson (Boston: Houghton Mifflin Company, 1987).

15. Dante Alighieri, *Inferno*, trans. Allen Mandelbaum (Berkeley: University of California Press, 1980).

16. See Winthrop Wetherbee, *Chaucer and the Poets: An Essay on "Troilus and Criseyde"* (Ithaca and London: Cornell University Press, 1984), 37–40, 98–100, and 174–76.

17. See Michel Zink, "The Allegorical Poem as Interior Memoir," in *Images of Power: Medieval History/Discourse/Literature*, guest ed. Kevin Brownlee and Stephen G. Nichols (*Yale French Studies* 70 [1986]), pp. 109–10, 113–15, for a discussion of troubadour *cansos* that hinge on this term.

18. See Morton W. Bloomfield, "A Grammatical Approach to Personification Allegory," *Modern Philology* 56 (1958): 73–81.

19. R. K. Gordon, trans. and ed., *The Story of Troilus*, Medieval Academy Reprints for Teaching 2 (Toronto: University of Toronto Press, 1978), 72.

20. Vitz, 64–95.

21. For a current and extensive discussion of the links between metamorphosis and allegory, see Bruce Clarke, *Allegories of Writing: The Subject of Metamorphosis* (Albany: SUNY Press, 1995), 23–51.

22. Although the word *bark*, signifying a commercial boat or ferry, did not enter common English usage until after the middle of the fifteenth century (see *OED* 1.672, col 1, "Bark, barque"), it had enjoyed long currency in Latin form (*barcus*, as indicated in Isidore's *Etymologies*; *OED* 1.672, col 2), which would have made it a candidate for sylleptical function in Chaucerian wordplay. For theoretical review of such parameters

regarding Chaucer's puns, see Laura Kendrick, *Chaucerian Play: Comedy and Control in the "Canterbury Tales"* (Berkeley and Los Angeles: University of California Press, 1988), 23, 159–60.

23. See note 17 above. See also James J. Paxson, *The Poetics of Personification* (Cambridge: Cambridge University Press, 1994), 93–103, on how the phenomenological diminishment of the allegorical narrator/protagonist's mind accompanies the reflexive and spontaneous generation of personified characters. Also see Paul Zumthor, "On the Circularity of Song," in *French Literary Theory Today*, ed. Tzvetan Todorov (Cambridge and New York: Cambridge University Press, 1982), 185, for a discussion of the initial generation of a discourse-level, personified character out of the *canso* singer's psychic condition.

24. See R. A. Shoaf, "*Troilus and Criseyde*: the Falcon in the Mew," in *Typology and English Medieval Literature*, ed. Hugh T. Keenan (New York: AMS Press, 1992), 149–68. Of further interest is the semiotic charge Shoaf teases out of the *mew* image in the *Troilus*: the mew, a compartment used for the keeping of hawks especially during molting, conveys the sense of confinement, dispersal (bird feathers, like those arboreal leaves, must be shed), and transformation (see especially 153–59).

25. Ovid, *Metamorphoses*, vol. 2, trans. Frank Justus Miller, Loeb Classical Library (Cambridge, Mass.: Harvard University Press, 1982).

26. For semiotic descriptions of how tropes and figures find logical or grammatical constitution, transformation, and interrelation, see Paul Ricoeur, *The Rule of Metaphor*, trans. Robert Czerny with Kathleen McLaughlin and John Costello (Toronto: University of Toronto Press, 1977); Jean DuBois, et. al., *A General Rhetoric*, trans. Paul B. Burell and Edgar Slotkin (Baltimore: Johns Hopkins University Press, 1981); and especially Tzvetan Todorov, *Theories of the Symbol*, trans. Catherine Porter (Ithaca: Cornell University Press, 1982), 84–110.

27. See Paxson, 53–54, 151–54, 160–66.

28. Jon Whitman, *Allegory: The Dynamics of an Ancient and Medieval Technique* (Cambridge, Mass.: Harvard University Press, 1987), 269–72.

29. I apologize for potential confusion in my taxonomical system of convenience: I have been using "reification" or "pragmapoeia" to denote the figural conversion of a human agent into a nonhuman thing, or *res*, while I have preferred "objectification" to denote the figural conversion of an essence or idea into any substantial form. See Paxson, 42–43.

30. R. A. Shoaf, ed., *Troilus and Criseyde* (East Lansing, Mich.: Colleagues Press, 1989), xxi–xxii.

31. Currently I am working on the obvious paucity of anachronisms in *Troilus and Criseyde*. This formal point of fact seems connected to the absence of pagan gods on the text's primary level of narrative action (the gods "act" only on the level of the Narrator's discourse; see 5.1–7, for example) as well as the absence of actual personifications (such as inhabit *The Parliament of Fowls* or *The House of Fame*). Such erasure or avoidance of the obvious mechanisms of allegory or medieval historiography could, of course, support the protomodern view of the *Troilus*, the view that this essay seeks to challenge.

32. Such botched assertion of idea finds expression, for instance, in Pandarus's distorted point concerning the Euclidean concept "dulcarnon," 3.933 ff.

33. Anacoluthon: the trope whereby two conceptually linked clauses fail in their grammatical or syntactical connection. In modern English, the dangling participle serves as a good example: "Walking down the street, my hat blew off my head."

34. Paul de Man's important discussions of face and prosopopoeia include "Autobiography as De-Facement," in *The Rhetoric of Romanticism* (New York:

Columbia University Press, 1984), 67–81; and "Hypogram and Inscription" and "Reading and History," in *The Resistance to Theory* (Minneapolis: University of Minnesota Press, 1986), 27–53, 54–72, respectively. See my discussion of metafigural defacement, Paxson, 66–70, regarding Prudentius's *Psychomachia*.

35. In Paxson, 52–53, I chart the quaternary structural relations of prosopopoeia, pragmapoeia, apostrophe or ecphonesis, and dialogism or sermocinatio using an illuminating Greimas Square. See the descriptions of the Greimas Square's analytical utility in Ronald Schleifer, *A. J. Greimas and the Nature of Meaning: Linguistics, Semiotics, and Discourse Theory* (Lincoln: University of Nebraska Press, 1987), passim.

36. See Jonathan Culler, "Apostrophe," in *The Pursuit of Signs* (Ithaca and New York: Cornell University Press, 1981), 135–54. That Chaucer's *sikes* are not just mere "sighs" or moans exhaled one after the other but rather lyrical apostrophes themselves is supported by the Narrator's recognition of the "thousand sikes, hotter than the gleede [that] / Out of [Troilus's] brest ech after other wente, / Medled with pleyntes new (4.337–39; my emphasis). Each mixture of *sike* and *pleynte* would thus equate to Culler's description of the complete "apostrophe" as the mixture or combination of the ecphonetic "O" and it's subsequent lyrical utterance. We have, of course, just witnessed a sample of the "thousand sikes" and their corresponding "pleyntes" in Troilus's apostrophic catalogue, ll. 250–336.

37. Although apostrophe of this variety usually implies wild emotional agitation, instability, and irrationality, the *sequence* of apostrophes reveals a tight logical progression, for it charts a reversed, etiological itinerary of the poem's plot or proairetic sequence. In terms of a narratological "move grammar," Calkas is the origin of action in the poem; he is, to use Thomas Pavel's terminology, the initial or prime "move" in a linear "move tree." Each element in the linear or syntagmatic chain of apostrophes represents a prior narrative node in the *Troilus*, the last of these nodes being the self-invoked death of Troilus—actually invoked here as a narrative prolepsis of events in 5.1806. See Thomas G. Pavel, *The Poetics of Plot: The Case of English Renaissance Drama* (Minneapolis: University of Minnesota Press, 1985), 3–24, for an exposition of generative plot-grammars and their utility in the narratology of Elizabethan tragedy.

38. Allen C. Koretsky, "Chaucer's Use of the Apostrophe in *Troilus and Criseyde*," *Chaucer Review* 4 (1970): 251.

39. Vance, 381.

40. Julian N. Wasserman, "Both Fixed and Free: Language and Destiny in Chaucer's *Knight's Tale* and *Troilus and Criseyde*," in *Sign, Sentence, and Discourse: Language in Medieval Thought and Literature*, ed. Julian N. Wasserman and Lois Roney (Syracuse: Syracuse University Press, 1989), 211.

41. On the Narrator's taxonomy of sighs both pleasurable and sorrowful, see 3.1360–65. Although space does not at this point permit me a full treatment of the poetics of apostrophe in the *Troilus*, I must mention at least one additional point that is of further importance to the framework I've so far employed: Chaucer's treatment of the apostrophic *sike* presages the whole Romantic structure of pathetic fallacy (as it would later be named by Ruskin), especially regarding Troilus's fantasy that the breeze (an external, natural phenomenon) he feels on the walls of Troy has its pneumatic source in Criseyde's distant sighs of suffering (an internal psychic condition; see 5.666–79). The moment conveys the sense that the apostrophic "O" is interchangeable with the *aura* (as Walter Benjamin termed it) identified with Nature conceived as a personified pan-presence in the Romantic theorization of the symbol.

42. Boccaccio also provides Troiolo's addresses to his soul and eyes; see Gordon, 74.

43. Barbara Johnson, *A World of Difference* (Baltimore and London: Johns Hopkins University Press, 1987), 185. Pandarus's own apostrophe to the tongue (3.302), which comes near the climax of his lecture on gossip, serves as an ironic, self-reflexive sign of apostrophe's urge to separate the vocal or pectoral ("O") from, quite literally, the *lingual* or linguistic. See my final paragraphs below on the deconstructive stakes inherent in such ironical dissection of voice and physiology.

44. Slavoj Žižek, *The Sublime Object of Ideology* (London: Verso, 1989), 18–19, 134–35, and 165.

45. John M. Steadman, *Disembodied Laughter: "Troilus" and the Apotheosis Tradition* (Berkeley: University of California Press, 1962), 128–29.

46. Alfred David, "Chaucerian Comedy and Criseyde," in *Essays on "Troilus and Criseyde,"* Chaucer Studies 3, ed. Mary Salu (Cambridge: D. S. Brewer, 1979), 91.

47. Although Troilus's final laugh is reported secondhand by the narrator, Chaucer wins the prize for two of the earliest graphic mimeses of laughter: Alison's "Tehee!" (*Miller's Tale*, 3740), and Criseyde's "Nay, therof spak I nought, ha, ha!" (2.589). Of course, Chaucer's direct meditation upon the semiotic status of speech conceived as "broken air" appears in *The House of Fame*, 2.765 ff.

48. Julia Kristeva, *Desire in Language: A Semiotic Approach to Literature and Art*, ed. Leon S. Roudiez, trans. Thomas Gora, Alice Jardine, and Leon S. Roudiez (New York: Columbia University Press, 1980), 281–83.

49. J. Hillis Miller, *Fiction and Repetition* (Cambridge, Mass.: Harvard University Press, 1982), 59.

50. See Dinshaw, *Chaucer's Sexual Poetics*, passim, and 144–48.

51. I have focused this discussion on the frenzy scene as one of the central, or more telling, passages in the figural characterization of Troilus. Criseyde's characterization, of course, deserves equal attention, which I abbreviate here only for want of space and time. Briefly, I take Criseyde's "swoon scene" in book 4 as the structural analog to Troilus's frenzy scene, which closely precedes it. Some acoustic echoes alert us to this analogy: Troilus's frenzy involves "a thousand sikes" (337), while the Narrator tells how Criseyde "cryed a thousand sithe" (753). But Criseyde's impassioned exclamations avoid any use of the apostrophic "O," even though the exclamations are addressed to an absent listener, to Troilus, who is her "deere herte" (759). Criseyde, in fact, utters not apostrophes but a battery of rhetorical questions at the moment she contemplates suicide. I would adduce Dinshaw's discussion, cited above, of the differences between masculine and feminine response, reading, and cognition in the *Troilus* in order to frame a future comparison of the figural structures comprising the two frenzy scenes.

52. See St. Thomas Aquinas, *Summa Theologica*, Ia.50.2, vol. 9, ed. Thomas Gilby (Cambridge and New York: Blackfriars and McGraw-Hill, 1964), 9–15, for the theological (or rather pneumatological) commonplace that angelic, demonic, or posthuman spirits could be said to *contain* rather than *be contained by* the bodies that they contact or coextend with spatially. For Thomas, the verbal metaphors of insides/outsides fails pneumatology from the start.

53. H. Marshall Leicester, "Oure Tonges *Differance*: Textuality and Deconstruction in Chaucer," in *Medieval Texts and Contemporary Readers*, ed. Laurie A. Finke and Martin B. Shichtman (Ithaca and London: Cornell University Press, 1987), 17.

54. See note 31, above.

Contributors

SIMON GAUNT is a fellow of St. Catharine's College, Cambridge, and a lecturer in the Department of French, University of Cambridge. He has published articles on the troubadours and medieval French culture and is the author of *Troubadours and Irony* and *Gender and Genre in Medieval French Literature*.

WARREN GINSBERG is Professor of English at the State University of New York at Albany. He has written about Latin literature, especially Ovid; medieval Italian, especially Dante and Boccaccio; and Middle English literature, especially Chaucer. His works include *The Cast of Character* and an edition of *Wynner and Wastoure and the Parlement of the Thre Ages*. He has just completed a new book entitled *Chaucer's Italian Tradition*.

CYNTHIA GRAVLEE received her Ph. D. in medieval literature from the University of Alabama in 1987. She is Associate Professor of English at the University of Montevallo, where she teaches World Literature, Arthurian Literature, and Irish Literature. Her scholarly work has centered on gender issues in medieval literature.

CHARLOTTE GROSS, Associate Professor of English at North Carolina State University, has published essays on troubadour lyric, Chaucer, the *Pearl* Poet, and twelfth-century thought. She is presently at work on a study of time in medieval philosophy and poetry, entitled *Cosmos and Canso*.

JOAN G. HAAHR, Professor of English at Yeshiva University, studied with Morton Bloomfield at Harvard University, from where she received her Ph.D. Her publications include articles on the medieval Ovidian tradition, on medieval historiography, and on Chaucer. In addition to working on a long-term project on medieval amatory literature and the growth of secularism, she has been trying her hand at writing fiction.

ROBERT W. HANNING has degrees from Columbia and Oxford universities. Since 1963, he has been a faculty member at Columbia University, where he is currently Professor of English and Comparative Literature; he has also taught as a visitor at Yale, Princeton, Johns Hopkins, and New York universities. He was for some years a member of the faculty of the Bread Loaf School of English, Middlebury College, and on three occasions directed the Bread Loaf program at Lincoln College, Oxford. The recipient of ACLS, Guggenheim, and NEH fellowships, he has directed three NEH-sponsored Summer Seminars for College Teachers (one of which served as the ultimate point of genesis for the present collection of essays). His publications include *The Vision of History in Early Britain*, *The Individual in Twelfth-Century Romance*, a translation (with Joan M. Ferrante) of *The Lais of Marie de France*, and essays on a variety of medieval and Italian Renaissance subjects. He is a Fellow of the Medieval Academy of America.

JAMES J. PAXSON is Associate Professor of English at the University of Florida. He is the author of *The Poetics of Personification* and is currently completing a book entitled *Theory's Master Tropes and the Institutional Imaginary*. He has also coedited a collection of essays entitled *The Performance of Middle English Culture: Essays on Chaucer and the Drama in Honor of Martin Stevens*, and has published articles on allegory, critical theory, rhetorical tropes, medieval drama, science and literature, and the institution of literary studies in America. He is Associate Editor of *EXEMPLARIA: A Journal of Theory in Medieval and Renaissance Studies*.

SANDRA PIERSON PRIOR is the author of two books on the *Pearl* poet: *The Pearl Poet Revisited*, and *the Fayre Formez of the Pearl Poet*. She has published several articles on both the *Pearl* poet and Chaucer. Her other scholarly interests include medieval drama, typology, and the apocalyptic tradition. Her essay on *Eliduc* for this volume is part of a larger study on the place of women in medieval narrative. Professor Prior directs the Composition Program and teaches medieval literature at Columbia University.

NANCY M. REALE is a Master Teacher of Humanities in the General Studies Program at New York University. She has published several articles on English, Italian, and Latin medieval texts, with an emphasis on

Boccaccio and Chaucer. Her major scholarly interest is the medieval use of *riscrittura* as a tool through which authors establish new aesthetic and political claims for their own work and the poetic process in general while simultaneously maintaining and asserting their connections with their literary inheritance. She is currently coediting a volume of essays entitled *Satura: Essays on Medieval Religion and Education in Honor of Robert R. Raymo*, which is forthcoming.

ANNE HOWLAND SCHOTTER is Professor of English and Chair of the Faculty of Humanities at Wagner College. Her published work includes *Ineffability: Naming the Unnamable from Dante to Beckett* (coedited with Peter S. Hawkins), "Woman's Song in Medieval Latin," "Rhetoric versus Rape in the Medieval Latin *Pamphilus*," and articles on the *Pearl* and *Sir Gawain and the Green Knight*. She is coeditor of the medieval section of a forthcoming anthology of British literature.

SARAH SPENCE is Associate Professor of Classics and Adjunct Professor of Comparative Literature at the University of Georgia. She has published widely on topics related to medieval literature and the classical tradition. Her books include *Rhetorics of Reason and Desire: Vergil, Augustine and the Troubadours* and *Texts and the Self in the Twelfth Century*.

ROBERT M. STEIN is Associate Professor of Language and Literature at Purchase College, State University of New York, and Adjunct Professor of English and Comparative Literature at Columbia University. He has published articles on medieval history and romance and on contemporary critical theory.

Index

Index of Authors

Abelard, Peter, 112–14, 120nn. 7, 8, 9, 10, and 12, 155n. 3
Abrams, M. H., 221–22n. 4
Acontius, 83
Aers, David, 22n. 13
Agrippa, 41
Alan of Lille, 13, 141, 155n. 4
Allen, Don Cameron, 69n. 1
Allen, Peter, 21n. 7
Alton, E. H., 69
Anderson, David, 203n. 5
Andreas Capellanus, 13–15, 22n. 10, 69, 77
Appel, Carl, 19, 90, 96–99, 101–2, 104–6, 107nn. 2 and 3, 108nn. 5 and 19, 109nn. 21 and 22, 110n. 37
Aquinas, Saint Thomas, 225n. 52
Aristotle, 217
Arnaut Daniel, 48–49
Aston, Margaret, 155n. 3
Athanasius, 68
Auerbach, Eric, 32, 38n. 14, 137n. 9
Augustine, Saint, 37n. 7, 62
Augustus Caesar, 41
Austin, John, 223n. 12

Bahti, Timothy, 22n. 17, 185n. 2
Bakhtin, M. M., 204n. 9
Bal, Mieke, 223n. 13
Baldwin, John, 154n. 2
Barkan, Leonard, 86n. 32
Baron, Dennis, 22n. 9
Baron, Hans, 59n. 38

Barthes, Roland, 14, 20, 22n. 12, 23n. 22
Baswell, Christopher, 156n. 10
Bede, 157n. 13
Benjamin, Walter, 225n. 41
Benkov, Edith Joyce, 84, 86n. 33
Bennett, C. E., 57n. 11
Benôit de Sainte-Maure, 52–53, 60n. 52, 200
Benson, C. David, 60nn. 50 and 51
Benson, Larry, 56n. 4, 158n. 18, 185n. 3, 203n. 2, 223n. 14
Benson, Robert, 119n. 3
Bernart de Ventadorn, 18–20, 89–90, 95–96, 99–101, 105, 107nn. 2 and 3, 108n. 5, 108–9n. 19, 109nn. 21 and 22, 110n. 37, 111, 115–17, 121nn. 26 and 27, 169
Bertini, Ferruccio, 84n. 2
Bisson, Thomas, 157n. 15, 203–4n. 8
Blamires, Alcuin, 155n. 3, 159n. 22
Blanch, Robert J., 85n. 7
Bloch, R. Howard, 22n. 16, 96, 108n. 16, 161n. 37
Bloom, Harold, 15, 22n. 15
Bloomfield, Morton W., 223n. 18
Blumenthal, Wilfred, 84n. 3, 85n. 20, 86nn. 25 and 27
Boccaccio, Giovanni, 15, 19, 53–55, 61n. 53, 165–68, 170–73, 173–74n. 3, 175–76n. 7, 176nn. 8 and 10, 198, 203n. 2, 205n. 15, 210, 216, 222–23n. 10, 225n. 42
Boheemen, Christine van, 223n. 13

Index of Subjects